REALISTIC EVALUATION

Ray Pawson and Nick Tilley

Los Angeles | London | New Delhi
Singapore | Washington DC

© Ray Pawson and Nick Tilley 1997

First published 1997

Reprinted 1998, 2000, 2001, 2002, 2003, 2004, 2005, 2006, 2007, 2008 (twice), 2014

SAGE Publications Ltd
1 Oliver's Yard
55 City Road
London EC1Y 1SP

SAGE Publications Inc.
2455 Teller Road
Thousand Oaks, California 91320

SAGE Publications India Pvt Ltd
B 1/I 1 Mohan Cooperative Industrial Area
Mathura Road
New Delhi 110 044

SAGE Publications Asia-Pacific Pte Ltd
3 Church Street
#10-04 Samsung Hub
Singapore 049483

Library of Congress Control Number: 97-065723

British Library Cataloguing in Publication data

A catalogue record for this book is available from the British Library

ISBN 978-0-7619-5008-0
ISBN 978-0-7619-5009-7 (pbk)

Typeset by M Rules
Printed and bound by CPI Group (UK) Ltd, Croydon, CRO 4YY
Printed on paper from sustainable resources

To:

Alice
Jenny
Jo
Joe
Peter
Sam
Wendy

CONTENTS

ACKNOWLEDGEMENTS

The authors would like to thank the following for help, advice and encouragement along the way:

Norman Blaikie for being Malaysia's only (closet) realist. *Debbie Westmoreland*, Ms Word, who would have processed the book had not some bright management spark come up with the idea that academics should do their own tpying. *Elliot Stern* who only expects to be 'a footnote in the history of evaluation' but could be the all-time hero if only he would ban constructivism from his journal. *Ken Pease*, realist evaluation incarnate, for being crazy enough to perceive that scientific progress takes the path from Rochdale to Huddersfield. *Gloria Laycock*, for having the best qualities of 'Frank Candour' and 'Emma Bluestocking', and for, perhaps, being the first exponent of the realist experiment in criminal justice evaluation. *Stephen Barr* and *Simon Ross* of Sage Publications, who dealt with the book with sensitivity amidst their takeover of world methodology. *Brian Goodale*, for knowing his Dutch towns and basic chemistry and traditional songs, as well as being the master of the hyphen. *Steven Duguid, Colleen Hawkey, Wayne Knights* and *Maureen Nicholson* who, without being bullied, made the transition from idealist practitioners to realist evaluators. *Paul Ekblom, Kate Painter,* and *Tim Hope,* who, as sympathetic sceptics, still need a bit more bullying. *Gary Henry, George Julnes* and *Mel Mark* for giving us hope that realism would be understood in North America even if our quaint, jolly-old terminology would not. Let us give them a little head start here – no, chaps, an 'agony aunt' is not a relative in pain. *Eleanor Chelimsky, Ray Rist* and *Frans Leeuw,* the agony aunts of 'global evaluation' who we trust to lead the way with plenty of realistic advice. *Gordon Parker* and *Masahiko Kaneko,* who saved us the fag of smoking out many of the references to Chapter 7, and whose very real contributions do not exculpate us from any remaining errors therein. *Paul Graham, Geoff Taylor* and *Paul Williams,* and *inmates of the HMP Full Sutton program,* the voices of Chapter 6, who from their respective sides of the criminal justice fence taught us about the value of the insider's wisdom.

R.P. gives thanks for the moment when manna came from heaven, and hereby acknowledges formally his debt to the *ESRC* for the award of a Senior Research Fellowship for the year 1995–1996. He would also like to record his deep gratitude to colleagues at Leeds who, in his absence, withstood the onslaughts of evaluation and assessment on the universities. He will always remember their charm and grace as they greeted his occasional appearances in the department.

N.T., lacking ESRC support, depended on the faith and charity of a long suffering wife and family.

Finally, this book's authorship, as with our previous efforts, puts Pawson before Tilley. The only significance of this is in the branding of our product. Just occasionally, we allowed ourselves to muse on becoming the Marks and Spencer, Smith and Wesson, or indeed the Fortnum and Mason of evaluation. Others, however, have made less kind suggestions – Laurel and Hardy, Jack and Jill . . .

Ray Pawson and Nick Tilley
Leeds and Nottingham

INTRODUCTION

Real . . . realist . . . realistic evaluation

Throughout history people have sought ways of understanding and improving their lot. Once upon a time such wisdom used to be dispensed in rather broad brush strokes and society somehow managed to get by under the harsh glare of a few sacred principles. Over the ages, responsibility for the task of providing well-being through wisdom has passed to and fro between aristocracy, church and state. The expectations of such a project have suffered momentous historical mood-swings from enlightenment to despair, dark age to renaissance. In more recent times such cycles have begun to quicken. Soothsayers have come and gone in all sorts of shapes and forms, from shaman to sociologist, priest to politician, philosopher king to agony aunt.

Nowadays, the task of improvement through understanding has become a profession. We live in the age of the specialist. The extremes of the modern division of labour have fetched up a new kind of sage and these particular technocrats go by the name of *evaluators*. Professionals, of course, acquire their capital (human and otherwise) through the possession of a 'secret knowledge'. The rest of society values, and perhaps even covets, this esoteric wisdom, so encouraging all good professionals to ration their skills and exclude the non-*cognoscenti*. The greatest opportunity for professional closure comes when the authority for the knowledge base rests on 'science' and, surely enough, evaluation has fought for its status on the basis of the rigour of its research strategies and methodologies. This book is both a stock-taking exercise and a manifesto concerning evaluation's quest for scientific status.

Evaluation is at a watershed. On the one hand we can see it as a sweepingly successful social movement. One is tempted by metaphors of bull markets, of messianic movements, even of orgies. However we view it, evaluators are piling in. The word has flown from North America to Europe, Australasia and Asia. The news has spread from ivory tower to senate, town hall and boardroom and on again to office, shop and sales floor. Evaluators roam both private and public sectors. They inhabit every facet of life from agriculture to zymurgy. The reason for this explosion of evaluators is no mystery at all. We live in a knowledge-centred, value-adding, information-processing, management-fixated world which has an obsession with decision making. As we write, managers and administrators have become the largest group of employees in Britain. There are 3,921,000 of them, 15.8% of the labour force, all charged with making judgements to better their organizations. Here lies the great promise of evaluation: it purports to offer the universal means with which to measure 'worth' and 'value'. Evaluation, in short, confers the power to justify decisions.

On the other hand, and paradoxically, we also live in an age of mass cynicism and cultural relativism. Across the hallways in the aforementioned ivory towers, other intellectuals are preaching their own self-destruction in advising us about the end of certainty in a postmodern culture. They perceive human understanding to be locked into the particular discourse which surrounds each social group. The rise of a global multiculturism and the fragmentation in local subculturism are said to have produced a world composed of a babble of incommensurable voices. No one, prophet, intellectual or evaluator, can claim to be in possession of the universal standpoint, that secret scientific key to the truth. No longer is it possible to claim a privileged prescription of how such a world of multiple social constructions should operate. In this climate, a rather different message is thrust on the would-be evaluator: stop feigning certainty and instead celebrate the free, instinctive play of imagination within decision making.

Evaluation, to repeat, is at a watershed. At its grandest the evaluation project seems to face the task of keeping the flame of reason and rational progress alive. There is a pressing need to justify once again the original goal expounded by the evaluation pioneers, namely that it is possible to research and learn from social policies, programs and initiatives in order to modify and improve their effectiveness. Against this, we have to be mindful of the lessons of history and the sticky ends of some predecessors. Evaluation could go the way of shamanism; it could be a philosophical kingdom without a court; it could turn out to have the shelf life of the typical agony aunt; it could be heading for a fall.

This book seeks to wrestle with these giant conundrums. We seek positive answers and a positive future for evaluation. We do so via a call to arms for *realistic evaluation*. In these introductory remarks it is appropriate to give the reader an indication of some of our conclusions, saving the body of the work for their justification. The simplest key to our ambitions is to be found by unpicking our title. *Realistic* is a lovely compound word, plugging together the three lego-bricks of *real . . . realist . . . realistic*. In our view, these terms mark the key domains of evaluation.

First, evaluation deals with the *real*. Let us think of some examples which will detain us later. We believe that burglars are real, so are prisons, and so are the programs which seek to reduce burglary and rehabilitate prisoners, and so too are the successes or failures of such initiatives. We do not accept that such components of the criminal justice system take their meaning narratively according to the political rhetoric and legal discourse which surrounds the key players. In making such a claim, we do not suppose that the examples mentioned above correspond to some elemental, self-explanatory level of social reality which can be grasped, measured and evaluated in some self-evident way. The reality we seek to explore is stratified. All social programs involve the interplay of individual and institution, and of structure and agency. All social programs involve disagreement and power-play. No social program removes all disagreement and power-play. All social interaction creates interdependencies and these interdependencies develop into real-world customs and practices, which are often quite independent of how people would wish them to be. These emergent processes are the realities which social programs seek to change. These are the realities assumed in our approach, which always begins with an attempt to come to a *sociological* understanding of the balance of resources and choices available to all participants involved in a program.

Secondly, evaluation should follow a *realist* methodology. We do not shrink from promoting the goals of 'detachment' and 'objectivity' in evaluation, and therefore do not balk at the need to establish a scientific methodology for evaluation. Historically, alas, evaluation attempted to establish its scientific credentials when the philosophical orthodoxy about science ran along over-simple positivistic lines. This resulted in early evaluation employing a rather mechanical experimental format and emerging with a disappointing mixed bag of findings. Nowadays, the philosophy of science is avowedly post-empiricist and rests on a view of explanation which is not simply driven by 'method' and 'measurement', but which suggests a more extensive role for 'theory'. The most powerful advocates of the privileged, progressive nature of science are the *scientific realists*. We suggest that it is high time to reassert the need for scientific evaluation and to do so under the banner of realism.

Thirdly, evaluation, perhaps above all, needs to be *realistic*. The whole point is that it is a form of applied research, *not* performed for the benefit of science as such, but pursued in order to inform the thinking of policy makers, practitioners, program participants and public. To be sure, there is little point to evaluation if it fails to extend the knowledge of such stakeholders, but the goal of being 'realistic' should be regarded as a decree forbidding evaluators from hiding behind those secret, scientific languages in delivering their verdicts. The first step in achieving such a task is for evaluation to take on a perhaps uncharacteristic modesty. To be realistic is to acknowledge that there is no universal 'logic of evaluation', no absolute 'science of valuing', no general 'warranty for decision making' applicable to all judgements. It needs to be made clear that the 'evaluation community' is an overblown fiction and that we can no longer corral together the 'action researcher' and the 'auditor', the 'experimentalist' and the 'ethnographer', the 'product' and the 'program' evaluator, the 'management consultant' and the 'mathematical modeller'. Being realistic means trying to perfect a particular method of evaluation which will work for a specific class of project in well-circumscribed circumstances. In our particular case, this betokens an attempt to return evaluation to its roots in examining the effectiveness of particular social programs targeted at specific social problems. We seek to find a way of engaging rigorously in piecemeal social reform.

A reader's guide to *Realistic Evaluation*

What follows is a long methodological argument about how to conduct evaluation research. We know from long, long experience in trying to develop research practice that methodological positions can become 'badges of honour'. One can easily be misunderstood, debating positions tend to become foreclosed too early, and straw men and red herrings galore litter the path to progress. Having set out our objectives, at least in terms of the 'headlines' of being real, realist and realistic, we move on by trying to make our lines of argument absolutely clear by offering the reader a user's guide to its staging points. In producing this manifesto, we have addressed concerns which take us far beyond the esoteric preoccupations of 'methods' specialists and we make a point of having something to say to the old hands (evaluators, evaluation users, practitioners, policy makers) as well as the newcomers (would-be evaluators, undergraduate and graduate students). We begin by setting down our own agenda, chapter by chapter.

Chapter 1 presents a history of evaluation research in 28½ pages. Yes, of course, we are making a little ironic play with the title here, for evaluation research is now so extensive and diverse that it would take a very fat book indeed to tell the whole story. Our history will thus speed polemically from 'experimental evaluation' to 'pragmatic evaluation' to 'naturalistic evaluation' to present-day 'pluralistic evaluation', calling in momentarily at some of the more interesting waystations and visiting some of the 'black boxes' and 'black holes' which evaluators have sought to avoid. The resulting picture is something of a paradox. On the one hand, with diversity came the 'paradigm wars' and the multifarious attempts to besmear all rivals in order to promote one particular set of first principles as representing the true path of evaluation. More recently, perhaps, the assuaging tones of the pluralists have come to dominate, encouraging evaluation to sit happily on the methodological fault lines and to swell in terms of ambition, audience, and applications. For us, neither of these positions represents a happy ending and we close with dire warnings about jacks of all trades being masters of none.

Chapter 2 continues our critical line of inquiry with a much more in-depth examination of experimental evaluation. It is important to make clear our motives here, since the reader may anticipate a dose of anti-empiricism when, quite frankly, evaluation needs another round of positivism bashing like a hole in the head. Ours is a constructive critique, and thus more of an attempt at paradigm liberation than a paradigm war. The experimental tradition in evaluation was founded in terms of what we see as the entirely praiseworthy goals of being 'objective' in pursuing an incremental program of 'social engineering'. We join with many other critics in recognizing that these ambitions remain thwarted, largely because experimentalists have pursued too single-mindedly the question of whether a program works at the expense of knowing why it works. The purpose (and originality, we trust) of the chapter is thus to extricate, minutely and exhaustively, the missing explanatory ingredients of this tradition.

Chapter 3 identifies, at length and for the first time in the book, the trade we do wish to master, namely realistic evaluation. Realism has become an important perspective in modern philosophy and social science but has been conspicuous by its absence in evaluation methodology. The chapter seeks to show that it will become an important presence, because it attends precisely to those explanatory elements overlooked by the experimentalists. This is a foundational chapter. It will trace the beginnings of realism in the philosophy of science, showing how it generates an entirely novel account of the function of the experiment in natural science. We then examine how causation in the social world should be construed and derive the basic realist formula:

$$mechanism + context = outcome$$

These terms form the conceptual backbone to realistic evaluation and drive all further arguments in the book. The chapter ends by demonstrating how the language of outcomes, mechanisms, and contexts can give us an initial explanatory 'fix' on any social program.

Chapter 4 begins the 'how to' section of the book. Here we tackle the issue of putting realist principles into practice, beginning with the notion of a realist research design. Design is the great act of imagination in methodology. Nowhere more than in this act of 'thinking through' the entire research process do we crystallize our thoughts on the basic rules of social explanation. The chapter will work through several realist designs using examples from evaluations in the criminal justice area. The examples are drawn from designs we ourselves have employed and from the previous work of other researchers which we feel has been implicitly or prototypically realist. The case studies are chosen to span the full panoply of social science strategies and methods, utilizing techniques qualitative and quantitative, contemporaneous and retroactive, active and passive. The point is that realist research design employs no one standard 'formula', other than the base strategy of producing a clear theory of program mechanisms, contexts and outcomes, and then using them to design the appropriate empirical measures and comparisons.

The common thread running through the designs is to produce ever more detailed answers to the question of *why* a program works for *whom* and in *what* circumstances.

Chapter 5 considers the potential for gaining transferable lessons from the findings of evaluation research. In particular, we wish to consider how evaluation might achieve an accumulation of results and a convergence of understanding with respect to a particular class of programs. This is perhaps the supreme challenge facing the evaluation community. Approaches that focus on program outcomes, and seek cumulation via 'replication' or 'meta-evaluation', are prone to disappoint, and tend typically to report inconsistency of outcomes across different initiatives. Other approaches which concentrate on the inner workings of programs are prone to dwell on the immediate ambitions of particular stakeholders, and often tend to celebrate the uniqueness of the situations studied. Scientific realism offers more hopeful messages since it starts with a fresh conception of the nature of cumulation in evaluation studies. Progress emerges through a process of theory building and theory testing. Such a process can be put in place on a planned basis through a programmed sequence of iterated evaluations which call systematically upon bodies of more abstract social science theory as well as the findings of other forms of empirical research. The process is illustrated through the success story of UK research on 'repeat victimization'.

Chapter 6 wades into further controversial waters in producing a realist account of the 'research relationship' between evaluator and stakeholder. At stake here is the practical issue of how to utilize the knowledge of program practitioners and participants in conducting an evaluation. Data collection is another feature of research on which the evaluation tribes most instinctively divide. Thus we have one camp aspiring to precise before-and-after measurement of program subjects in closely controlled conditions, and another camp seeking empathetic understanding of program participants by sharing in their own natural settings. We spurn these as choices because what is under test in realist evaluation are theories of how programs work. In distinguishing the different mechanisms, contexts and outcomes operating within programs, these theories will identify different groups of practitioners and subjects, who play quite different roles in the routine performance of the program. Knowledge of how the program works will thus differ from participant to participant, and indeed between researcher and subjects. The matter of 'what to ask the subject?' and 'how to ask them?' is thus a matter of a division of expertise. Realism generates clear expectations about the balance of expertise within programs and thus generates a new theory-driven account of data collection.

Chapter 7 is an (entirely free) realistic evaluation consultation. Its function is to broaden the substantive base of the book. By this stage we have argued that the realistic approach can reach every corner of evaluation methodology from design to data collection to analysis to cumulation.

For consistency's sake, we have used the same body of programs about policing and prisons in pursuing and illustrating the argument. We also believe that realistic evaluation can reach every corner of the programming and policy field. This chapter is thus designed to demonstrate the utility of the approach to an entirely different example – smoking cessation programs. The chapter is written in the form of an imaginary dialogue between a policy maker and her assistant (who are keen to implement a new program to reduce smoking but sorely perplexed as to the implications of current research) and an evaluation consultant (whose views we admire).

Chapter 8 turns to realistic evaluation, policy making and the policy maker. It argues that in order to conduct a realistic evaluation, researchers must learn the policy maker's overall theories of how the program will yield specific benefits, as well as maybe unwanted effects, in the contexts in which it is being introduced. Findings about the program theory – including confirmation, refutation or more often refinement to the theory – can then be fed back to the policy maker, who can adjust existing programs or devise new ones accordingly. The chapter goes on to formulate a model of the teaching and learning process between the evaluator and the program as a whole. This includes not only the policy maker but also the practitioner and the participants. We argue that this culminates in a process of program 'realization', by which we mean a growing understanding of how programs may accomplish objectives by actualizing causal potentials.

Chapter 9 is a summary of the case for *realistic evaluation*.

1
A HISTORY OF EVALUATION IN 28½ PAGES

Where we stand

Our brief history of evaluation research begins at the end with an instant observation on the here and now. A metaphor comes to mind. Evaluation is still a young discipline. It has grown massively in recent years. There can be no doubt about it – evaluation is a vast, lumbering, overgrown adolescent. It has the typical problems associated with this age group too. It does not know quite where it is going and it is prone to bouts of despair. But it is the future after all, so it is well worth beginning our evaluation journey by trying to get to the bottom of this obesity and angst.

The enterprise of evaluation is a perfect example of what Kaplan (1964) once called the 'law of the hammer'. Its premise is that if you give a child a hammer then he or she will soon discover the universal truth that *everything needs pounding*. In a similar manner, it has become axiomatic as we move towards the millennium that *everything, but everything, needs evaluating*. The nature of surveillance in post-industrial society has changed. The army of evaluators continues to grow. Instead of hands-on-the-shoulder control from the centre, the modern bureaucracy is managed by opening its every activity to 'review', 'appraisal', 'audit', 'quality assurance', 'performance rating' and indeed 'evaluation'. These activities can take on a plethora of different forms including 'self-appraisal' and 'peer appraisal', 'developmental reviews', the creation of 'management information systems', scrutiny by outside 'expert consultants', 'total quality management' and indeed formal, social scientific 'evaluation research'. The monitoring and evaluation process touches us all.

This sense of exponential growth and widening diversity is deepened if one examines change in the academic literature on evaluation. Once upon a time, the evaluation researcher needed only the 'Bible' ('Old Testament', Campbell and Stanley, 1963; 'New Testament', Cook and Campbell, 1979) to look up an appropriate research design and, hey presto, be out into the field. Nowadays, tyro investigators have to burrow their way through 'Sage' advice on 'summative evaluation', 'formative evaluation', 'cost-free evaluation', 'goal-free evaluation', 'functional evaluation', 'tailored evaluation', 'comprehensive evaluation', 'theory-driven evaluation', 'stakeholder-based evaluation', 'naturalistic evaluation', 'utilization-focused evaluation', 'pre-ordinate evaluation', 'responsive evaluation', and finally 'meta-evaluation' before they even get their hands on a social program. Worse still, adopting one of these approaches often means taking sides in the 'paradigm wars'. Whilst much of the rest of social science has attempted to transcend the positivism versus phenomenology debates (Bryman, 1988), evaluation research is still developing its own fundamentalist sects, which are prone to make declarations of the type: first-, second- and third-wave evaluation is dead . . . long live fourth-generation evaluation (Guba and Lincoln, 1989)!

The sense of bewilderment grows when one considers what it is that evaluators actually seek to evaluate. In the beginning (the 1960s), 'evaluation research' referred to the appraisal of the great social programs of the 'great society' (the US). In this period, the cost of social welfare soared through the roof (Bell, 1983) and financial, managerial, professional and academic interest groups conspired to follow. Thus what began as 'social research' into specific corrections and educational policies soon became an 'evaluation movement' which swept through the entire spectrum of social sectors (Shadish et al., 1991). Even when federal funding fell, activity levels were more than compensated for as it became appreciated that one could go down the scale and down the ranks and 'evaluate' any function of any functionary. Such a history has repeated itself elsewhere, cumulating with the UK, European, and Australian Evaluation Societies being founded in quick succession in 1994–1995. The ultimate step of 'having to face up to the process of globalisation' (Stern, 1995) has been taken with the publication of the first 'international' *Evaluation* journal and a conference in Vancouver billed grandly as the 'first evaluation summit'.

We can thus say, without too much hyperbole, that 'evaluation' has become a mantra of modernity. Ambition is further fuelled by gurus like Scriven who, in describing the scope of what can be evaluated, declares, 'Everything. One can begin at the beginning of a dictionary and go through to the end, and every noun, common or proper, calls to mind a context in which evaluation would be appropriate' (1980, p. 4). Here then lies a danger for anyone intent on refining the practice of evaluation (as we are): the term now carries so much baggage that one is in danger of dealing not so much with a methodology as with an incantation.

A corollary of believing oneself to be a jack of all trades is that one often ends up as a master of none. This brings us to the second of our initial observations, to the effect that evaluation research has not exactly lived up to its promise: its stock is not high. The initial expectation was clearly of a great society made greater by dint of research-driven policy making. Since all policies were capable of evaluation, those which failed could be weeded out, and those which worked could be further refined as part of an ongoing, progressive research program. This is a brave scenario which (to put it kindly) has failed to come to pass.

Such a remark is, of course, an evaluation. We have reached 'e' in

Scrivèn's alphabet of nouns and seem to have found ourselves engaged in an instant evaluation of evaluation. We hope to persuade readers of the merits of a rather more scholarly approach to our topic in the course of the book. For now, we rest content with a little burst of punditry by casting our net around some of the recent overviews of the findings on community policing, 'progressive' primary teaching and health education (smoking prevention) programs:

> The question is, is it [community policing] more than rhetoric? Above I have documented that community policing is proceeding at a halting pace. There are ample examples of failed experiments, and huge American cities where the whole concept has gone awry. On the other hand, there is evidence in many evaluations that a public hungry for attention has a great deal to tell the police and are grateful for the opportunity to do so. (Skogan, 1992)

> There are a number of studies that have investigated the relationship between teaching style and pupil progress . . . Most of the severe methodological problems that arose with research on teaching styles, for example surrounding the operationalisation of concepts and the establishment of causal effects . . . have not yet been satisfactorily resolved. This means that we should treat with great caution claims made about the effects of particular teaching strategies on pupils' progress. (Hammersley and Scarth, 1993)

> In recent years, we have seen a number of well-conducted, large-scale trials involving entire communities and enormous effort. These trials have tested the capacity of public health interventions to change various forms of behavior, most often to ward off risks of cardiovascular disease. Although a few have had a degree of success, several have ended in disappointment. Generally the size of effects has been meagre in relation to the effort expended. (Susser, 1995)

A sense of disappointment is etched on all of these quotations. Self-evidently, there is still a problem in distinguishing between program failure and program success in even these stock-in-trade areas of policy making. This state of affairs naturally leads to a sense of impotence when it comes to influencing real decision making, a sense which has come to pervade the writings of even the great and the good in the world of professional evaluation:

> We are often disappointed. After all the *Sturm und Drang* of running an evaluation, and analysing and reporting its results, we do not see much notice taken of it. Things usually seem to go along much as they would have gone if the evaluation had never been done. What is going wrong here? And what can we do about it? (Weiss, 1990, p. 171)

Clearly any body of knowledge which is capable of producing such a cry for help is capable of being *ignored* and this perhaps is the ultimate ignominy for the evaluator. Perhaps the best example of such disregard that we can bring to mind is the pronouncement of the present UK Home Secretary when he declared, a couple of years back, that 'Prisons Work'. Now, political slogans uttered in the context of party conferences are normally regarded as no more than part of the rolling rhetoric of 'crusades

against criminals', 'crackdowns on crime' and the like. This pronouncement was particularly hurtful, however, because it deliberately used the
'w' word and thus trod directly upon the territory of the evaluation
researchers whose *raison d'être* is to discover whether and to what extent
programs *work*. Mr Howard's instincts in these matters did not rely on the
bedrock of empirical evidence produced by the ranks of criminologists,
penologists and evaluators at his disposal. Instead, he figured that armed
robbers, muggers, rapists, and so on, safely locked away, cannot therefore
be at liberty to pursue their deeds. What we have here then is policy
making on the basis of a tautology (and one, moreover, involving rather
interesting implications for prison overcrowding). *The research is nowhere to
be seen.* Whilst this is beginning to sound like a cheap jibe at the expense of
the politician, it is in fact part of the 'dismal vision' (Patton, 1990) that
periodically grips the evaluation community. So whilst the view that 'prisons work' through incapacitation glides over several decades of hard data
on reconviction rates, it is much more difficult to make the case that a
policy of incarceration is opposed by secure, consistent and telling evaluations on 'alternatives to custody'.

So there we have it – the paradoxical predicament of present-day evaluation. On the one hand we have seen an elastic, burgeoning presence
stretching its way around the A to Z of human institutions. On the other,
we have seen lack-lustre research, a lack of cumulation of results and a lack
of a voice in policy making. Picture again our obese, recumbent adolescent.
The world lies at his feet (for some reason we cannot help seeing the male
of the species). Resources are waiting. Expectations are high. But he is still
not quite sure how to get off that couch.

How has this come to pass? A full answer to our own question would
have us delve into the organization, professionalization, politics, psychology and sociology of the evaluation movement. In the remaining pages
here, we commit ourselves only to a history of evaluation research from the
point of view of methodological change. We identify four main perspectives on evaluation, namely *the experimental, the pragmatic, the naturalistic*
and *the pluralist*. An outline and critique of each is provided in turn, allowing us to end the review with some important pointers to the future. We
begin at the beginning in the age of certainty.

Go forth and experiment

Underlying everything in the early days was the *logic of experimentation*. Its
basic framework is desperately simple and disarmingly familiar to us all.
Take two more or less matched groups (if they are really matched through
random allocation, you call it real experimentation; quasi-experimentation follows from the impracticality of this in many cases). Treat one group
and not the other. Measure both groups before and after the treatment of

the one. Compare the changes in the treated and untreated groups, and lo and behold, you have a clear measure of the impact of the program. The practitioner, policy adviser, and social scientist are at one in appreciating the beauty of the design. At one level it has the deepest roots in philosophical discourse on the nature of explanation, as in John Stuart Mill's *A System of Logic* (1961); at another it is the hallmark of common sense, ingrained into advertising campaigns telling us that Washo is superior to Sudz. The basic design (untreated control group with pre-test and post-test, which is discussed in detail in Chapter 2) is set down as Figure 1.1 using Campbell's classic *OXO* notation (Campbell and Stanley, 1963).

	Pre-test	Treatment	Post-test
Experimental group	O_1	X	O_2
Control group	O_1		O_2

Figure 1.1　*The classic experimental design*

The sheet anchor of the method is thus a *theory of causation*. Since the experimental and control groups are identical to begin with, the only difference between them is the application of the program and it is, therefore, only the program which can be responsible for the outcomes. On this simple and elegant basis was constructed the whole edifice of experimental and quasi-experimental evaluation. This way of thinking about causality is known in the epistemological literature as a 'successionist' or 'molar' understanding of causality. The basic idea is that one cannot observe 'causation' in the way one observes teaching schemes and changes in reading standards, or burglar alarms and changes in crime rates. Causation between treatment and outcome has to be *inferred* from the repeated succession of one such event by another. The point of the method, therefore, is to attempt to exclude every conceivable rival causal agent from the experiment so that we are left with one, secure causal link.

At this juncture experimentalists acknowledge a fundamental distinction between their work in the laboratory and in the field. A simple ontological distinction is drawn which regards the social world as inherently 'complex', 'open', 'dynamic' and so forth. This renders the clear-cut 'program causes outcome' conclusion much more problematic in the messy world of field experiments. Additional safeguards thus have to be called up to protect the 'internal validity' of causal inferences in such situations. For instance, there is the problem of 'history', where during the application of the program an unexpected event happens which is not part of the intended treatment but which could be responsible for the outcome. An example might be the comparisons of localities with and without neighbourhood watch schemes, during which police activity suddenly increases in one in response to some local policy directive. The neat experimental comparison is thus broken and needs to be supplemented with additional monitoring and statistical controls in order that we can be sure the scheme rather than the increased patrols is the vital causal agent. Such an example can be thought of as a shorthand for the development of the entire quasi-experimental method. The whole point is to wrestle with the design and analysis of field experimentation to achieve sufficient *control* to make the basic causal inference secure.

Following these principles of method comes a theory of *policy implementation*. In Campbell's case we can properly call this a 'vision' of the *experimenting society* – a standpoint which is best summed up in the famous opening passage from his 'Reforms as experiments' (1969):

> The United States and other modern nations should be ready for an experimental approach to social reform, an approach in which we try out new programs designed to cure specific social problems, in which we learn whether or not these programs are effective, and in which we retain, imitate, modify or discard them on the basis of their apparent effectiveness on the multiple imperfect criteria available.

What we have here, then, is a clear-cut Popperian (1945) view of the open society, always at the ready to engage in piecemeal social engineering, and to do so on the basis of cold, rational calculations which evaluate bold initiatives.

This then was the unashamedly scientific and rational inspiration brought to bear in the first-wave studies such as the Sesame Street (Bogatz and Ball, 1971) and New Jersey Negative Income Tax experiments (Rossi and Lyall, 1978). These are worthy of a brief description, if only to give an indication of the *nature* of the initiatives under test. The background to the first was the then radical notion referred to in the States as 'Head Start', which we tend to think of more prosaically in the UK as 'pre-schooling'. The guiding notion, which educationalists are very fond of telling us, is that there is far more cognitive change going on in our little brains between the ages of two and five than at any other interval throughout the life span, and that if we want to reduce social disparity through education, we have to 'get in there quickly before the rot sets in'. One of the fruits of this notion was the production of a series of educational television programs designed for this age group, which many readers will have doubtless seen and will remember as being very serious about their playful approach to learning. The second example stands as the heavyweight champion, costing $8,000,000 (at 1968 prices) and which itself spawned a variety of replication studies. The core policy under scrutiny was another radical idea, involving scrapping the benefit and social security system and then

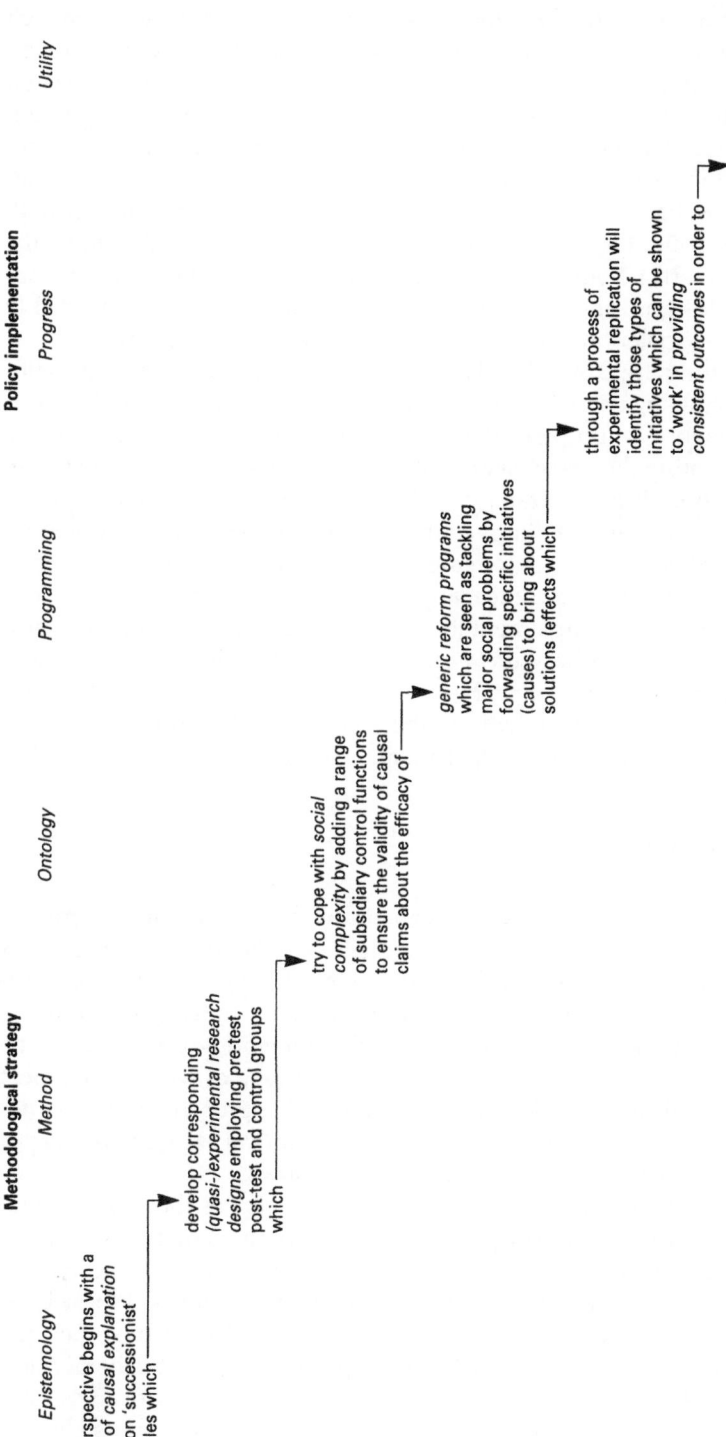

Methodological strategy

| Epistemology | Method | Ontology | Programming | Progress | Utility |

Epistemology

The perspective begins with a theory of *causal explanation* based on 'successionist' principles which

Method

develop corresponding *(quasi-)experimental research designs* employing pre-test, post-test and control groups which

Ontology

try to cope with *social complexity* by adding a range of subsidiary control functions to ensure the validity of causal claims about the efficacy of

Programming

generic reform programs which are seen as tackling major social problems by forwarding specific initiatives (causes) to bring about solutions (effects which

Policy implementation

Progress

through a process of experimental replication will identify those types of initiatives which can be shown to 'work' in *providing consistent outcomes* in order to

Utility

inform the policy making process which is a matter of coming to *rational choices* amongst potential policy reforms on the basis of hard data from successful programs

Figure 1.2   *An overview of experimental evaluation*

enlarging the role of the taxation system so that when family income fell below a certain level the 'tax' went the other way. The design involved comparing a control group under the standard tax/benefit regime with eight experimental groups which experienced a different balance of 'guaranteed incomes'. Under test was the notion that 'taxation rates' and 'safety nets' were the very basis of the family economy, and changing them might affect a whole battery of moral, attitudinal and behavioural variables. Both evaluations sought to address core issues of social policy and change (the 'war' on poverty), both were put in place using expensive, complex randomized designs and, in the case of the latter, some remarkably imaginative legislation was needed to allow the trials to take place.

We can summarize our already brief description of experimental evaluation by extracting its main ingredients in Figure 1.2. Since we will use this same framework to compare all the various schools of evaluation research, it is worth noting the key elements. We make a broad distinction between (a) the methodological strategy and (b) the assumptions about policy implementation which are implicit in a research program. Methodology is further subdivided in order to tease out the basic tenets on the nature of explanation, on the key technical apparatus, and on the make-up of social reality. Under policy implementation, we list the essentials on what programs seek to do, on how they get refined, and on how knowledge of them feeds into policy making. Figure 1.2 is actually just one (rather long) sentence. The idea is to show how the whole model is infused with the search for causation through experimental control.

But does it work?

For us, the experimental paradigm constitutes a heroic failure, promising so much and yet ending up in ironic anticlimax. The underlying logic (as above) seems meticulous, clear-headed and militarily precise, and yet findings seem to emerge in a typically non-cumulative, low-impact, prone-to-equivocation sort of way. We will be devoting the whole of the next chapter to explaining this paradox in a critique of some of the most advanced applications of the quasi-experimental approach. In this chapter we will satisfy ourselves with describing the historical record in terms of a couple of the most significant shots across the bows.

This first wound is in fact self-inflicted, in as much as the experimental approach has always been gripped by anxiety about its own track record. To pick up again our tale about the Sesame Street and Negative Income Tax experiments, it is interesting to note that secondary accounts of these have mushroomed (Cook et al., 1975; Nathan, 1989) and they have become almost as legendary as the Hawthorne experiments (Roethlisberger and Dickson, 1939) in terms of tales of 'what really went on'. Historically speaking, however, these difficulties resemble only preliminary tremors; the real 'quake occurred with the publication of Martinson's 'What works? Questions and answers about prison reform' (1974).

Martinson's paper is the most cited in the history of evaluation research. Such pre-eminence should serve as a warning for any true believers in academic performance indicators, however, for the paper is more or less universally derided. Indeed, as is commonly known, even Martinson (1979) eventually turned his back on his original paper with its seemingly bleak 'nothing works' conclusion. It is well worth raking over these old coals once again because the great debate around 'what, if anything, works?' reveals a great deal about how evaluation research has come to understand the *nature* of program efficacy.

Martinson's (1974) paper is a summary of a 1,400 page manuscript which itself was a summary of *all* published reports in English on attempts at the rehabilitation of offenders from 1945 to 1967. These programs are sorted into a series of broad 'treatments', so that Martinson reviews, in turn, educational and vocational training, individual counselling, milieu therapy, drug and surgical treatment, sentence variation, decarceration, community psychotherapy, probation and parole, and intensive supervision. Curiously, he never uttered the verdict 'nothing works' directly in the whole paper, yet he managed to flatten the aspirations of reformers in fields way beyond his own with these words:

> I am bound to say that these data, involving over two hundred studies and hundreds of thousands of individuals as they do, are the best available and give us very little reason to hope that we have in fact found a sure way of reducing recidivism through rehabilitation. This is not to say that we have found no instances of success or partial success; it is only to say that these instances have been isolated, producing no clear pattern to indicate the efficacy of any particular method of treatment. (1974, p. 49)

Reading Martinson's paper (or indeed this very passage) from the point of view of the rhetorical practices involved, we can say that *it works* through the construction of an impossibly stringent criterion for 'success'. To count as a body of treatment that 'works', such programs have to provide positive changes in favour of the experimental group in all trials in all contexts. He is thus able to discount successful experiments by dint of them being 'isolated' and thus producing an 'inconsistent' pattern of outcomes.

Thanks to this loaded logic Martinson managed to throw a spanner in the works of evaluation which has rattled around ever since. He certainly hit the spot in terms of political reaction, for indeed, in the 1970s, 'reaction' was growing. The merest possibility that 'nothing works' was just the spur needed for a backlash demanding 'retribution' and 'just deserts' as the proper engines of criminal justice, a clamour which students of the political ebb and flow report as lasting comfortably into the 1980s (Nuttall, 1992).

Although overshadowed politically, the 'mainstream' evaluation community never took Martinson's pessimism seriously. Palmer (1975) 'revisited' Martinson's study in the year following its publication and pointed to the skulduggery involved in bundling programs into broad treatment groups which would inevitably show mixed results. Palmer observes that, if programs are taken on an individual basis, Martinson details and actually uses the term 'success' to describe dozens of conditional positive achievements in which certain portions of programs had worked for a portion of their clientele. Following the same example through, we note that 'revivification' of faith in rehabilitation was symbolized with the publication of two massive, Martinson-like overviews of corrections programs (Ross and Gendreau, 1980; Gendreau and Ross, 1987). On the basis of fresher but much the same types of evidence as that surveyed by their gloomy predecessor, they opined (hopefully) to the effect that *most things have been found sometimes to work.*

What was at issue through these decades was a debate about weight of evidence, about the level of empirical support necessary before one can recommend with some certainty that a particular program works. What is being assumed, therefore, is a sort of *counting model of efficacy.* In the end we shall know what works according to the drip, drip, drip of empirical evidence, and in many ways the original debate was about whether the bottle was half full (Gendreau and Ross, Palmer) *or* was half empty (Martinson). Most decidedly *not* at issue in this debate was the ability of the experimental approach to evaluate each individual study or even its capacity to bring home (eventually) the weight of evidence needed to sustain policy making. Martinson (1974) did not even consider studies worthy for inclusion in his meta-analysis unless they carried 'true comparability between the treated and untreated groups'. A decade or so later, Gendreau and Ross (1987) erected a similar methodological barrier and thus reviewed only inquiries with 'post-treatment follow up with central group comparison'.

What came out of the furore, in short, was the oldest yarn in academe: *more research is needed.* Keep faith with the experimental approach, and eventually outcome patterns will become clearer and, in time, predictive ability will grow. So the story developed. Writing, as we are, 30 years on from the opening blows of the 'what works?' debate, we are privileged to be in a position to apply a bit of hindsight to this point of consensus, to this prediction that inconsistency would be eventually eradicated. In fact we have already delivered the verdict in our earlier triplet of quotations: the bottle is still half empty / full. In three decades we have lumbered on from 'inconsistency is bad', to 'inconsistency is (partly) good', to 'inconsistency is ubiquitous.'

Palmer cocks the gun for our second blast at the experimental approach, in his recommendation, following his review of Martinson, that:

> Rather than ask 'What works for offenders as a whole?' we must increasingly ask, 'Which methods work best for which types of offenders and under what conditions or in what types of settings? (1975, p. 150)

Reviewing a rather different literature, Rosenbaum makes a remarkably similar point when he says in relation to crime prevention:

> [There is] a compelling need to open up the black box ... and test the many presumed causal links in our theoretical models. We are past the point of wanting to report that crime prevention does or does not work, and now are interested in specifying the conditions under which particular outcomes are observed.' (1988, p. 382)

These are indeed words of wisdom for evaluators and we shall spend much of this book trying to throw light into the black box. Festering away in both these challenges is the dilemma that experimental evaluation might be incapable of asking the right question. The aim of *OXO* outcome investigation is to achieve sufficient control to tell us in any particular trial whether an initiative has 'worked' or not. To understand why there is inconsistency of outcomes we need to ask the rather different question of 'why' or 'how' the measure has its effect. We need a method which seeks to understand what the program actually does to change behaviours and why not every situation is conducive to that particular process.

The impatience represented by these quotations left a lingering doubt in the evaluation community as to whether there was any room within constant conjunction logic and the apparatus of experimentation for these deeper explanatory functions. We have no such hesitations about the limits of that method, which we will explore further in Chapter 2. For the moment, we need to go back to the history and describe some of the alternative futures to evaluation which have been espoused, responding in their different ways to the lack of progress documented to this point. In outlining these byways, we basically draw a US map. In the UK, until very recently, there has been significantly less movement from the quasi-experimental orthodoxy. In America, by contrast, they 'love a good paradigm debate' (Patton, 1990, p. 205), and so in Kuhnian mode we now travel back to inspect the practical turn.

Enter politics

We are still awaiting the experimenting society, with (quasi-) experimental evaluation proving slow and cautionary, and constant in one thing only: its call for *more time*. This state of affairs led many in the evaluation movement to question whether the experimental approach constituted part of the problem rather than providing the solution to making sound policy decisions. The consequence was a powerful call, which began alongside but independently of the 'nothing works' episode, and which demanded that evaluators stop being naive about the organizational and political contexts in which all policy making takes place.

This political 'bottom line' to evaluation can be expressed in two ways. The first is to acknowledge that the very act of engaging in evaluation constitutes a political statement. By and large, evaluation research is *reformist*; its basic goal is to develop initiatives which help to solve 'social problems'. Social problems get the inverted commas treatment here, of course, since views of what constitutes such problems are politically coloured. As we have seen, an interest in evaluating 'prison reform' will evaporate if criminality rather than rehabilitation is seen as the problem. Likewise the substance of, or even the need for, AIDS prevention programs will vary according to whether it is conceived of as a 'gay plague' or another sexually transmitted disease.

Evaluations are also patently *petty political*. That is to say, they tend to treat certain social/historical/political configurations as given, and the ambitions of the programs which get evaluated are directed at 'reducing' problems within 'systems' or ensuring the better operation of those systems. Thus 'corrections' evaluations involve themselves with 'treatments' rather than a radical agenda on decarceration. AIDS prevention evaluations involve themselves with condom awareness rather than questioning the cultural or moral basis of sexual activity.

We utter no secrets here. Most evaluators and most practitioners know full well that the programs in which they are involved are engaged in reform of a not too radical kind. They do not suppose that poverty, inequality, injustice, ill-health are going to be eliminated by a few programs. They do not suppose that they can do anything to change fundamentally the cultural and community roots which give rise to social disadvantage. The practical turn, then, turned not so much on the discovery of politics amidst programs, but on the idea that *research ought to be constructed so that it is better able to be used in the actual processes of policy making*. The various writings of Weiss (1976; 1987) embody the change from a knowledge-driven to a use-led model of research. Some of her wisest words on matters such as 'decision accretion', 'issue networks' and 'truth tests' have become the standard vocabulary to describe the policy making process.

Thus she argues that policies are not made at a single point in time according to whether they 'work' or not. Rather there are gradual accretions, with one choice after another being made, which narrow policy options so that rationality gives way to fear of the political U-turn (Weiss, 1976). Politicians don't read research. Members of the House of Representatives spend about eleven minutes a day reading (Weiss, 1987). They rely for the exchange of new ideas on networks comprising lobbyists, agencies, consultants, think-tanks, correspondents and perhaps the odd academic. Accordingly, research functions not as a valid, tested, body of propositions based on causal logic, but as ammunition for debate and intraorganizational arguments (Weiss, 1980).

Readers new to all this should not be carried away with the scepticism. Social science is not reduced to the role of producing little soundbite-sized factoids for the press release – 'my independent statisticians' report bla bla bla'. Rather Weiss's reading of the evaluation/policy interface leads her to the famous 'enlightenment' or 'knowledge creep' theory of the role of evaluation research:

> As the decision makers whom we interview reported, a much more common mode of research use is the diffuse and undirected infiltration of research ideas into their understanding of the world. They reported few deliberate and targeted uses of the findings from individual studies. Rather, they absorbed the concepts and generalizations from many studies over extended periods of time and they integrated research ideas, along with other information, into their interpretation of events. This gradual sensitization to the perspectives of social science, they believe, has important consequences. (Weiss and Bucuvalas, 1980)

Weiss's observations here concern capital P 'Politics' and 'Policy Making'. The sentiments, though, were widely influential and passed into the hands of evaluators charged with researching much more localized initiatives. Eventually the utilization-focused approach became *canonized* as a fully fledged alternative to the 'traditional paradigms'. The new foundations are most memorably espoused by Stufflebeam in summarizing the 'standards' published by the US Joint Committee on Standards for Educational Evaluation:

> The standards . . . call for evaluations that have four features. These are *utility, feasibility, propriety* and *accuracy*. And I think it is interesting that the Joint Committee decided on that particular order. Their rationale is that an evaluation should not be done at all if there is no prospect for its being useful to some audience. Second, it should not be done if it is not feasible to conduct it in political terms, or practicality terms, or cost effectiveness terms. Third, they do not think it should be done if we cannot demonstrate that it will be conducted fairly and ethically. Finally, if we can demonstrate that an evaluation will have utility, will be feasible and will be proper in its conduct then they said we could turn to the difficult matters of the technical adequacy of the evaluation, and they have included an extensive set of standards in this area. (1980, p. 90)

This quotation gives us the foundation for our diagrammatic summary of pragmatic evaluation. Ideas on the nature of policy making are washed through to give the goal of 'technical adequacy' to method. This phrase is most instructive for it gets us right to the heart of the feet-on-the-ground view of methodology which characterizes this perspective. Patton's (1978; 1980; 1982) writings are pragmatism incarnate in their presentation of research method in the classic 'toolbox' manner. Evaluation research is a collection of standard research tasks (sampling, interviews, questionnaires, data analysis, etc.) which are best learned through exemplars (such as confessional tales from his own research) and which depend for their success on the application of sheer craft (every page intones the needs for 'skill', 'sensitivity', 'discipline', 'clarity', 'creativity', 'competence', 'care', etc.). Patton is not prone to fretting about the ultimate truths that will emerge from such craftwork. For him the real test bed is not the following of certain epistemological axioms but the matter of whether the practical cause of policy making is forwarded. Although others have railed against 'foundationalism' and 'methodolatry' in social science (Bell and Newby, 1977), nowhere will one see such an extreme reduction of research to the form of a 'style book'.

Figure 1.3 brings the whole model together. Pragmatic evaluation is cast upon the same set of features as in our original model but one can see at a glance that the flow of knowledge is deemed to work in basically the opposite direction from that depicted by the experimentalists. The exception of course is the all-important feedback loop of 'enlightenment'.

Exit veracity

A historian of ideas, here, would be alert to one of those typical lurches between *foundationalism* and *pragmatism* which have characterized the development of the social sciences. Campbell and colleagues founded evaluation on an epistemology. The experimental method and the view of policy formation rested on certain rules deemed to be axiomatic in the production of valid (causal) explanations. Utilization-focused evaluation, by contrast, is focused (naturally enough) on ends rather than rules, and in reading its literature (we can promise) one has a much harder time in deciphering 'how to do it' and 'why to do so' in ways which are consistent with the stress on utility. As Shadish et al. (1991, p. 205) report, Weiss's own position on research strategy is hard to pin down. She starts with a preference for experimental and quasi-experimental method (Weiss, 1972). Latterly she becomes a pluralist, accepting diverse methods including the 'experiment, survey, historical case study, observation or whatever', but more and more tends towards the methodological empty generalization and ultimately, like Patton, just counsels 'careful and sound research' (Weiss, 1981). Perhaps this is not so surprising: if any of us were entrusted with the task of providing *enlightenment*, then we too might lack certainty about how to make the first step.

The most critical issue for utilization-focused evaluation is whether 'he who pays the researcher calls the methodological tune.' Ever since the term 'pragmatism' was first coined by C. S. Peirce (1931), its notion of the 'truth' (ideas which promote satisfactory relations with other parts of our experience) has been assailed as obscurantist and relativistic. In the last analysis, it rests on a theory of the social acceptability of ideas, rather than on their 'correctness'. Our view is that once researchers abdicate the claim for privileged knowledge based upon their methodological strategy, then someone else will claim the warrant for them. We speak from the heart here since the usurpation of the criteria for knowledge is happening in the UK as we speak:

> The main principle governing any Government funding of R&D is the Rothschild principle, laid down in Cmd 4814 and reiterated in the White Paper 'Realising Our Potential: A Strategy for Science, Engineering and Technology': *'the customer says what he wants, the contractor does it, if he can, and the customer pays'*. (Department of Health, Code of Practice, 1993, our italics)

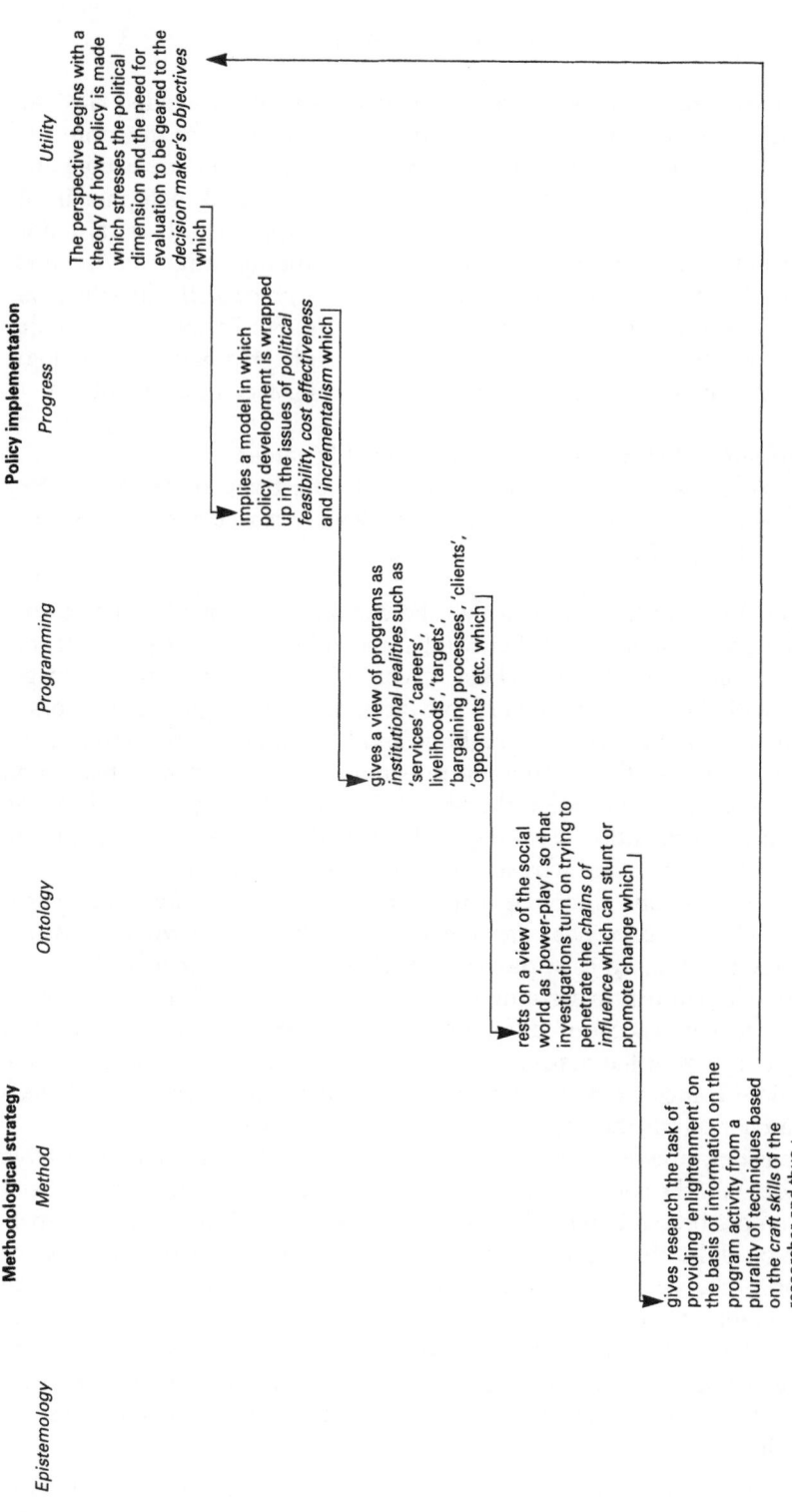

Methodological strategy

Epistemology　　*Method*　　*Ontology*　　*Programming*

Policy implementation

Progress　　*Utility*

regards as valid that knowledge which is *pragmatically acceptable* since it falls into the prevailing framework in which the policy is set

gives research the task of providing 'enlightenment' on the basis of information on the program activity from a plurality of techniques based on the *craft skills* of the researcher and thus

rests on a view of the social world as 'power-play', so that investigations turn on trying to penetrate the *chains of influence* which can stunt or promote change which

gives a view of programs as *institutional realities* such as 'services', 'careers', 'livelihoods', 'targets', 'bargaining processes', 'clients', 'opponents', etc. which

implies a model in which policy development is wrapped up in the issues of *political feasibility, cost effectiveness and incrementalism* which

The perspective begins with a theory of how policy is made which stresses the political dimension and the need for evaluation to be geared to the *decision maker's objectives* which

Figure 1.3　*An overview of pragmatic evaluation*

Our unease about the potential tension between 'technical adequacy' and 'crowd pleasing' deepens further with a closer reading of the aforementioned doyen of the user-friendly school of evaluation. Patton is the Lewis Carroll of evaluators, and uses every analogy, tale and metaphor in the book in order to promote a more skilful approach to evaluation. Anticipating our worry that user-driven evaluation might be methodologically rootless, he booms (in italics), *'the prerequisite for situational responsiveness is a firm grounding in fundamentals.'* For Patton, however, this does not refer to the platform provided by epistemology and ontology; rather he invokes the spirit of artistic or sporting accomplishment:

Sportswriter: How are you preparing for the big game?

Coach: The way we prepare for every game, by practising fundamentals. If we execute the way I know we can, and avoid mistakes and injuries, we'll win. (1982, p. 20)

Despite his erudition, we fear that there is one old adage that he has not come upon, namely Sir Walter Scott's 'metaphors are no arguments, my pretty maiden.' (1842) So, whilst it would be very nice if we could get away with the incorporation of some fundamentally English metaphors in evaluation training (bowl a good line and length, play with a straight bat etc.) we suppose that matters of research design and data construction need to be rooted in a very clear-headed understanding of social change and social explanation. Evoking 'skill' in method is never enough; it can never tell us when and why to utilize a particular approach.

Let us make absolutely clear the nature of this little offensive against Patton's line, since he has pushed hardest with the 'it ain't what you do it's the way that you do it' approach to evaluation. His instincts are those of the classic pluralist in assuming that selection of research method should always take into account 'different situations, different purposes, different people, different languages' (1982, p. 49). The rule of thumb is that the mandate comes from the policy maker and the sensitive, experienced researcher selects the appropriate tools from the available kit.

Consider, however, the range of possible clients and their respective mandates. If the contract is, say, for 'an evaluation' of the efficacy of a jelly diet on prisoner rehabilitation, the researcher can indeed use a full repertoire of skills throughout the entire investigation process and so, for instance, choose from structured or unstructured interviews, psychological testing, feminist interviews, vignettes and so on as the best instrument to reveal the vital data. Suppose, however, the decision maker's wants are expressed at the level of a preference for a particular methodological strategy, for example 'a quasi-experimental investigation' of the outcomes of a jelly diet. Patton is quite clear on this:

> If a funding mandate calls for a summative outcomes evaluation, then the evaluator had better be prepared to produce such an animal, complete with a final

report that includes that terminology right there on the front page, in big letters, in the title. (1982, p. 49)

Research skills would still, of course, be applied in doing the deed but other strategic considerations would have been foreclosed, giving us a general rule of pragmatic evaluation: *the more explicit the policy mandate, the more compressed and purely technical the researcher's role.* The ultimate squeeze, of course, is when the policy maker demands 'evaluation results': show us that the jelly diet works! Here we have the Rothschildian vision with research skills for hire – skills, moreover, which are closer in esteem to those of the caterer or plumber than those of the scientist.

Assembling constructivism

In the 1970s, many social science disciplines were gripped with a 'debate on positivism' and witnessed the rise of 'oppositional' perspectives known variously as the 'interpre(ta)tive' approach, 'phenomenology', 'hermeneutics', 'naturalism' and so on. This tide coincided with the pragmatic turn in evaluation and the two swept along to form an approach we shall refer to as *constructivism*. This offers yet a different organizational focus for evaluation, which moves the lead item on the agenda from the political to the social.

The core idea urges us to consider again the nature of what it is we are evaluating. The argument goes that the initiatives and programs which go under the microscope cannot and should not be treated as 'independent variables', as 'things', as 'treatments', as 'dosages'. Rather, all social programs are constituted in complex processes of human understanding and interaction. The key claim is that whatever the program, in whatever the circumstances, it will 'work' through a process of reasoning, change, influence, negotiation, battle of wills, persuasion, choice increase (or decrease), arbitration or some such like. A neighbourhood watch scheme, for instance, will involve a whole chain of negotiations. One group (initiators and police) will come to a particular understanding of crime, of which they would apprise another group (neighbours) in the hope of changing collective ways of acting in such a way as to persuade a third group (potential criminals) that they should reconsider the odds of being observed and arrested. Even those schemes which turn on the adaptation of the physical environment (say, increasing street lighting to reduce crime) depend for their success (or otherwise) on how well they impinge on the reasoning process. Do they encourage dwellers to recognize and enlarge upon 'safe territories'? Do they influence potential criminals to prefer 'safer cover'?

Such insights led to many important developments in evaluation research. The first was a transfer of gaze from outputs to processes. Instead of concentrating on questions such as 'does the program improve reading standards?', 'is the health of the target population improved by the initiative?', research is directed primarily to the internal dynamics of such schemes, by seeking the views of those present on why (if at all) the implicit ideas behind a scheme have crossed their paths and changed their reasoning. This emphasis on the actor's point of view tends to have gone hand in hand with a rather more sensitive outlook on the number of influential players in a program. Thus whilst the experimentalist might only have eyes for experimental and control subjects, and the pragmatists would look in the main towards policy makers, constructivism attempts to accommodate 'stakeholders' by the dozen. Guba and Lincoln (1981), for instance, differentiate between 'agents', 'beneficiaries' and 'victims', each category itself being finely subdivided to number fourteen in all, so that a proper evaluation should reach everywhere from the pockets of the providers to the pens of the publishers of any given venture.

Following the lines of advance of this particular perspective takes us next to the specific research methods employed in the name of evaluation. The step is neatness itself. The social world is fundamentally a process of negotiation, so are programs – and so, therefore, should be the research act. Evaluators, in short, are the 'orchestrators' of a negotiation process. We paraphrase Guba and Lincoln here by describing the staves of the score as follows: identify key 'stakeholders' (all of 'em); establish their (not the researchers') 'constructions' about a program via a prolonged period of field observation; arrange for these claims, concerns and issues to be negotiated in a 'hermeneutic dialectic circle' (act as a go-between); generate consensus with respect to as many 'joint constructions' as possible by creating a 'forum' (an evaluation arbitration and conciliation service); attempt to reconsider unresolved constructions by 'recycling' until 'enlightenment' is obtained (co-op 'til they drop).

The internal logic of constructivist evaluation, too, can be set down on the grid which we have already. A dramatic contrast stares one in the face. In this case we return to a fountainhead based in a methodological imperative, but one which is considered classically as the 'opposite' of the experimentalist's search for causal laws. Constructivism has always stipulated that the quest to understand human meaning is the defining feature of social inquiry. The same stress on meaning works its way into the core of evaluation, as a view both of programs and of the research act. The engine of the method is thus an exchange of meaning between the researcher and all program participants. The outliers on this model of inquiry are viewpoints on the nature of social knowledge and on what it is programs are supposed to achieve. Note that even these carry the hallmark of the negotiation process. Figure 1.4 summarizes how the word is spread.

The baby and the bathwater

So there we have it – the evaluator as ethnographer/ringmaster. Lest the reader detects a note of cynicism creeping in here, we should point out that

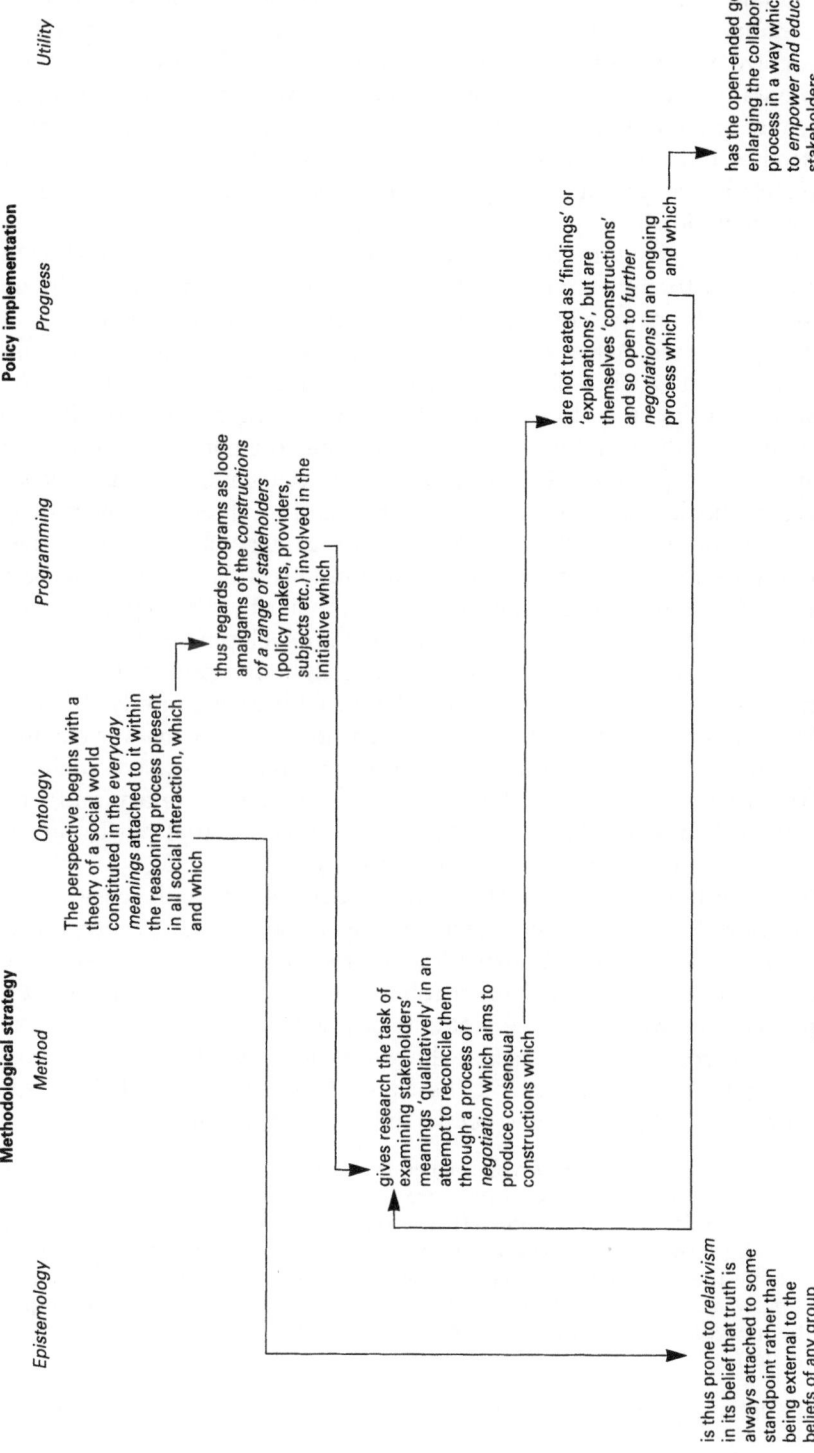

Methodological strategy

Epistemology Method Ontology Programming **Policy implementation** Progress Utility

The perspective begins with a theory of a social world constituted in the everyday *meanings* attached to it within the reasoning process present in all social interaction, which and which

gives research the task of examining stakeholders' meanings 'qualitatively' in an attempt to reconcile them through a process of *negotiation* which aims to produce consensual constructions which

thus regards programs as loose amalgams of the *constructions of a range of stakeholders* (policy makers, providers, subjects etc.) involved in the initiative which

is thus prone to *relativism* in its belief that truth is always attached to some standpoint rather than being external to the beliefs of any group

are not treated as 'findings' or 'explanations', but are themselves 'constructions' and so open to *further negotiations* in an ongoing process which   and which

has the open-ended goal of enlarging the collaborative process in a way which seeks to *empower and educate* all stakeholders

Figure 1.4   *An overview of constructivist evaluation*

important conceptual distinctions about evaluation have flowed from the apparatus described here. For instance, it is now fairly commonplace to recognize the long chains of command and diversity of expectations about a program as we flow from policy maker to practitioner to participant. Thus for any program we might anticipate not only a variety of potential outcomes, but a plethora of parties responsible for those outcomes. One of the most interesting outcome permutations is so-called 'theory–success/implementation–failure'.

When push comes to shove, however, we have to admit an inclination to dismiss constructivist/naturalistic/fourth-generation evaluation as mere casuistry. It is not merely a matter of the misplaced pseudo-scholarship of the language associated with the paradigm, though it is hard not to snigger when Guba and Lincoln (1989, pp. 191–204) talk about getting stakeholders to agree to and formally sign 'conditions for a productive hermeneutic dialectic' (one wonders whether the contract in question comes with the standard '21 days to change one's mind' cooling-down clause). This language, however, is merely an indication of a more deep seated air of unreality about the evaluations-as-negotiations perspective, namely its failure to appreciate the asymmetries of power which are assumed in and left untouched by the vast majority of policy initiatives. We find it difficult to imagine, for instance, the development of a 'joint construction' of the claims and concerns of neighbourhood watchers and neighbourhood burglars, since they begin with uncommonly different assumptions about the legitimacy of this particular way of making a living. The imagination leaps further in regarding the productive dialectic hermeneutic between the above-mentioned Home Secretary and, say, Reginald 'Hacksaw' Molloy as they develop conceptual parity on the merits of a new program in sentence planning.

Guba and Lincoln's negotiations, we suspect, belong to the cosy suburban world of the meeting between school governors, teachers and parents in which they thrash out homework policy for the fifth grade. The splendid irony about their self-proclaimed commitment to negotiation is that it is trumpeted between the covers of a monograph whose foreword remonstrates, 'there are some persons who, we believe, would not profit from reading this book' (1989, p. 15). These are, of course, the 'true-believers in positivism' (1989, p. 16), who get the following welcome:

> We have argued that *no accommodation is possible* between positivist and constructivist belief systems as they are now formulated. We do not see any possibility for accommodation if that accommodation is to occur by having one paradigm overwhelm the other by the sheer power of its arguments, or by having the paradigms play complementary roles, or by showing that one is simply a special case of the other. We do see the possibility that, through a hermeneutic dialectic process, a new construction will emerge. (1989, p. 17, our italics)

This 'let's negotiate on our terms' philosophy stems from a beguiling epistemological split which has opened within the phenomenological school. The original methodological 'calling' for ethnographic understanding was espoused by the likes of Becker (1971) and Blumer (1969). Let us call this hermeneutics I. It stressed that by being witness to the day-to-day reasoning of their research subjects, by engaging in their life world, by participating in their decision making, the researcher would be that much closer to reality. The hermeneutic approach, it was assumed, almost literally, placed one in touch with the truth (much more closely, anyway, than those arcane positivists with their hygienic, dehumanizing, pseudoscientific measuring instruments).

All this has changed, however, since today there is a new worst enemy within the phenomenological approach, and these are . . . phenomenologists (Hammersley, 1992). Hermeneutics II again starts from the point of view that all beliefs are 'constructions' *but* adds the twist that we cannot, therefore, get beyond constructions. It insists, in other words, that there are no neutral/factual/definitive accounts to be made of the social world. Every claim, description or explanation about social life carries with it the assumptions of the individual making the claim, description or explanation. This applies as much to ordinary folk coming to their own accounts of the world as it does to social scientists giving their account of other people's accounts. To put this matter in a slightly more practical vein, we can say of any prolonged period of field observation or of any cycle of evaluation negotiations that they will generate thousands upon thousands of separate thoughts and actions which are open to an infinite number of descriptions. The researcher's account of such an open-ended reality must therefore be selective and rest upon his or her preferred assumptions, pet theories, cherished values and so on. Since on this view there is no single objective reality to report upon, hermeneutic dialectic circles (not surprisingly) go round in circles, rather than constituting a linear advance on the truth.

Note, if you please, that we are not attempting to spread vile propaganda here. This methodological demur would come as no surprise to Guba and Lincoln. Indeed, the eleventh bullet point in their summary of constructivist methodology states:

> Evaluation data derived from constructivist inquiry have neither special status nor legitimation; they represent simply another construction to be taken into account in the move toward consensus. (1989, p. 45)

We rather suspect, however, that this throwing out of the objectivist baby with the relativist bathwater would deliver a shock even to some potential admirers of the radical agenda of fourth-generation evaluation. Many qualitative researchers who have been inspired to engage in 'process evaluation' in the hope of seeking the truth about the subtleties (and realities) of decision making and choice within programs might be disappointed to learn that they have presented simply another 'version'.

Funders of evaluations might also be somewhat surprised to have paid for the privilege of entering a world which denies the privilege of any particular point of view.

There is worse to come. Not only does constructivism preach a militant agnosticism on *truth*, it urges a dismal minimalism on *scope*:

> Phenomena can be understood only within the context in which they are studied; findings from one context cannot be generalized to another; neither problems nor their solutions can be generalized from one setting to another. (1989, p. 45)

The roots of such situational relativism are worth tracking down. Madness it may be, but there is method to it. Part of the story lies in the failure of alternative paradigms with respect to a point noted earlier. The muddle over 'what works?' stems from the track record of the experimental approach in which replications have tended to indicate program success in some respects here but not there, and in other respects there but not here. Guba and Lincoln put their fingers right on this one. Experimentation tries to minimalize all the differences (except one) between experimental and control groups and thus 'effectively *strips away the context* and yields results that are valid only in other contextless situations' (1989, p. 60, italics in original).

Naturalists thus acknowledge the significance of the context on constraining the actions, standpoints and negotiations of stakeholders. They regard these circumstantial features as being likely to vary between the past, present, and future as well as the here, there, and everywhere and they seek to resolve the dilemma by trying to cope only with the here and now. This is utterly perverse. One of the useful lessons we learn from the pragmatists is that policy making and program development are part of a vast intersection of ideas and interests. We can all paraphrase the typical moment programs come into life: 'so that's what they are doing over there, is it – and they get funded – let's have a go before it's too late.' Social initiatives are thus begged, stolen and borrowed the world over, and the notion that this process is devoid of learning beggars belief.

For instance, if we think again of neighbourhood watch schemes, it is patently obvious that they involve a range of interactions between neighbours – to be used in (1) co-operation/surveillance within a scheme and (2) organization/promotion of the scheme. We certainly know enough by now to understand that communities will differ in their abilities to deliver on these desiderata. To lapse into shorthand, we can say that the extended families, the terraced housing and the lack of executive experience of traditional working class communities make them better at the former rather than the latter pair, whilst the privatized lifestyles, tall hedges and boardroom blitzes of the middle classes render their communities long on the second pair but short on the first.

Crude as it is, this attempt to begin to understand the nature of neighbourhoods in neighbourhood watch schemes illustrates a general model of contextual understanding – namely that one has to hypothesize upon, identify, conceptualize and eventually measure contextual similarities and difference. Thinking about context without comparison is unthinkable. Guba and Lincoln would deny all this and forbid the transfer of intelligence from one context to another. So where are they left? Their notion of context amounts to *those circumstantial features which happen to turn up in a particular investigation*. Context is simply the current background circumstances which encourage or enable a particular group of stakeholders to be assembled for negotiation. So whilst they are happy to accuse experimentalists of 'context-stripping', they only manage to replace it with 'context-hopping'. Context appears with the fall of the dice. Solipsism rules.

In summary, we can say that the naturalistic approach brought people's reckoning back into the reckoning in evaluation research, and thus proved a valuable corrective to perspectives which were obsessed with behavioural outcomes. As often happens in the paradigm wars, however, the swing of the pendulum was too momentous and other vital items were lost from the agenda. Constructivism suffers from what veterans of 'perspectivism' in social science regard as the standard weakness of phenomenological approaches – namely, the inability to grasp those structural and institutional features of society which are in some respects independent of the individuals' reasoning and desires. The social world (and thus policies and programs) consists of more than the sum of people's beliefs, hopes and expectations. The 'conceptual parity' to which Guba and Lincoln aspire fails to recognize the asymmetries of power which allow some people to advance their ideas whilst others have choices foreclosed.

This is no place to explicate how evaluation research should be based on a view which respects the 'duality of structure and agency' (Giddens, 1984). What might be a more useful practical starting point, however, is to begin evaluation with the expectation that there will be disparity in knowledge of, and control over, any program, and this will be a permanent condition. There is always likely to be an 'escape' of outcomes within a program from people's intentions for that program. This may lead to a variety of end-products, quite different from Guba and Lincoln's vision of enlightenment for all. It may be, for instance, that programs work with the subjects being blithely unaware of the intentions behind the initiative (as, perhaps, with the introduction of new teaching schemes). It may be that a program fails because subjects are too well informed about its intentions (as, perhaps, with the many crime reduction schemes). To establish propositions such as these, of course, requires the researcher to generate some means of making *independent* judgements about the institutional structure and power relations within a program, and this is a role constructivism cannot contemplate.

Only connect

Our history has told the tale of the good ship *Evaluation* being tossed back and forth on a sea of favourable and ill tides. Paradigms have come and stayed, and swept protagonists into mutually antagonistic waters. Now, it may already have struck crew members that what is needed at this juncture is the arrival of a good Captain Sensible to get things shipshape by attempting a synthesis to connect up some of the best lessons from each approach. One can imagine the attractions of a perspective which combines the rigour of experimentation with the practical nous on policy making of the pragmatists, and with the empathy for the views of the stakeholders of the constructivists. Several well-known evaluators have shared this pluralist vision and our history would be incomplete without a record (and evaluation) of their efforts.

A good name for what we are describing might be *comprehensive evaluation* and the copyright, on the name at least, belongs to Rossi. His best known statement on the issue begins with a threefold distinction of evaluation activities:

1 'analysis related to the conceptualization and design of interventions';
2 'monitoring of program implementation'; and
3 'assessment of program utility' (Rossi and Freeman, 1985, p. 380).

Rossi takes a sociological view of programs and sees them customarily as attempting to deal with individual deficiencies that spring from inequalities of social condition. For programs to be an appropriate response requires them to contain a proper institutional *and* individual diagnosis of the problem, and some of the labour of evaluation needs to be exercised in monitoring the adequacy of program conceptualization. Programs are delivered by institutions. Rossi is a great believer in their fallibility, and sees a key role of evaluation in terms of troubleshooting and correcting administrative faults, failed delivery systems, and good old human error. Finally, and unlike the aforementioned evaluators who also have a keen eye for process, Rossi remains keen on outcome effectiveness. 'Unless programs have a demonstrable impact, it is hard to defend their implementation and continuation' (1985, p. 40). By this he not only demands positive results from experimental-type impact studies, but also anticipates the need to be hard-headed about economic costs and benefits.

Another proponent of a more pluralist vision of evaluation is Cronbach (1963; 1982). Whilst, as far as we are aware, he never coined a term for the multiple functions he requires of evaluation, he, much more than other methodologists, emphasized the depth of interrelated activities that comprise the programs which are encountered in evaluation. His field is educational evaluation and he writes of the typical task as follows:

The program may be a set of instructional materials distributed nationally, the instructional activities of a single school, or the educational experience of a single pupil. Many types of decisions are to be made, and many variations of information are useful. It becomes immediately apparent that no one set of principles will suffice for all situations. (1963, p. 672)

So there we have it: calls for *breadth* and then *depth* in program evaluation. It is quite impossible to deny the good sense of any of this, yet we blanch at the prospect of declaring ourselves champions of pluralism. We also, incidentally, have scratched our heads in attempting to set down a diagrammatic summary of 'comprehensive evaluation'. Unlike our other efforts (Figures 1.2, 1.3, 1.4) everything seemed to get crowded up at the top. The reasons for the stultification of pluralism (and the lack of a diagram) are actually quite mundane – a matter of never having sufficient resources to research everything, a matter of not being able to see the wood for the trees, a matter of not knowing exactly where to start. We can hide our lack of enthusiasm here by having others make the point for us:

To the extent that evaluators try to do everything Rossi recommends, they will do little well. To the extent that they pick and choose among the options, they will not be comprehensive. Some priorities are needed. (Shadish et al., 1991, p. 425)

These uncharacteristically pithy words of wisdom belong to a monograph which, incidentally, we recommend as the place to go if you wish to read a fine history of evaluation methodology in 484½ pages.

Rossi and Cronbach have not been introduced here merely to give pluralist evaluation a small pat on the head in order to wave it goodbye. For, in coming to their respective views on the need for breadth and depth in evaluation research, these two authors made much more specific contributions to the basic strategy and it is these we would like to celebrate here. Both authors began their work when experimental evaluation was the norm. They were amongst the first to recognize (in their own work) some of the failures we charted in the section on the *OXO* approach. More significantly, in suggesting remedies, they did in fact establish some alternative evaluation priorities which, in due course, we would like to incorporate in our own model.

The first of these is referred to as 'theory-driven' evaluation. The notion was introduced in a paper by Chen and Rossi (1981) and we should be clear in giving Chen (1990) much of the credit for its development. Their starting point, perversely enough, comes from thinking about an experimental evaluation which 'works'. Suppose everything has gone well and the experimental group have clearly outperformed the controls. Whilst by the lights of experimental logic we can claim the program a 'success', we actually learn *nothing* about why it works:

The domination of the experimental paradigm in the program evaluation literature has unfortunately drawn attention away from a more important task in gaining understanding of social programs, namely, developing theoretical models of social interventions. A very seductive and attractive feature of controlled experiments is that it is not necessary to understand how a social program works in order to estimate its net effects though randomized experiments. (Chen and Rossi, 1983, p. 284)

An evaluation priority is shouting from the rooftops here, namely that what we need to know is *what it is about a program which makes it work* (cf. Palmer's earlier remarks on Martinson). In a typical initiative, there are scores of potential devices at work in the delivery of a program. For example, as Cronbach has just told us, the typical educational innovation might involve a nationally developed curriculum and teaching scheme, but it will be implemented locally via a school with a range of classroom cultures and teaching resources, as well as a range of individual teaching and learning styles. Here is where a bit of theory comes in useful. By theory, by the way, Chen and Rossi do not mean that grandiose sociological speculation which purports to explain life, the universe, and everything. They refer to the mundane distinctions about such matters as classroom cultures and teaching style, the likes of which are inextricably bound up in the delivery of any 'program' and the detail of which will make an enormous difference to its success. What they suggest, therefore, is that the evaluator should use prior knowledge of the varying circumstances of the delivery of any program and of its track record, and build this into the investigation. Experimental evaluation is basically committed to perfecting one comparison – that between the presence and the absence of a program. Theory-driven evaluation anticipates considerable variation in the delivery of programs, even in those cases where the program is 'present', and thus is able to build alternative within-program comparisons into the design and analysis. In 'theory', here, we have the germ of an understanding of why the results of experimental evaluation are so inconsistent and why, in spite of this, cumulation of findings might be possible.

Theory-driven evaluation by itself, of course, is no panacea. One problem which has divided even its proponents (see Rossi's introduction to Chen, 1990) is what exactly is meant by 'theory' in such proposals. Shadish et al. (1991, p. 431) argue that Rossi's formulation restricts the usage to multiple 'X causes Y' type propositions and thus barely takes us further than the experimental/statistical orthodoxy. Costner (1991) argues that in Chen's hands usage of the term 'theory' roams over different forms of knowledge such as 'values', 'common sense', 'first-hand experience', 'collected academic wisdom' and so offers little new beyond a level-headed pluralism. Our instinct is that evaluation should be explicitly theory-led rather than generally theory-laden, and in Chapter 3 we will come up with a precise prescription for the form of explanatory proposition which we believe should drive evaluation.

Cronbach was responsible for hammering a rather different nail into the coffin of narrow experimental evaluation. His concern was with identifying the proper *domain* of evaluation studies. The core of his criticism is that experimental evaluation generates an obsession with *internal validity*. The experimentalist's basic goal is to show that the treatment and only the treatment is responsible for a particular outcome. For example, if the experimental and control comparison shows that a new reading scheme apparently generates faster progress in reading ability, the experimentalist's propensity is to make damn sure that the difference was not really due to other unforeseen differences between the settings, such as teacher experience, pupil backgrounds, staffing problems, quality of the school dinners, etc.

Cronbach argues that *users* of evaluations will bring a completely different set of priorities and worries to the issue of whether treatment really causes outcome. To make his case he introduces a whole nomenclature, abbreviated as u.t.o.s. The acronym describes the different facets of an evaluation: u is the unit of analysis (such as the individual, the school); t is the treatment (the program as it is applied); o refers to the observations made (various input and output measures); s is the setting (the particular locality and its programming needs). In short we can say that utos (lower case) describes the case study actually investigated. This case, of course, is but one of a whole potential population of units, treatments, observations, and settings in and around which the said program could be developed. UTOS (upper case) thus represents the total population of all conceivable combinations of these elements which could be relevant to our knowledge of a given program. *UTOS (say it 'star UTOS') represents the particular subdomains from this total population which will be relevant to *other* audiences interested in the evaluation.

In short, says Cronbach, by concentrating on internal validity, evaluators will merely scratch at a surface issue, namely whether t is really linked to o. Evaluations only really become useful if they attempt the jump from utos to UTOS or indeed to *UTOS. Rendering this in more common evaluation parlance, Cronbach is saying that the typical audience will rarely read a report on gains from a new reading scheme with a keen eye on whether extraneous differences in lunch nutritional levels have been properly controlled. What they are interested in is – 'would it work on my patch?' In utos language this means investigators should make an attempt to specify how their results might transfer from u to U*. In general there is a whole raft of equivalent puzzles as we try to generalize back and forth across different units, treatments, observations and settings. Consider Cronbach's (1982) own example concerning T*:

> When the first returns on compensatory education came in, few discussants confined attention to the conclusion about the UTO on which data were collected. One reaction contemplated a change in treatment: 'It is all very well to report negatively on Head Start (T); but does not that show that compensatory treatment needs to continue for a longer time (T*)?' So follow through was mounted as a T* (and later evaluated directly).

Cronbach is undoubtedly correct in his overall sensibility to the importance of external validity. Again, we should balance our enthusiasm for the idea by noting that UTOS terminology is not the talk of the ministry of education, the town hall or indeed St John's Church of England Primary School. To be frank, it has not even taken hold in 'academic' evaluation. This is largely because UTOS language describes the problem rather than setting in motion the solution to the issue of external validity. It could even be said that it describes the problem too well. Cronbach (1982) again:

> No investigation can answer all questions. The variety of U*, T*, and O* that will concern the different sectors of the audience is endless, and future settings can be only dimly foreseen. The planner seeking relevance, aims at a target that becomes visible only after he has fired off his best shot. The task is so demanding as to make the aspiration seem almost foolish.

He goes on to say, however, there is room for optimism. We share it and we hope to tackle external validity in a more modest way by showing that, with proper attention to the *contextual features* of every case, evaluation research can be more than the sum of the individual cases.

Our brief history is now complete save for a summary of what (we suppose) it has achieved. History is not neutral reportage; one inevitably evaluates, one irresistibly takes sides. So for us, evaluation, which should have the mature confidence of a 34-year-old (recall we started with Campbell and Stanley), looks more like a confused teenager. Experimentation and its derivatives still constitute the kernel idea but continue to go round in never increasing circles. Pragmatism and constructivism rather turned out to be leaps from frying-pan to fire. Pluralism makes sense to everyone and satisfies no one. On the other hand, we have acknowledged the elemental good sense which spawned each of these approaches and we have expressed positive excitement at some recent departures. What is more, and whilst such sentiments can sound trite, the recognition of the pitfalls of any method is obviously the prerequisite for thinking about remedies. Rossi and Cronbach, remember, learned the hard way. With this thought, we issue our end of term report:

Evaluation research 1963–1997

Must do better. Too easily distracted by silly ideas. Ought to have a clearer sense of priorities and to work more systematically to see them through. Will yet go on to do great things.

R.P./N.T.

Our primary concern from this point onwards is with the future of evaluation and any worthwhile view of that future must be based on positive messages. The new dawn actually belongs within our weasel words on experimental evaluation. We noted earlier its ambition for evaluation to have a scientific basis but have shown, largely as a matter of reportage, that it has failed to deliver the goods in terms of productive, cumulative findings. So, in this case, we refrain from instant dismissal since the need for a scientific base for evaluation is not under challenge from us, merely the particular application. We find it very difficult to conceive that evaluation, of all things, should *not* strive for objectivity.

We say this with an awareness of the centuries of despair that philosophers have experienced in trying to set down the 'formula' for achieving objective knowledge. Perhaps, at this stage, we can rest content with installing 'objectivity' as our ideal and rely on Gordon's (1992) brilliant quip for preserving this as a goal:

> That these ideals cannot be attained is not a reason for disregarding them. Perfect cleanliness is also impossible, but it does not serve as a warrant for not washing, much less for rolling in a manure pile.

We have had our say about the manure piles in evaluation. We have also identified two extremely well-washed evaluation theorists whose insights we aim to modify and develop. This completes our initial effort to 'position' our perspective and we pass on to our attempt to capture the scientific high ground in evaluation. Readers who would like instantly to scale the heights might like to peek at Figure 9.1, which gives a one-sentence summary of our efforts in a way that parallels Figures 1.2, 1.3 and 1.4.

2

OUT WITH THE OLD: WEAKNESSES IN EXPERIMENTAL EVALUATION

This chapter will provide a constructive critique of the experimental tradition in evaluation. We will confront experimental evaluation for its weakness *as science*. We will concentrate our fire on the epistemological assumptions about causation and their lack of fit with the nature of social programs. Experimental evaluation has struggled because of a basically 'positivist' understanding of the nature of social causation. We hesitate to put it like this, since the term 'positivism' these days has been reduced to a crude term of abuse. It is used as an evil totem by those intent on musing about there being no place for scientism in understanding the rich, meaningful, emotional world of human intercourse. You will hear no such romanticism from us in this chapter, for we seek to discuss a wrong-headed notion of scientific explanation in order to pave the way for a *realist* understanding of science. We are indeed the courtiers at the palace of scientific evaluation, announcing that the king is dead – long live the king!

To pursue this task we want to begin by picking up, *and explaining*, some of the well-recognized failures of experimental evaluation already noted in our 'brief history'. The first of these one might refer to as the *Martinson problem*. Why, from the 'nothing works' days to the present, has experimental evaluation continued to produce inconsistent findings? The second methodological issue we seek to explore is the *black box problem*. We have hinted previously that experimental evaluation only produces descriptions of outcomes, rather than explanations of why programs work (or fail). We will use this chapter to highlight the missing explanatory ingredients in the traditional experimental approach. This is the task on which we seek to be judged here: we will show precisely which causal agents are omitted within traditional experimental designs and why they cannot be so incorporated. This will then leave us in a position to put a realist remedy in place.

The structure of the chapter is as follows. We begin by examining the fundamental causal logic of evaluation. We appraise the two great scientific metatheories of causation, the 'successionist' and the 'generative', with the aim of showing that experimental evaluation has been drawn inexorably to the former, when it should have been embracing the latter.

We then move to a discussion of two major applications of the method in order to pinpoint the consequences of this erroneous choice. The first of these examples involves heading back to Martinson territory and reviewing the nature of corrections programs in order to show why they will inevitably be misunderstood when manipulated under traditional experimental logic. We will examine in some detail the experimental trials involved in the evaluation of the Cognitive Skills Training Program (Porporino and Robinson, 1995). This is probably the grandest initiative ever undertaken by the Correctional Services of Canada, and one that has been much imitated the world over. Subjects come onto such initiatives with a range of resources at their disposal, willing and able to make a range of different choices. We will show that the same program will thus work in quite different ways for different subjects and that the experimental method is simply not designed to appreciate such subtleties.

We then shift our attention to the opposite end of the criminal justice system and examine a form of initiative which has provoked evaluation interest world-wide, namely 'community policing' programs. In this case we put the microscope to a specific, state-of-the-art example of experimental evaluation, namely Bennett's (1991) study of 'contact patrols' in London and Birmingham. Our purpose here is to show that the explanatory capacity of experimental evaluation rests on an irresolvable paradox. Community policing initiatives, of the type studied here, work by persuading residents that it is in their best interests to alter their own actions in respect of reducing crime. The likelihood of such a change in reasoning will vary greatly according to the social composition of the neighbourhoods in question. Experimental logic, however, marches to a very different tune. The idea is to match the circumstances of experimental and control groups. The method thus seeks to discount in design and evidence precisely that which needs to be addressed in explanation. An examination of Bennett's (failed) attempts to wrestle with this paradox will be very instructive for us in establishing a new set of priorities.

The two examples together demonstrate the need for a basic shift in social explanation from a 'successionist' to a 'generative' theory of causation and thus prefigure a parallel move in evaluation from an 'experimental' to a 'realist' paradigm.

Experiments and causation

Evaluation is saturated with a vocabulary of *causation*. We ask: did the program work, did it make the subjects brighter, healthier, richer, safer, saner etc.? In doing so, we are attempting to demonstrate an unequivocal causal relationship between program and outcome. The bottom line, as they say, is to show that it really was the program which was responsible for changing the subjects' lot. This seemingly simple matter of establishing causal propositions has had philosophers in dispute for centuries. Many of the most momentous disputes in natural and social science have turned on the matter of whether cause has been well and truly established. It is perhaps not surprising, therefore, that causation remains an academic *cause célèbre*, and that we feel the need to add a couple more chapters to the debate in the context of evaluation research.

Our framework is established by Harré's (1972) well-known distinction between 'successionist' and 'generative' theories of causation. These two reconstructions summarize much of what is in dispute in our understanding of causality. Both of these great metatheories start with the supposition that causal explanation in science is a matter of having a method which will distinguish those cases in which X is linked to Y in some regular, lawful fashion from those in which the association comes about by accident or happenstance. What is at issue between the perspectives is how one brings forth evidence to support such a claim.

Successionists follow Hume (1739) in his view that causation is unobservable (a 'perception of the mind') and that one can only make such inferences on the basis of observational data. The key is to establish a controlled sequence of observations which differentiate the causal relationship from the spurious association. The logical framework behind this observational approach was established in Mill's (1961) celebrated *methods*: the method of agreement, the method of difference and the method of concomitant variation. This is a fabulous piece of thinking which has flown forward hundreds of years to end up as the inspiration to evaluation's seminal work, *Quasi-Experimentation*. In their first chapter, we find Cook and Campbell (1979) savouring Mill's canons and showing how they implicitly contain the modern-day notions of experimental manipulation, control groups, and before-and-after comparisons. From here, it is just a few short steps to the logic of what the textbooks call the 'classic experimental design', which we have already depicted as Figure 1.1 but reproduce here for easy reference as Figure 2.1.

	Pre-test	Treatment	Post-test
Experimental group	O_1	X	O_2
Control group	O_1		O_2

Figure 2.1   *The classic experimental design*

The sequence of steps here is probably too familiar to require much recapitulation; we anticipate that most readers will have been drilled in the basic ideas of random allocation of subjects to experimental and control groups, the exposure of the former but not the latter to the experimental treatment, and the application of pre-treatment/post-treatment measures in order to compare the rates of change in the two groups. The key stroke of logic in this classical design is that, being identical to begin with, the only difference between the experimental and control groups lies in the application of the initiative. Any difference in behavioural outcomes between the groups is thus accounted for in terms of the action of the treatment. If the researcher has managed to put into place this regime of manipulation, control and observation, then we require no further information to infer that treatment (cause) and outcome (effect) are linked. Accordingly, it can be said that the foundational ideas of experimental logic are successionist. Causation is 'external' in that we do not and cannot observe certain causal forces at work. In terms of actual programs, this would correspond to the claim that one does not need to witness the cognitive leap when the prisoner 'rehabilitates' or the burglar is 'deterred' in order to recognize that such changes have occurred. Evaluators can do no more than apply the measures and controls as rigorously and systematically as possible and then sit in experimental judgement awaiting *constant conjunction* in the form of some net differences in outcomes between subjects and non-subjects.

The other great metaphysical theory of causality can also be said to stretch back into philosophical antiquity but has witnessed more sustained development in the last three decades. It also stresses the need to observe regular patterns between inputs and outputs, between causes and their effects, but seeks to establish the connection in quite a different way. Generative theory holds that there is a *real* connection between events which we understand to be connected causally. We can capture the basic idea in the language customarily used in making many 'everyday' causal references. In such cases we often speak of a 'case', 'system', 'thing', 'person' in *transformation*. Thus we say that gunpowder exploded, we say that the economy went into recession, we say that the prisoner was rehabilitated. In explaining these transitions we often point to an external observable cause (such as a spark, an oil crisis, a boot camp) but we also rely, as part of the explanation, on some *internal* feature of that which is changed (such as the 'state' or chemical 'composition' of the gunpowder, the 'structure' and level of 'development' of the economy, the 'character' or 'disposition' of the prisoner). These internal *liabilities* or *powers* are deemed important in scientific, as well as everyday, explanation because they allow us to make sense of those occasions when the causal relationship is absent (as when the spark fails to ignite gunpowder which is not compacted, or when an oil crisis leaves oil-producing or subsistence economies unaffected, or when the boot camp merely toughens the already tough offender).

In short, the generative theory sees causation as acting internally as well as externally. Cause describes the transformative *potential* of phenomena. One happening may well trigger another but only if it is in the right condition in the right circumstances. Unless explanation penetrates to these real underlying levels, it is deemed to be incomplete. In the next chapter, we will show how this fundamental imagery can be developed into a fully fledged model of scientific explanation. For the time being, we trust that this initial explication of the philosophies of causation allows us to make plain our charge against experimental evaluation, which can be stated as follows. In pursuing causal explanation via a constant conjunction model, with its stress on that which can be observed and controlled, it has tended to overlook the liabilities, powers, and potentialities of the programs and subjects whose behaviour it seeks to explain.

Let us also make the manner of the argument plain. The above-drawn dualism between successionist and generative causation is a brief, pen-picture example of what philosophers call 'rational reconstructions'. These are pared-down ideal types which try to capture the abstract essentials of explanatory logic. When it comes to real research, the actual 'logic-in-use', of course, is a good deal more messy. We do not suppose, for instance, that there are evaluators out there working through Mill's rulebook, pondering on when to enact the second inductivist canon. Real research, however, does involve choosing between explanatory priorities, and it is at this level of immediate, deliberate, strategic priorities that we make our claim. In the following examples, we will show how ideas of controlled observation, classical design, *OXO* conceptualization and so on have proved so compelling that attention has been drawn away from certain crucial causal agents. The other main reason for descending from abstraction and pursuing our case with real research examples is that it will allow us to build a sustained, substantive picture of just what we take the missing causal 'liabilities, powers and potentialities' to be.

Corrections and causation

In this section we want to consider the nature of change sought in 'corrections' programs. We want to show that the very nature of rehabilitative change is such that it cannot be captured in *OXO* terminology. This is a task of some conceptual precision. It is not a question of ranting about being in the 'wrong narrative', with the language of randomization, controlled trials and so on failing to convey the smell of fear, sweat, slop and semen of hundreds of confined bodies. We want to examine some of the cherished strategies of the experimental tradition, and then focus on the nature of the causal agents which might make a prisoner change, so as to locate in detail where the explanatory tensions lie.

Since we wish to make our case by exploring the limitations of a real evaluation rather than producing an artificially manufactured catalogue of woes, we also clearly need to use a well-resourced example of best practice rather than picking upon the partial, shoe-string efforts which tend to characterize this less than glamorous quarter of the criminal justice system. Given these requirements, our case study virtually chooses itself, namely the evaluation of the Cognitive Skills Training Program which was introduced by the Correctional Services of Canada in 1989. This is probably the most ambitious and comprehensive rehabilitation program ever attempted by this or any other prison service. By the end of March 1993, 2,500 offenders had been assessed as suitable cases for treatment and 1,400 had completed the program. The underlying theory is that much criminal behaviour is rooted in 'cognitive deficiency' (Ross and Fabiano, 1985). The program itself thus focuses on six areas of deficit: self-control, cognitive style, interpersonal problem solving, social perspective taking, critical reasoning, and values. The initiative was implemented methodically to a clear program theory which involved the production of staff training manuals, teaching handbooks, line staff involvement, as well as considerable regime changes in order to recruit inmates and service the provision. The course itself lasts for eight to twelve weeks and consists of audio-visual presentations, games, puzzles, reasoning exercises, role-playing, group discussion etc. In summary, the program 'incorporates a variety of psycho-educational and social-learning techniques to assist offenders in rehearsing both new behaviour and new thinking skills' (Porporino and Robinson, 1995). Last but not least we must mention the evaluations (Fabiano et al., 1990; Porporino and Robinson, 1995). These were funded in the manner fitting a program with national implementation and, crucially, were carried out by a team committed to a rigorous experimental strategy.

Volition and volunteers

Let us begin with the tribulations of random allocation. At once we meet a series of jarring problems. The random allocation of prison subjects to experimental and control groups is often regarded as being beset with too many ethical dilemmas and practical difficulties to make it feasible. The moral dilemma is self-evident. Programs are planned social situations, which carry a set of hopes and expectations and thus produce, like it or not, superior and inferior conditions between experimental and control groups. With this in mind evaluators have often been reluctant to 'play God' in casting people's lives randomly into channels over which they have no choice. Let us not over-dramatize here: the choice between being on or not on a corrections program is clearly not as life-threatening as, say, being allocated to drug or placebo in certain medical trials. Nevertheless, given certain sordid historical episodes of experimenting on confined people, most corrections evaluators are reluctant to forbid subjects a say on whether they enter a program.

On top of this, there are some immensely good practical reasons why random allocation to programs would be disastrous. Without some element of subject self-selection, the nature of the programs themselves would change dramatically. Programs depend for their daily existence on the co-operation of subjects and without it one rapidly heads toward the revision of provision, the ejection of malingerers, or, in the extreme, the curtailment of the initiative. Common sense provides the reason here. Co-operation and non-disruption are the very minimal requirements for the basic operation of any sustained social interaction, and one is much more likely to get it if the subjects have chosen to be there. A counsellor on an 'anger management' course once put this to us very nicely: 'the last thing you see on my course is anger.'

Our point, however, is that the true perils of randomization in corrections evaluations do not lie with the *ethical* or the *practical*, but belong at the even more fundamental level of the *causal*. To get at the issue we need to probe a little deeper into the nature of the personal change contemplated on such programs. As we have seen, for the most part subjects enter programs voluntarily. The people who are drawn into, lend support to, and are (perhaps) changed by the experience of a program are those for whom it has salience. One of our students, discussing a thin period of recruitment to a prison education program, put it rather more vividly: 'you can lead a horse to water, but you can't. . . .' He found no need to finish the couplet and neither should anyone else involved in evaluation, since it is another way of saying that *choice is the very condition of social and individual change and not some sort of practical hindrance to understanding that change*.

Our argument with experimental evaluation now begins to crystallize a little. One might summarize the point by saying that it is not programs which work, as such, but people co-operating and choosing to make them work. In the language of generative causation, we would say that programs work *through* their subjects' liabilities. Now, it is all too easy for us to imagine an experimentalist reading through the argument to this point with blood boiling; all this would be regarded as very old news indeed. The problem is regarded as a genuine one, but has already been filed away as one of the standard threats to internal validity, under the name of the 'volunteer effect'. The recommended solution is to run volunteer-only experiments. If we get inmates to volunteer for a program, and *at that point* assign them to experimental and control conditions, we erase the problem since the motivational levels will then correspond between the two groups, and the general levels of co-operation and compliance should be no better or worse than for any other program.

Let us see how this works in practice. The 'Cog Skills' program was subjected to a range of pilot and core studies, each very much wedded to the experimental approach using random allocation. The actual method of allocation works through a process of producing what Porporino and Robinson (1995) call a 'waiting list control group'. This operates as follows.

The general population of inmates is screened in broad terms to select those with well-established criminal patterns, the program is offered to those who are deemed to fall into this category, and inmates then volunteer. The courses are, however, oversubscribed. This allows a mock 'waiting list' to be created which, rather than operating on a 'last come, last served' basis, gives the opportunity for random assignment to the actual program or to the 'queue'. The prison system itself also creates a regular tide of transfers and so the researchers were able to create a control group composed of volunteers who happened to be transferees and those who were randomly assigned to wait. And thus, with a little ingenuity, the basic experimental design is regained.

This is a working instance of what we earlier termed 'logic-in-use'. In cracking a practical research problem, researchers actually reaffirm a broader set of methodological principles. Thus when Porporino and Robinson insist that 'the only defensible manner to assess the effects of an intervention is to have a control group that is equivalent on pre-selection factors' (1995, p. 176), they are establishing priorities given in successionist logic. Such choices govern what gets attention in research (as well as what gets omitted) which in the present case led to even more ingenuity being expended on the matter of group equivalence. For instance, some new worries on this score developed as a fuller sample grew, when the situation arose in which some 'waiting listers' actually did make it onto the program, thus losing 'control' status and becoming 'experimentees'. Are we to assume that their capacity to wait indicates a still higher level of motivation? Another 'operational reality' in some prisons was that the programs began without an excess of candidates and so the trials had to begin before the achievement of the control quota, and thus without true random assignment. In the event, our researchers' considered assessment was that these problems were small enough not to compromise the normal margins of experimental error and so could be ignored. We raise these issues not for the purpose of questioning these decisions, but rather to demonstrate the tremendous eye for detail that can go into the construction of experimental and control groups.

The difficulty is that an eye for such a set of details is an eye drawn away from quite another way of understanding the problem. What we are trying to address here is the issue of the volition of the subject and how this contributes to the working of social programs. This is no technical quibble but an argument about the very way in which social programs enable subjects to change. Our point is basically that programs should be considered as learning situations, and, as with all learning situations, we should understand that progress is triggered by the purposeful actions of subjects. Programmes will, in one way and another, offer a range of opportunities. Whether they are cashed in depends on the potentialities and volition of the subject. We are thus claiming, in this fundamental sense, that choice making *is* the agent which engineers change within social initiatives.

Our interest in this chapter is in the causal vocabulary needed to describe such a process of change. This is where the generative paradigm comes in with its terminology of 'transformation' and its concentration on the 'liabilities' and 'powers' of subjects. Such a framework enables us to shake off those conceptual habits which allow us to speak of a program 'producing outcomes' and to replace them with an imagery which sees the program offering chances which may (or may not) be triggered into action via the subject's capacity to make choices. Social programs involve a continual round of interactions and opportunities and decisions. Regardless of whether they are born of inspiration or ignorance, the subject's choices at each of these junctures will frame the extent and nature of change. What we are describing here is not just the moment when the subject signs up to enter a program but the entire learning process. The act of volunteering merely marks a moment in a whole evolving pattern of choice. Potential subjects will consider a program (or not), volunteer for it (or not), co-operate closely (or not), stay the course (or not), learn lessons (or not), retain the lessons (or not), apply the lessons (or not). Each one of these decisions will be internally complex and take its meaning according to the chooser's circumstances. Thus the act of volunteering for a program such as 'Cog Skills' might represent an interest in rehabilitation, a desire for improvement in thinking skills, an opportunity for a good skive, a respite from the terror or boredom of the wings, an opening to display a talent in those reputedly hilarious role-plays, a chance to ogle a glamorous trainer, a way of playing the system to fast-track for early parole, and so on.

What this suggests to us is that corrections evaluation needs to develop a much more comprehensive model of the way that different subjects make choices in response to the range of opportunities offered in the course of a program. Experimental evaluation is simply not attuned to grasping this challenge. We have already seen the basic instincts at work. The volition of the subject has to be treated in the same way as any other threat to the integrity of the basic design. That is to say, it is to be regarded as 'noise', as a 'confounding variable' which has to be controlled by supplementing the basic design in order to allow the real experimental apparatus to get rolled into place. Experimental logic gobbles up the problem by first of all treating an entire conceptual domain (choice making) as a variable (motivation), then coming up with a ready-made measure of motivation (volunteering), and then introducing the standard apparatus of random allocation (pre-selection equivalence) to ensure the 'volunteer effect' is controlled out of the explanatory equation. We suggest, moreover, that the experimental approach is unlikely to be diverted from such conceptual steerage because the logical routing just described brings on board a mighty series of other commitments, namely dealing with the 'operational realities' described above such as coping with transfers, unequal waiting lists and so on. Our charge here is thus basically that experimental evaluation deals with a problem by changing it, and that the issue of the

'transformative capacity' of subjects is squeezed back into the successionist framework of manipulate, control, and observe.

So far we have pursued our argument on the basis of some first-hand
(but one might say, intuitive) knowledge of how prisoners find their way
onto programs. Is there a rather more solid empirical foundation for our
claim that the subject's choice making capacity cuts right across and thus
undermines the volunteer/non-volunteer distinction? We need look no
further than the data from Porporino and Robinson's pilot investigation of
the first 50 men through the Cognitive Skills Training Program which we
reproduce as Figure 2.2. The three histograms compare the readmission
rates of (from the left): volunteers who made it onto the program (treatment group); volunteers who 'waited' or were dispersed (control group);
the base rate of readmissions for the correctional system as a whole. What
do the data reveal?

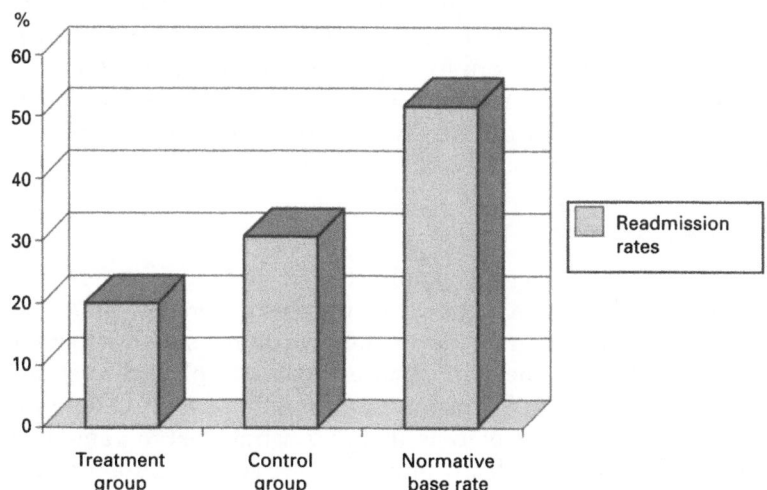

Figure 2.2 *Comparison of readmission rates for experimental,
control and base rate groups*

Let us offer three readings:

1 *The experimentalist's lesson.* The experimental and control groups are
   identical right down to the fact that all have volunteered. The results
   thus show that the program seems to be working and further evidence
   should be sought by replication of this procedure on a larger scale.
2 *The bureaucrat's lesson.* The biggest 'improvement' (compare the control
   and base rate histograms) seems to be in the men who volunteered for

the course but did not undertake it. A way forward for corrections would be to offer lots of courses attracting lots of volunteers but then not bother to run them.

3 *The realist's lesson.* The course seems to have made a difference but for a self-selected group. Exploring the difference between the control group and the base rate is just as vital, however, because we need knowledge of the make-up of the volunteers if the success is to be replicated.

Reading 1 requires no further explanation. Reading 2, we should say very rapidly, is just us being facetious. It assumes, of course, a bogus equivalence between the population and the volunteers. Yet in a way it is just half a joke, for readings 1 and 2 have some unfortunate parallels. Both of these readings are products of attending to evaluation by only having eyes for comparisons involving 'inputs' and 'outputs' with scant regard for just who is experiencing the 'throughput'. We thus reach our conclusion that the realistic lesson (reading 3) of 'volunteer-only' experiments is that *they encourage us to make a pronouncement on whether a program works, without knowledge of the make-up of the volunteers.* One is alerted to the crucial point that programs tend to work for some groups more than others, but the methodology then directs attention away from an investigation of these characteristics and towards (as we have seen) the battle to maintain the equivalence of the two subsets of this self-selected group.

Horses and courses

This brings us to another key feature of a transformative understanding of rehabilitative change. In arguing that prisoners exercise volition in benefiting from what a program has to offer, we do not suppose that they are free agents (forgive the pun) who exercise complete discretion as to whether they benefit from the provision, and thus simply choose whether they go straight or not. Choice is always constrained. Programs are learning processes and, as with any other learning activity, certain groups and certain individuals are more likely to have the appropriate characteristics to allow them to profit from the experience. It is one of the commonest experiences of program practitioners that they have a sense of the 'type' of subjects for whom a program is particularly salient. This is a rather every-day piece of wisdom, the significance of which will be returned to throughout the book. For now, we only wish to use it to pass on the next broad charge against standard experimental designs, namely that the concentration on the comparison between the two broadly equivalent aggregates of experimentees and controls makes it an extremely poor instrument for picking up these harmonious marriages of subject and provision through which programs really work.

Picking up our example again, we note that, quite typically, the only subsets of prisoners initially distinguished are the group which happens to volunteer (which is further subdivided into experimentees and controls) and those who do not. Applying our horses-for-courses argument, we can speculate that there will be some people for whom Cognitive Skills may well have a particular salience, as well as others for whom it constitutes a poor choice. Assuming that this 'informed guess' about this particular trial is correct, we have a result of great potential significance for evaluation methodology in corrections. Experimental outcomes are likely to be much influenced by the overall 'balance' of the group which happens to volunteer. On one occasion we may have a group who find the program particularly felicitous; on another, many volunteers may turn out to have backed the wrong course (or horse). The great worry underlying all this, of course, is that experimental results are likely to vary if this balance shifts much from trial to trial.

This may sound familiar. This inconsistency of results is precisely what led us to place the microscope upon the experimental tradition in evaluation, and we find ourselves back with the 'Martinson problem'. The reasons for this lack of certainty in evaluation research have been much speculated upon and we would concur with other commentators that incompetence in implementation, death by political cross-fire, insufficiently articulated goals, as well as some downright bad ideas in the conception of programs have led to the topsy-turvy outcome patterns noted several times previously. Ponder for a moment, however, on where the finger points in all these 'excuses' for lack of progress. About the only 'stakeholders' not to get it in the neck are the members of the research community. The significant difference between this and previous accounts of why evaluation findings are so capricious is that our explanation will point the finger of suspicion at methodological failure. Could it be that research languor rather than policy blight lies at the root of the problem?

Alas, the cognitive skills evaluation also follows the typical tortured path of boom and bust. The pilot experiment, with its rather encouraging data reported above, was followed up by a full-scale evaluation having much the same methodological characteristics. This followed the national implementation of the program by which time 1,400 inmates had completed the program. The full-scale evaluation followed a subsample of 757 cases, of which 446 cases had actually completed the program, 104 were program drop-outs, and 207 men were used as waiting list controls in the manner previously described. The overall result is depicted as Figure 2.3.

Two 'outcome' measures were examined. The percentage of former inmates who are 'convicted' of a new offence actually shows a 1% increase for the treatment group over the controls (15% – 14%). Offenders assigned to Cognitive Skills were 'readmitted' at a rate of 32% compared with 37% for the control group. This is a movement in the right direction but not a statistically significant one. Such variation could quite reasonably occur by chance. Porporino and Robinson revert to some distinctly non-experimental language in order to disguise their disappointment here. At least, they say, the program is 'an overture that makes sense to offenders', given only

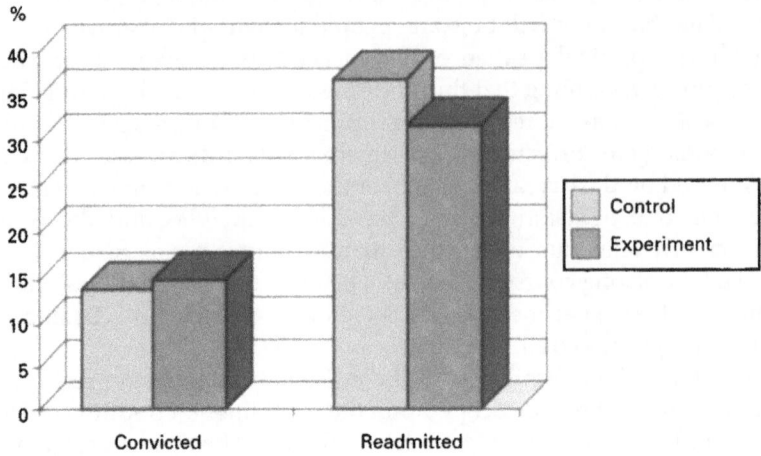

Figure 2.3   *Conviction and readmission rates in the main experiment*

a 20% drop-out rate. They also come up with a neat explanation of lack of success which concedes a point or two about inmate volition. Entrenched criminals, they point out, 'may have learned new skills, but they prefer their old habits'. In the end, though, they are driven to regret the lacunae of evaluation knowledge and perhaps the demise of the latest programming brain-child:

> Administrators and policy-makers, unaware or misinformed about these issues [the indeterminacies of evaluation], and the considerable efforts needed to address them, may rush first into wholesale buy-in, as the promises of impact on recidivism are made, but then into wholesale sell-out, as the generalized reductions in recidivism seem not to be realized. (1995, p. 186)

One wonders just who is hoisting whose petard here? For us, this sequence of events is typical of the lack of progress of experimental evaluation. Our explanation for the turnaround in success in this instance is that 'pilot' and 'full' experiments have picked up a different balance of subgroups of offenders in terms of their potentialities with respect to Cognitive Skills. Recalling our suspicions above about the mighty range of reasons which might bring a prisoner into a program (from repentance to skiving), it is not difficult to imagine that these motivations might alter and multiply as we move from trial to national implementation. It may well be that inmates enter because they are displaced from programs removed to make way for the new 'buy-in'; it may well be that more parole-chasers are willing to place their bets on the major program carrying the clout of the Ottawa policy makers; it may well be that the attractions of being in the 'showcase' initial trial are not there for the 2,501st volunteer.

These are simply speculations on our part. The range of inducements to enter a course will vary with local conditions. What is more, we are certainly not suggesting that such potential motivations be stirred into the 'pre-selection equivalence' pot, since there is no way of achieving control over the mass of judgements made during the typical program. What we are suggesting is that the engine for program success comes when the right horse chooses the right course, and experimentalists have been remarkably poor at playing this particular field. To escape the problem (as well as our wretched racing metaphor), we can rephrase the contention by going back to the basic proposition about *why* a program works. This will identify *some* program aspect which meets *some* existing need of a program subject. Our argument is that the best way to get at the crucial causal harmonies is to hypothesize and test within-program variation in the success rates of different subgroups of subjects. Alas, as we are about to see, the apparatus of the OXO experiment, with all its other priorities, tends to suppress such an insight.

The classic experimental design distinguishes only two subgroups – experimentees and controls. A volunteer-only experiment distinguishes three – experimentees, controls and non-volunteers (see Figure 2.2). Porporino and Robinson's experiments take us a couple of steps further. The underlying program theory is that the cognitively deficient are those in need of cognitive skills. The program is thus offered not to all and sundry but only to those having 'high' cognitive deficits as identified by case managers. Those familiar with penal systems will know that our prisons and penitentiaries do not deal with the world's best and brightest. The pre-selection to a high-volume program like Cognitive Skills thus involves quite a generous cut of the prison population. The experiment also takes on board what is often regarded as the 'first law' of prison initiatives, namely 'Andrews's principle' (Andrews et al., 1990) which asserts that programs work best when aimed at 'high-risk' offenders. Again, case managers tried to ensure that offenders who had the greatest risk of reoffending – as measured by the statistical information on recidivism (SIR) scale – were invited to volunteer for the course. This is easily enough measured: certain factors such as 'number of previous incarcerations', 'age at first incarceration' and so on are part of a well-established pattern of reoffence and have been put together in the SIR prediction instrument which is able to band prisoners broadly into five increasing levels of risk of return. Selection went roughly to plan in this respect, with 61% of Porporino and Robinson's subjects falling in the 'fair to poor' or 'poor' risk categories.

Our argument is that programs work when suitable cases are brought for apt treatment. We can see if the 'Cog Skills' evaluation made any progress on this score by following through the results on 'risk'. Andrews's principle is a loathsome creature from our point of view. It is what we would describe as a 'successionist law', that is to say it is hacked around the literature as a mere empirical regularity which happens to have cropped up as an outcome across a range of experiments with offenders. The problem is that it remains short on explanations on *why* this pattern regularly emerges. Before we would accept it as a 'principle' we would want something established about the 'tendencies' or 'liabilities' of high-risk offenders which made them conducive to change under programs. Those who in the normal bleak course of prison events tend to be reoffenders might do well on programs for a variety of reasons: 'ceiling effects' (they can't get much worse), 'high project availability' (they tend to be around for some time), 'last chancers' (they have reached the point where they can't take any more), 'lost souls' (they have lacked any previous attention). These (bracketed) thoughts are merely top-of-the-head possibilities, of course. The whole point is to circumscribe which of these processes trigger in which kind of program in which kind of circumstance. Without knowledge of these real causal agents the principle is a sitting duck, just waiting to be shot down (falsified) at the next empirical trial . . . which brings us back to Porporino and Robinson's experiments. In thinking about differential effects according to risk, they went further than targeted pre-selection, and followed a (potentially realist) path of examining outcomes for different subsets of prisoners. Experimental and control comparisons are thus made for two groups of 'low-risk' and 'high-risk' prisoners, as defined by breaking the sample at the median SIR score. The results are given in Figure 2.4.

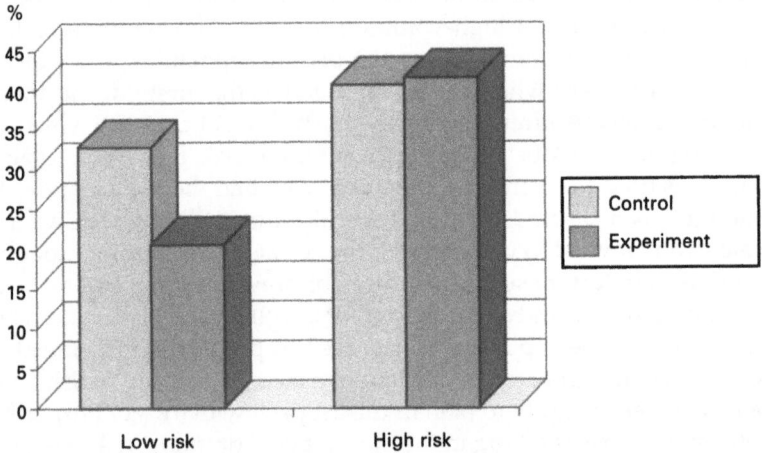

Figure 2.4   *Comparison of readmission rates for low-risk and high-risk groups*

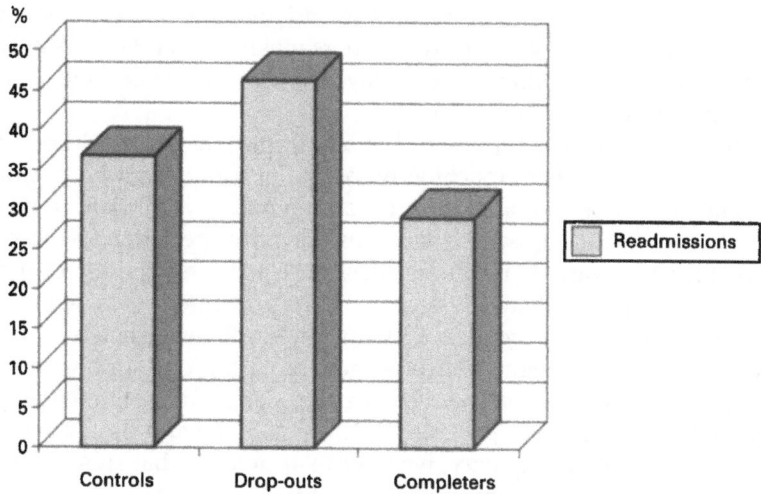

Figure 2.5 *Comparison of readmission rates for controls, drop-outs and completers*

This represents more gloom and despondency for Porporino and Robinson. The results are 'unambiguous'. Cognitive Skills has brought about a statistically significant improvement for the low-riskers, and has had no effect whatsoever for the high-riskers. Andrews's principle has been hit with a dose of salts. Porporino and Robinson (1995, p. 185) set off at this point into *ad hoc* principle-saving speculation that 'risk' is a relative term and that their 'low-riskers' can be considered, well, 'high-riskers' in the grander scale of criminal activity. What, perhaps, they might have considered is that this accidental discovery of a subgroup for whom the program worked is a model for how the initiative as a whole should have been evaluated. It may be that these federal low-risk inmates (stinking with the original designation) are somehow more open-minded in their receptivity to thinking skills than the real old lags who may tinker with their new-found abilities with ne'er a thought that they will be applied. This is all *post hoc* speculation, of course, and therein lies our methodological case. Programs work through a process of constrained choice and, without some clear initial theorizing about what the potentially successful pathways may be, we will never be able to capture and understand them with the standard experimental categories.

A final example of this comes from a 'successful' sorting of within-program 'winners' and 'losers' by Porporino and Robinson. Yet another 'equivalence problem' arose when they confronted the classic problem of course 'drop-outs'. Are these to be excluded from consideration in the experimental group on the grounds that they did not complete the treatment, or should they be included on the grounds that the experimental group comprising only 'completers' would effectively select a well-motivated cream? In the event our researchers make the standard decision that separate data are required on both stayers and withdrawers, and we reproduce the findings as Figure 2.5.

This is a somewhat typical and vitally important result. Drop-outs are readmitted at a rate approaching twice that of completers! Porporino and Robinson's experimentalist instincts on the matter lead them to pose the question of what happens if we consider only the latter as the proper experimental group. No joy here, alas, since even this self-selected group does not enjoy a statistically significant improvement over the controls. These results do deserve their exclamation mark, nevertheless, if we consider the broader lesson, which is that 'dropping out' and 'completing' merely mark two poles of the subject group's encounter with the program. Rather than imagining a program is a fixed X in the middle of a controlled OXO observational sequence, we have to appreciate that subjects come to programs with a compendium and continuum of anticipations – expectantly, open-mindedly, half-heartedly, cynically. Such hopes will render the initiative, on a daily basis, into a different kind of encounter. Experimental horses, it might be said, choose their own courses. What this points to is the need to conceive programs as a series of different *pathways*, consisting of a variety of modes of engagement with a course and a whole structure of opportunities offered by a course. If we begin to hypothesize about some of these potential routes, in advance of empirical work, then the real causal agents within programs would begin to appear systematically on the research agenda.

The implications of our battle with this particular case study should now be clear. In its search for evidence, experimental evaluation works with a logic which prioritizes a certain set of observational categories and sequences. This framework tends to overlook the real engine for change in social programs which is the process of differently resourced subjects making constrained choices amongst the range of opportunities provided. On the two occasions in the above research when such mechanisms have been contemplated, the results sprang into statistical significance. This is no small irony: the Cognitive Skills research comes to life the moment we recognize that the subjects are already cognitively skilled.

Causation and community policing

Our second case study moves us to the opposite end of the criminal justice system. We 'rewind' from the period when the criminal is behind bars to consider those programs aimed at reducing the fear of crime. We also focus deliberately on a type of initiative with the opposite *scope*, moving from courses aimed at changing individual behaviour to projects targeted at the community. Futhermore, we move into the realm of *quasi-experimentation*, in which cases are chosen by matching rather than random assignment. Methodologically speaking, however, our objectives are similar, in that we wish to drive home the lesson about programs consisting of myriad pathways of constrained choice which get missed on the high road of experimentation. In particular, we will use this case study to illustrate the weakness of the experimental paradigm in understanding the explanatory import of the social context in which a program operates.

A word, first of all, on the target for our criticism here. We are acutely aware in the choice of both case studies of the danger of setting up some kind of Aunt Sally, ready-made for a knocking exercise. We thus choose Bennett's 'The effectiveness of a police-initiated fear-reducing strategy' (1991) for several reasons, most of them due to its excellence. His study is a thorough, technically proficient, indeed statistically sophisticated evaluation. It is carried out by an experienced, independent researcher at an elite institution. It was carried out with the enthusiastic co-operation of the key stakeholders (notably the police) and was supported by the financial and political clout of the Home Office Research and Planning Unit. The results, furthermore, were deemed significant enough for publication in a leading journal, *The British Journal of Criminology*. All this is about as far as it is possible to be from *post hoc* shoe-string efforts by the untrained and self-interested practitioner which is the case in much work which passes for evaluation. In short, it is the leader in its particular field, especially since, as Bennett notes, there were very few precedents for this type of study in Britain.

Let us now briefly outline Bennett's method. In Cook and Campbell terminology, it might be labelled multiple outcome, composite control design, employing pre- and post-test, panel and cross-sectional samples, incorporating process evaluation (repeated twice!). We (somewhat bravely) attempt to represent the design in Figure 2.6.

Two experimental areas (*E*) in Southwark, London, and in south Birmingham were selected for study. These were estates comprising about 2,000 households which were expected to be characterized by high levels of fear of crime on the basis of high and comparable existing victimization rates and on the basis of site visits which revealed similar 'visual indicators' of disorder such as graffiti, broken windows, criminal damage and amount of litter. Neighbouring 'control' areas were chosen which were deemed to be similar by dint of the same set of characteristics. A subtlety here was the fact that these were 'composite control areas' (C_1, C_2, C_3) – that is to say amalgamations of a number of non-program locations, a tactic which serves to lessen the potential extraneous effect of unpredictable *local* crises in crime and policing of the kind which have been known to disturb the best conceived field experiments. Three nearby areas in London and two neighbouring areas in Birmingham were thus selected for the control sample. Samples were drawn using about a third of the households in the chosen areas, the particular member to be interviewed being selected randomly.

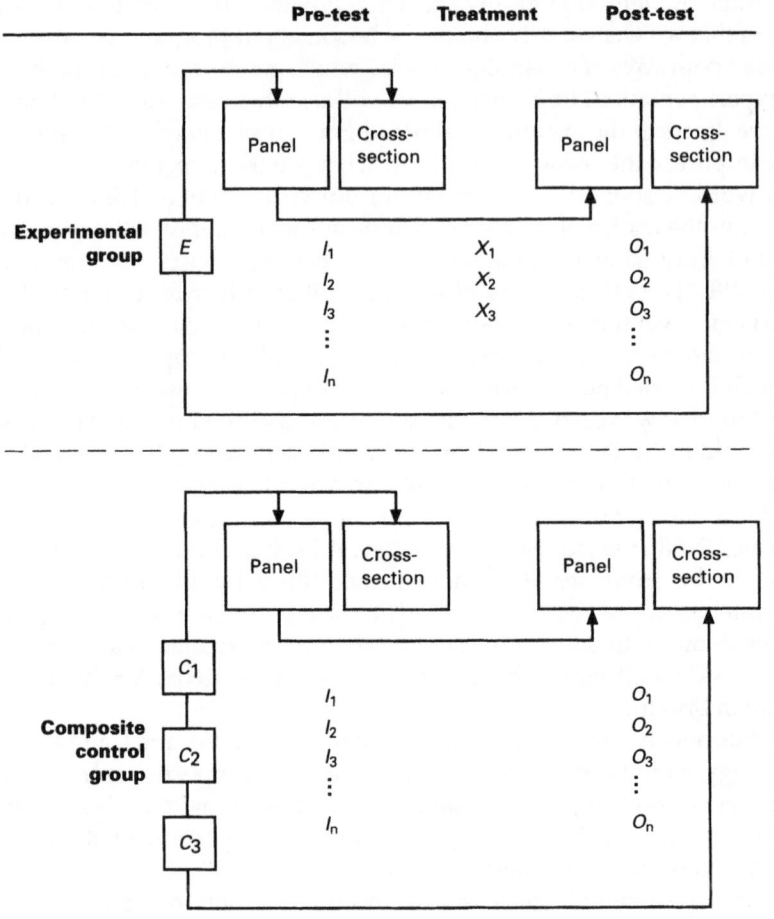

Figure 2.6   *Bennett's design*

Further methodological rigour is evident in the use of both cross-sectional and panel samples to provide the pre- and post-treatment data (though as it turned out, little difference accrued from the two strategies). Program effectiveness was measured by making comparisons over time $(I - O)$ of 'change in victimization', 'change in fear of victimization', 'perceptions of the area', 'informal social control' and 'satisfaction with police'. Each of these items was represented by several items which themselves were derived from a factor analysis of a large number of separate questions which had been 'tried and tested' in the British Crime Survey.

Another bugbear of evaluation research is that programs often do not perform as expected because of failures in implementation rather than conception. Once again, we have no immediate argument with Bennett on this score for, in addition to the above, he carried out a 'process' evaluation to check that the program had actually been conducted as planned. It is worth noting carefully, however, the precise *mechanics* of the program which were inspected, namely 'contact rate' and 'duration'. Ultimately a total of 88% of Birmingham and 87% of London households were contacted (X_1). Contacted dwellings were checked (X_2) to ensure that they had the same demographic characteristics as the estate population as a whole (more rigour). On average, over the one-year program, at least one police officer was in the area for 10.6 hours per day in Birmingham and 10.4 hours per day in London (X_3), with only two days in the former and eleven in the latter during which there were no officers on patrol. On this basis Bennett pronounces that the 'the main programme elements were implemented effectively and constitute a programme capable of being evaluated in terms of its outcome effectiveness.'

So there we have it – a particularly well-researched sledgehammer of an evaluation. We will proceed to explain why we think the sledgehammer missed the nut shortly, but first let us outline Bennett's results.

1 The program was noticed. Thus, the percentage of residents who 'know some police officer by name or sight' increased by 35% in the Birmingham experimental area and by 20% in the London experimental area. This contrasts with an increase of only 3% in the Birmingham control area and a decrease of 4% in the London control area. There was an increase of 34% in those in the Birmingham experimental area who had seen a police officer in the past two weeks, though no change in this in the experimental area in London (1991, p. 6).

2 Actual changes in rates of criminal victimization, as Bennett expected, did not vary between experimental and control areas (1991, p. 7).

3 Somewhat against expectations created by previous work, there were no positive net changes in 'fear of victimization'. The small improvements that did occur were matched by improvements in the control area (1991, p. 8).

4 One aspect of 'perceptions of the area', 'satisfaction with area', showed statistically significant improvement in the Birmingham experimental area, and another aspect, 'sense of community', did so in London (1991, pp. 9–10).

5 With regard to 'informal social control practices', the Birmingham experimental group evidenced positive change in 'control of crime' through 'taking action in response to burglary' and 'asking neighbours to watch property when away', whilst the London experimental sample registered improvement only in the latter (1991, p. 10).

6 'Satisfaction' and 'contact' with police improved substantially in both experimental areas (1991, p. 11).

To repeat, a rigorous design, followed painstakingly, producing as far as we are concerned some trustworthy results. What is wrong with this? From the policy maker's perspective – quite a lot. Nothing much follows at all so far as policing practices go. We are left in the dark about whether, where or how we might take community policing forward. The 'Martinson problem' rears its unwelcome head in this corner of the literature too. Some results were expected, some not. Some findings follow those of previous studies, some do not. No generalizable conclusions are forthcoming. No progression is evident. It is hard to see that previous uncertainties have been lessened or that a future program to reduce remaining uncertainties is suggested. One can imagine police chiefs reading through the report and wondering about implications for their patch. They would find no help even in deciding whether they would suffer the fate of the London or the Birmingham experiment, since the considerable differences in outcomes receive no comment by Bennett.

Doses and suggestions

Thus we return to our key question: *what is it about experimental evaluation, or in this case quasi-experimental evaluation, which leads even the very best of it to yield so little?* The central problem lies, once again, in the deficient and defective conception of the program which is built into the methodology. From the point of view of those delivering the program, it is reduced to a set of mechanical operations: contacts with the public, and days and average hours on the estate. This is a stark description of what is likely to be rather more complex and multifaceted. In practice, it transpires that the program was indeed rather more than what is suggested in the minimal measured features. A range of activities other than mere contact were encouraged, including leafleting, counselling, problem identification, monitoring actions taken, offering security advice and so on. Most significantly, 'beat officers were encouraged to manage their daily schedules as much as possible and to devise methods of achieving their own and team objectives' (Bennett, 1989, p. 30). This is highly suggestive of implementation differences which may well explain some of the variations in outcome pattern.

Our complaint here, however, is not merely the technical one that we have uncovered a bit of unconsidered variation. Our point is that by reducing the program to a series of mechanical steps, a series of performance targets (X_1, X_2, X_3) as in Figure 2.6, *OXO* gazes directly past the real question: what it is about the patrols which might lead them to cause a reduction in crime rates, fear of crime, improved community spirit and so on. As we stressed earlier, social programs are the product of volition, skilled action and negotiation by human agents and are not reducible to the facticity of a given event (frequency, duration etc.). What Bennett needed to be investigating is the *character of the contact*.

Crime exists within certain communities because it is tolerated, supported, overlooked, disowned, engaged in, despaired of, fought against in different measures by various groupings within that community. In the language of generative causation we can say that existing levels of crime are conditioned 'internally' by the overall balance of such sentiments within the locality. Contact policing will attempt to work by changing the balance of reasoning. Such programs should therefore be considered not as a given level of 'dosage' applied to the sick community but as 'suggestions' for future action. They will work (or not) according to whether these suggestions enter the reasoning of subjects, so changing that reasoning and subsequent action. As we discovered with the prison example, these chains of reasoning can be expected to be long, complex and diverse.

What evaluation research of this ilk should be testing, therefore, is a series of *implicit hypotheses* about how police presence may be persuasive in changing local patterns of thought and deed on crime. Contact patrols might work with the police and the more positively inclined members of the locality developing mutual trust to form the eyes and ears of the community, by such surveillance reducing the inclination of criminals and their supporters to pursue crime in the district. Success might follow because such schemes increase informal social bonds between those who had fought against crime and those who had tolerated it or despaired of change. A positive effort to increase neighbourly activities might be reckoned to reduce social isolation upon which fear of crime feeds. Patrols might work by countering the prevailing local mood (or propaganda) about the inevitability of victimization. This would foster a more active interest in crime prevention measures amongst those groups which had become resigned to the breaking-and-entering status quo. No doubt a range of other mechanisms are possible but this gives us a start, at paragraph length, in setting down some potential engines for change in such programs.

What is astonishing about Bennett's approach is its complete failure to put any such propositions to empirical test. And why does such research fail to get on to the real and obvious questions? Our answer should by now be clear, namely that evaluation research tends to be *method-driven*. Everything needs to be apportioned as an 'input' or 'output', so that the program itself becomes a 'variable', and the chief research interest in it is to inspect the dosage in order to see that a good proper spoonful has been applied (to repeat Bennett's words, 'the main program elements were implemented effectively and constitute a program capable of being evaluated in terms of its outcome effectiveness').

Communities and composites

Let us turn to the other side of the equation, switching attention from the delivery of the program to its reception within the community. The quasi-experimental conception is again deficient. Communities clearly differ. They also have attributes that are not reducible to those of the individual members.

These include cultures (for example religious beliefs), structures (for example employment patterns), and relationships (for example contacts between ethnic groups). In the language of generative causation, we would say that communities have 'powers' and 'liabilities'. It is these internal characteristics which allow them to accept or resist change. A particular program will only 'work' if the contextual conditions into which it is inserted are conducive to its operation, as it is implemented. Remember that programs are 'suggestions' and that suggestions go down much better in some localities than others. Quasi-experimentation's method of random allocation, or efforts to mimic it as closely as possible, represents an endeavour to cancel out differences, to find out whether a program will work without the added advantage of special conditions liable to enable it to do so. This is absurd. It is an effort to write out what is essential to a program – social conditions favourable to its success. These are of critical importance to sensible evaluation, and the policy maker needs to know about them. Making no attempt to identify especially conducive conditions, and in effect ensuring that the general and therefore the unconducive are fully written into the program, almost guarantee the mixed results we characteristically find.

In the case of Bennett's study we learn virtually nothing of the communities acting either as experimental sites or as controls. Here, the issue of what might operate to facilitate or impede effectiveness of the programs is not addressed. The design makes it irrelevant, so its exclusion is neither surprising nor culpable. All we know is that the experimental 'estates' are small (of about 2,000 households), are well bounded, and had high crime rates and similar amounts of graffiti and litter. We know nothing of the *character of the community* into which the community policing experiment was introduced. Variations in levels of street and commercial activity, internal division on the basis of age or race, estate design and density, rates of unemployment, isolation or otherwise from the city centre, population turnover and so on are not considered but in a fairly obvious way mark differences in community which may inform how a social program is received. We know even less of the 'control' estates. Indeed, whilst the device of using *unreal* 'composite' groups within quasi-experimental terms is excellent, in our terms it reveals a crucial weakness, since particular communities and their cultures and values obviously exert a profound and *real* influence on what police contact will be able to achieve. *Our argument is that precisely what needs to be understood is what it is about given communities which will facilitate the effectiveness of a program!* And this is what is written out.

For example, the one community feature we do learn of with clarity in regard to the experimental communities is overlooked in the analysis. Using Bennett's scoring system, initial 'level of satisfaction' with area rates 1.84 in Birmingham, but only 1.54 in London. 'Sense of community' rates 1.96 in Birmingham, but 1.71 in London. These 10–20% differences are indicative of real differences in the estates and presumably stem from such collective factors as social and ethnic divisions, amounts of community and street activity, level of friendship and kinship ties, turnover and tradition and so on. Bennett, however, views these scores as input variables with an eye to whether they change. But it is just these sorts of differences, combined perhaps with implementation differences, which may explain whether a program works. For instance, looking back to the basic results, we note the substantially higher rate at which the program was 'experienced' in Birmingham compared with London (Bennett, 1991, p. 6). The extent to which an officer is 'seen' on the streets depends somewhat self-evidently on the amount of street activity in the community. This is one of the several such matters neither commented on nor considered in Bennett's own study since his method directs him away from it.

Again we need to ponder closely the question of why there is such stunning oversight. We need to remind the reader that this is not a one-off case of technical ineptitude. Far from it: this is technical excellence. The real reason why Bennett tried to learn about community policing without considering the community is that evaluation research continues to be method-driven. As we have seen, there are powerful glimpses from the demographic data and the attitudinal patterns that there are significant differences in the localities investigated here. The quasi-experimental instinct is always to attempt to 'flatten' them out, to regard them as confounding variables and to attempt to remove their influence so that we are left with the 'pure' impact of the program on outcomes.

We trust we have made it clear why such quasi-experimental evidence cannot speak for itself, why its conjunctions are never constant, and why we find ourselves back at square one sharing Skogan's bewilderment (recall Chapter 1) at the disparity of such program effects the world over. The remedy is to give contextual factors their proper place in investigation. For instance, if we take the example of a program whose aim is to promote 'confidence' that crime is under control, several contextual conditions need to exist for this mechanism to come into operation. There must (obviously) not already be high levels of such confidence; the community must not be so fractured that the initiative could itself become a focus of friction; there will probably need to be some existing grouping within which the notion of confidence can be seeded; there should be no powerful oppositional groupings espousing credible alternative messages; the population needs to be stable enough for channels of communication and points of leadership to develop. Our hunch is that it is precisely such features which the community worker or the bobby on the beat would have to attend to in order to make the contact program work. It is not asking too much that evaluators should pay attention too.

Conclusion

Our closing remarks should begin on a note of reconciliation. In its first line, this chapter is described as a 'constructive critique' of the experimental tradition in evaluation. Experience has taught us that some readers will have found the arguments destructive. Bennett (1996), for instance, has responded to a fuller version (Pawson and Tilley, 1994) of the above criticisms, finding them 'exasperated and disdainful'. Readers interested in our views on just whose arguments are *ad hominem* should consult Pawson and Tilley (1996). Here, it is appropriate to give a reminder of why we chose the two case studies discussed in this chapter. They represent the best of the experimental tradition, and it is *only* the usage of the experimental strategy and its attendant weaknesses in which we have been interested. The above discussion is thus *not* intended to be a comprehensive critique of the studies in question, or of the massive range of the further evaluation work of Porporino, Robinson and Bennett.

We examined two programs which are completely different in scope and content. Yet we discovered that their evaluations missed out on a similar range of causal agents, the lack of consideration of which rendered the research findings arbitrary and inconsistent. In both cases the initiatives were fired by offering subjects a range of 'ideas', 'opportunities', and 'suggestions'. These are met with the 'volition', 'choice', and 'decision making facilities' of the subjects, and it is the operation of these reasoning processes which sets the program along the road to success or failure. Subjects, of course, do not simply have a free choice on whether they respond to the initiative, and the scope for change is limited by their 'powers', 'liabilities', and 'capacities'. These will vary between subjects. If the subject is an individual, the program through all its phases may be met with variation in 'entrenchment of habits', 'levels of risk', and 'capacity for learning'. If the subject is a locality, limiting factors might be the extent of internal 'division', the availability of existing 'resources', or the level of 'communal activity'. The overall fate of any provision will be set by the balance of such pathways of constrained choice as they exist through the duration of the program.

The little forest of inverted commas in the above paragraph gives a general picture of the 'missing ingredients' of experimental evaluation. The more microscopic examination of each case study has provided illustrations galore of these various concepts at the everyday level of provision and practice. It is our contention that by its very logic, experimental evaluation either ignores these underlying process, or treats them incorrectly as inputs, outputs or confounding variables, or deals with them in a *post hoc* and thus arbitrary fashion. Evaluators, of course, are much like their subjects, not all of whom can be convinced to change. We thus resist any reading which says that we have been talking about 'bad practice' here. It is not a matter of the more 'sensitive experimentalist' being able to incorporate such features within yet more complex designs. Research will look quite different if we commence inquiry on these pathways of constrained choice. It remains to show and tell.

3

IN WITH THE NEW: INTRODUCING SCIENTIFIC REALISM

This chapter represents the pivot and the base of the book. Our particular contribution to evaluation is distinctive in that it is the first to rest on realist principles. In this chapter we attempt to enunciate these foundations in some detail. Inquiry is always an amalgam of principle and practice, and our aim here is to demonstrate the broad potential of realist investigation. As a philosophy of science, realism can be said to be one of the dominant axes in modern European thinking. It thus can provide a powerful abstract language to resolve the problems of explanation we started to wrestle with in the previous chapter concerning the nature and operation of 'causal' forces. Metaphysical victories count for little outside the corridors of philosophy departments, however, and evaluators will be impatient to see the practical payoffs of this supposed epistemological potential. The chapter will thus cover considerable ground in sweeping from the philosophy of science to the car park. In what might sound a rather bizarre leap of imagination, we will claim that understanding the principles of generative causation is the key to knowing whether closed-circuit television might prevent your parked car from being stolen. Such is the scope of realist thinking and such is the scope of this chapter.

Claiming to be a 'realist' can sometimes feel like choosing to bat on the side of the 'good'. Too many people, in too many walks of life, have argued for their cause under the banner of 'realism' for the concept to perform any wonders of clarification (cf. Julnes, 1996). We find the epithet to be irresistible, nonetheless, because it forms the second of our three targets of producing a real, realist, and realistic evaluation. Moreover, we have no real choice in the terminological matter, since the roots of our perspective can be traced directly back to the influential *realist* tradition in the philosophy of science, as identified in the writing of Hesse (1974), Lakatos (1970), Bhaskar (1975) and Harré (1972; 1986). Without going into the details for the moment, we can say that realism has sought to position itself as a model of scientific explanation which avoids the traditional epistemological poles of positivism and relativism. Realism's key feature is its stress on the mechanics of explanation, and its attempt to show that the usage of such explanatory strategies can lead to a progressive body of scientific knowledge.

In social science (most particularly sociology, geography, psychology) there have been a number of attempts to make the leap from scientific realist explanation to realist social explanation. Amongst the best known works of this ilk are Keat and Urry (1975), Bhaskar (1979), Harré (1978), Sayer (1984), Layder (1990), Greenwood (1994), and Archer (1995). Over the years some of these realist social scientists have forced their gaze down from the initial, rather metatheoretical concerns to the workaday practicalities of doing empirical work (Layder, 1993). In this light we would mention a previous effort of one of the present authors (Pawson, 1989) in a book which attempted a scientific realist account of measurement and data construction in sociology. The work you are now reading should be seen as a continuation along this road of driving realism into research practice.

The structure of this chapter is as follows. In the first section, we pick up the argument about the advantages of the generative model of causation and show that this very basic idea on 'how things change' requires a wholesale shift in our thinking about explanatory priorities and a major revision in how we organize empirical work. In particular, we produce a realist reading of certain famous episodes in natural science explanation in order to show that the working model of the experiment bears little resemblance to the experimental and control group model which is regarded as 'classical' in social science. We demonstrate that experimental apparatus and logic get put into place only after, and only because of, the production of theories of how physical systems are shaped by underlying causal forces. Physical scientists manufacture *regular, law-like outcomes* in their empirical work by creating experimental *contexts* which put into effect their knowledge of underlying molecular and kinetic *mechanisms*. This research strategy is summarized with our introduction in this section of the basic realist explanatory formula: *regularity = mechanism + context*.

In the second section, we turn to a general theory of change in social systems. Social programs are merely a special case of social change, which always comes in a spiral of new ideas and transforming social conditions. The social conditions which confront any group or generation of people are not of their own making. Whilst their choices are therefore limited, the new ideas of that particular group do go to transform and set the conditions for the next generation. This understanding of the 'duality of structure and agency' forms the basis of the *structurationist* model which sociologists try to use to reconstruct episodes of social change. Policy makers try to engineer episodes of social change, and the success (or otherwise) of these initiatives depends upon the extent to which the program theory has been able to predict and control this interpretative spiral of ideas and social conditions. Just as a theory of physical change precedes the natural science experiment, the careful enunciation of program theory is the prerequisite to sound evaluation. We demonstrate that one can use broadly the same formal and general conceptual matrix with which to express those program theories, namely: *outcome = mechanism + context*. In other words, programs work (have successful 'outcomes') only in so far as they introduce the appropriate ideas and opportunities ('mechanisms') to groups in the appropriate social and cultural conditions ('contexts'). All else in realist evaluation follows from such explanatory propositions.

In the third section of the chapter, we enter the car park in order to give an operational illustration of this explanatory matrix. We select the example of the CCTV program in city centre car parks because what might seem like a rather technical attempt to reduce crime turns out to fire a whole range of potential mechanisms whose effectiveness will be modified in different contexts. We list some nine potential explanatory mechanisms and some six possible limiting contexts, giving together a multitude of variations on a program theme. Successful evaluation is shown to require a planned program of empirical testing of these different propositions.

Realist explanation and real experiments

Let us begin with some provocative questions. How many experiments in natural science use experimental/control-group logic? Do we understand the action of gravity on a falling body by observing the motion of a cannon ball dropped from a leaning tower and comparing it with the motion of one that remains atop? Do we understand the behaviour of atoms smashed in a particle accelerator by comparing them with the actions of those not so treated? One does not need to be a historian of science to answer these questions.

The questions sound perverse because they accentuate a profound difference in thinking about the linkage between causality and the experimental method which divides natural and social science. *Experiments in natural science tend to follow generative logic, whereas social science experiments are, in the main, successionist.* The main exception to the former part of this rule is certain sectors of medical science (Elwood, 1988) which are still strongholds of the experimental and control group tradition. This book is intended to prove the exception to the latter half of the rule since we will urge that the move to a generative approach will transform the utility of experimental thinking in evaluation.

We trust we have said sufficient about successionism and its over-simplifications in the previous chapter, so we turn immediately to the business of building on our model of generative causation. In that chapter we introduced the latter model of causation by concentrating on a terminology which stressed that causality was a matter of the internal potential of a system or substance being activated in the right conditions. To repeat an example, we know that gunpowder *doesn't* always ignite when the flame is applied (we've all seen some close shaves on this in the movies). The causal connection involved is thus not established by constant conjunction, nor is it a Humean perception of the mind. Rather we know that spark causes explosion because of the chemical composition of the gunpowder (if we were chemists, we would be able to put this in terms of the molecular structure of the mixture of potassium nitrate, charcoal and sulphur having the capacity to produce exothermic reactions etc.). We also know that there will be no explosion if the conditions are not right – if the mixture is damp, if there is insufficient powder, if it is not adequately compacted, if there is no oxygen present, if the duration for which heat applied is too short, and so on.

This bit of popular science is useful to us in that it contains all the ingredients of a realist causal proposition. Our basic concern is still, of course, the *outcome* (the spark causing the explosion). But what does the explanatory work is first of all the *mechanism* (the chemical composition of the substance which allows the reaction), and secondly the *context* (the physical conditions which allow the mechanism to come into operation). This proposition – *causal outcomes follow from mechanisms acting in contexts* – is the axiomatic base upon which all realist explanation builds and which we present diagrammatically in Figure 3.1.

This explanatory format is ubiquitous in the physical sciences. For instance, think of perhaps the best known of all regularities in physics, that governing the relationship between the temperature, volume and pressure of a fixed mass of gas (PV/T = constant). We regard this as the 'gas law' even though we know that this equation of the constant conjunction between these variables holds for only a limited range of their values. We are nevertheless prepared to speak without hesitation of, say, an increase in pressure causing an increase in temperature, and are persuaded that such a relationship comprises a 'law of nature' because we have established a

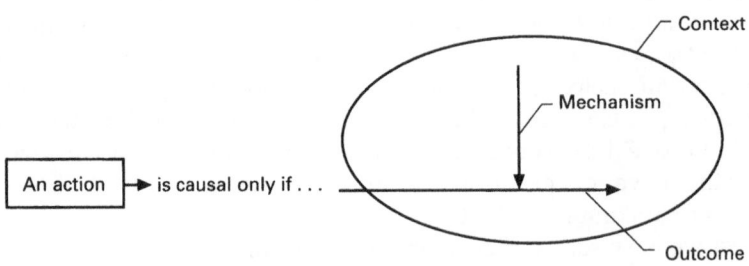

... its outcome is triggered by a mechanism acting in context

Figure 3.1   *Generative causation*

comprehensive model of the mechanisms and contextual conditions which bind together these elements of a system.

We have Bernoulli to thank for asking the question of why a gas had the potential for changing pressure and coming up with the notion that the *generative mechanism* is molecular motion. The properties of a gas thus come to be understood 'internally' as aspects of the behaviour of a swarm of microscopic, perfectly elastic particles in motion in a confined space. The motion of the particles generates *pressure* by bombarding the walls of the container, and *temperature* is related to the extent of molecular motion (or kinetic energy). As kinetic theory developed, it was discovered how to use the laws of classical mechanics to extend the swarm analogy to create a mathematical model which provided an entirely theoretical derivation of the gas laws. This model also builds in a variety of *contextual conditions* such as those noted above about perfect elasticity and the infinitely small size of molecules in relation to the volume occupied by the gas. As the theory became further refined this contextual understanding was put to use to explain empirical anomalies in the gas 'laws'. The laws 'fail' when a gas is near liquefaction, but the model is able to predict this changing empirical outcome by postulating how the contextual conditions may no longer be operational. In simple terms, we can say that gas molecules are relatively compressed at low temperatures, that they do not take up the hypothesized infinitely small space, and so the nature of the container bombardment changes, a correction being needed to be applied in relation to an increasing proportion of intermolecular collisions.

Whilst such an example hardly sets realistic standards for explanation in evaluation, it does have a skeletal structure which can be imitated. Outcomes are explained by the action of particular mechanisms in particular contexts, and this explanatory structure is put in place over time by a combination of theory and experimental observation. It is the precise nature of the realist interpretation of the interrelationship between theory and observation that we need to establish next. What is the role of experimental work as envisaged in realist methodology? We want to draw a sharp contrast here with the control-based strategy as envisaged in the so-called classic experimental design (Figures 1.1 and 2.1). The logic of *OXO* is to control a situation so that only change in the treatment can be responsible for the observed outcomes. The realist does not work with such one-dimensional logic, and a true (or should we say 'real') experiment has the following characteristics:

> The experimental scientist must perform two essential functions in an experiment. First, he must trigger the mechanism under study to ensure that it is active; and secondly, he must prevent any interference with the operation of the mechanism. These activities could be designated as 'experimental production' and 'experimental control'. (Bhaskar, 1979, p. 53)

One's view of the laboratory experiment shifts fundamentally if one starts

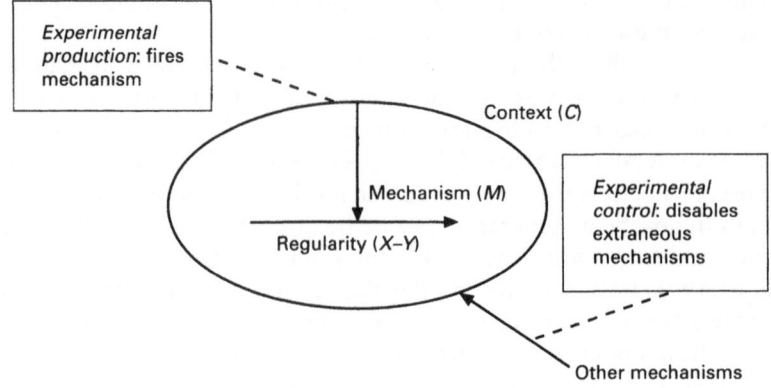

Figure 3.2 *The realist experiment*

from this vantage point (and by this we do not refer to the shock of discovering that all experimental scientists are male). Bhaskar seems to be
suggesting here that, instead of simply activating an independent variable and watching for its effect, the experimentalist's task is to manipulate
the entire experimental system, so as to *manufacture* the desired interrelationship between independent and dependent variable. The
experimentalist is indeed a *system builder* and the crucial evidence is produced not by controlled observation but by *work*.

A more complete, realist picture of the experimentalist's task would
thus go as follows. Experimentalists have a good deal of knowledge about
the *mechanism* (M) likely to bring about an empirical *regularity* (X–Y). They
put this theory to use in 'producing' (cf. Bhaskar) a *context* (C) which is
believed to sustain the ideal conditions to bring the mechanism into action.
The operation of the mechanism has the effect of shifting the physical
system out of equilibrium, causing change in its component properties
such as X and Y. Shifts in X and Y are recorded to see if they follow the predicted regularity. All this takes place under a situation of experimental
'control' (cf. Bhaskar). In the physical sciences, this has nothing to do with
control groups, but takes the form of 'laboratory control'. This amounts to
erecting some kind of physical barrier to ward off extraneous but anticipated causal forces or, more routinely, just carrying out the experiment in
otherwise stable conditions. This model of the experiment is summarized
in Figure 3.2. As well as noting the complete contrast with the *OXO* model,
the reader will not fail to register the similarity with Figure 3.1, and thus
the point we are attempting to illustrate, which is that realist experiments
are realist explanation incarnate.

At the risk of turning the chapter into a physics primer, we attempt to draw out some further consequences of this view of realist explanation via Koyré's (1968) realist reconstruction of some seventeenth century experiments on pendular motion. We enter the era of Galilean science and the attempts to understand the seemingly regular beats of a pendulum. Following Galileo's model, it was assumed that a simple pendulum consisted of motion caused by the action of a force (the gravitational constant) upon an object (the bob) as constrained by another force (the restraining influence of the string). Experiments were thus performed to discover the laws of pendular motion and, in particular, the relation between the period of oscillation and the length of the string, the ultimate aim being to devise a pendulum with a period of exactly one second.

Koyré describes lovingly the apparatus devised in pursuit of this task. We have to remember the rather difficult circumstances of the empirical work, there being no accurate timepiece then available to measure short intervals. This was something of a problem given the inclination, before too long, of the simple pendulum to draw to a halt. The most famous trials were those of Ricciole who used a team of Jesuit fathers trained to counteract the normal retardation of the pendulum by giving it a precise push after a given number of beats. This strategy aims for what the modern-day evaluator would call 'implementation effectiveness' and thus allowed the pendulum to complete a sufficient number of oscillations for its period to be timed by the then state-of-the-art waterclock. Despite the Jesuits being selected for their 'gift for music' which was hoped would allow them to keep in time with the precise rhythm of the pendulum, the experiments were not a success. Results could not be replicated, and Koyré chronicles the further frustrated efforts (some heroic, some fraudulent) to achieve reliability. Our imagination leaps at this point as we imagine the meta-evaluator, Father Doubting Thomas Martinson, surveying pendular programs and declaring that nothing works!

Eventually the experiments did work (and indeed pendulum clocks superseded waterclocks). What it took was a fresh look at the problem by Huygens, who we can say, without a shade of irony, applied some realist thinking to the problem. Instead of trying to discover the 'outcome' of the relationship between length and period of oscillation by attempting to perfect the existing experimental methods, he began by producing a model of the underlying 'mechanisms' of pendular motion. In 1659 Huygens produced a mathematical model which demonstrated that motion along the arc of a circle (as in a simple pendulum) was not regular; rather the quickest and most uniform line of descent followed a different geometrical pattern (the cycloid). We can follow the first steps in the theory by consulting Figure 3.3.

There are two forces acting on a simple pendulum – the downward force of gravity and the retaining tension in the string (Figure 3.3a). We can also think of the force in the string as having two components (Figure 3.3b) – one counteracting the downward force of gravity (that is, holding

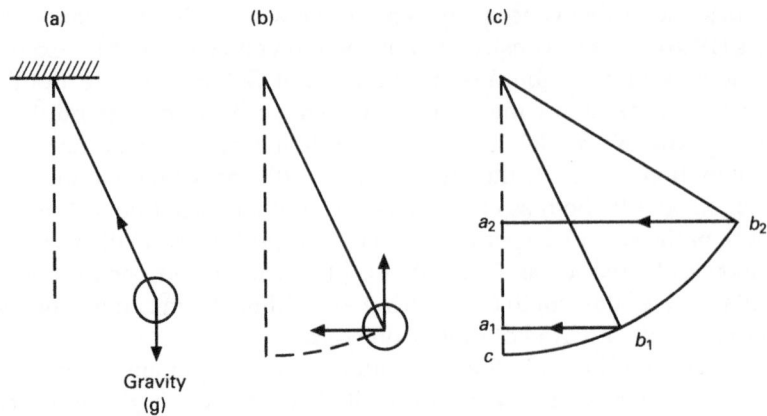

Figure 3.3   *Pendulum 'theory'*

the bob up) and one providing an inward force (that is, causing it to oscillate). At any particular moment, this inward force on the pendulum is proportional to the horizontal displacement of the bob ($a_1 b_1$, $a_2 b_2$ in Figure 3.3c). For small amplitudes this force is more or less equal to the displacement along the arc ($a_1 b_1 = b_1 c$ approximately). However, for large swings this approximation is a bad one ($a_2 b_2 \neq b_2 c$). Thus the inward force on the pendulum does not vary proportionally with the displacement along the arc, and the simple pendulum is not isochronous. This model of force mechanisms can be developed further to show that the 'cycloid' is the most regular line of descent (Bos, 1980).

Now we have the theory, it is possible to carry out experiments properly. What is needed is the production of an apparatus (the context) which will control the system so that a precise balance of forces (the mechanism) is fired to produce isochronous motion (the requisite outcome). Figure 3.3 provides us with a simple way to think about the experimental options. We now know that motion along the arc of a circle is not regular, but the distortion is minimized with short amplitude swings. Such a theory is immediately open to corroboration by comparing the periods of pendulums of the same length but oscillating with different amplitudes. Alternatively, we might hope to help the musical Jesuits and provide more reliable outcomes with the simple pendulum by advising them to stick to small amplitude experiments. More ambitiously, we can try to constrain the pendulum so that it follows the isochronous, cycloidal path. This was first achieved by having symmetrically shaped 'jaws' fixed to either side of the plane of motion, so that the string wraps itself partially onto one cheek and then the other. This enabled further experiments to be carried out comparing the speed and regularity of jaws and simple pendulums. The historical record demonstrates that there were in fact hundreds of variations on such experimental themes, all driven by increasing mastery of the mechanisms and contexts of pendular motion. We end our physics tutorial by quoting Kuhn:

> Because most scientific laws have so few points of contact with nature, because investigations of these contact points usually demand such laborious instrumentation and approximation, and because nature itself needs to be forced to yield the approximate results, the route from theory or law to measurement can almost never be travelled backwards. Numbers gathered without some knowledge of the results to be expected almost never speak for themselves. Almost certainly they remain just numbers. (1961, p. 174)

Experimentation is the vehicle that carries us on the route from law to measurement. Our illustration follows Kuhn's directional sense impeccably in showing that progress along this road is not method-driven. Progress is not a matter of careful replication of controlled trials which will arrive at empirical regularities. Such a process is more likely to end in error and inconsistency. Scientific progress occurs when experiments incorporate and test theory. Progress in theory development occurs by explicating the mechanisms and contexts which sustain law-like regularities. Progress in experimental method occurs when designs, comparisons and controls are put in place to manufacture the mechanisms and contexts which yield the expected outcomes.

If evaluators wish to be sincere in their imitation of the experimental method, we suggest some changes in the ranks of those who should be flattered. Perhaps it is time to abandon Hume and Mill (and their model of the experimentalist-as-logician), and celebrate Galileo and Huygens (and their practice of the theoretician-as-experimentalist).

Social reality, social causation and social change

What are social programs? It is useful to begin with such a stunningly simple question because much misunderstanding about the nature of the change engendered by programs has followed from an over-simple understanding of how such initiatives are themselves constituted. For us, there is no particular mystery about what one might term the 'ontology' of the policy initiative. Social programs are undeniably, unequivocally, unexceptionally *social systems*. They comprise, as with any social system, the interplays of individual and institution, of agency and structure, and of micro and macro social processes. Much is to be learned from inspecting the 'social nature' of programs. Realism has a standard set of concepts for describing the operation of any social system and the purpose of this section of the chapter is to draw parallels across into the explanation of *program systems*. We attempt this under five headings: 'embeddedness', 'mechanisms', 'contexts', 'regularities', and 'change'.

Embeddedness

Realists refer to the embeddedness of all human action within a wider range of social processes as the *stratified nature of social reality*. Even the most mundane actions only make sense because they contain in-built assumptions about a wider set of social rules and institutions. Thus, to use a favourite realist example, the act of signing a cheque is accepted routinely as payment, only because we take for granted its place within the social organization known as the banking system. If we think of this in causal language, it means that causal powers reside not in particular objects (cheques) or individuals (cashiers) but in the social relations and organizational structures which they form. One action leads to another because of their accepted place in the whole. This need to understand human action in terms of its location within different layers of social reality explains why realists shun the successionist view of causation as a relationship between discrete events (that is, cause and effect).

This simple principle is our starting point for understanding program systems. What we want to resist here is the notion that programs are targeted at subjects and that as a consequence program efficacy is simply a matter of changing the individual subject. Think of the examples which detained us in the previous chapter. The delivery of a 'treatment' for offenders such as the Cognitive Skills Training Program turns on a complex sequence of events and activities. At one level, it can be understood simply as a 'curriculum', a specific set of ideas and skills introduced into the minds of the prisoners. The ideas, however, are delivered in classroom interaction, and so are forged within a wider web of expectations about how prisoners should be treated. Programs are thus also 'work'. The instructor will be bound by one set of rules of behaviour, the prisoner by another. The instructor will have one set of aims, the inmate may choose another. Programs are also about 'people'. Practitioners have one particular set of backgrounds, experiences, and loyalties, inmates another; and the nature and success of the exchange of ideas will in turn be mediated by these characteristics. Programs, moreover, carry a 'history'. Prisoners and instructors will fetch into and out of programs a wider set of social resources and cultural expectations customarily given over to the treatment of the 'criminal classes'. Programs inevitably assume a 'future' and the impact of any initiative will depend on a rigid pattern of opportunities and constraints awaiting the inmate on release.

We have already told a similar tale about community policing programs. In one sense the program can be said to be the 'contact' achieved on patrol. Such interaction, however, can take on many different forms and range over a variety of ideas. The reception of the ideas will in turn depend on the cultural, social and economic circumstances in which the patrols are embedded. The ontological picture thus repeats itself, and we would submit that all social programs are encapsulated in this manner, a fact we can embody in the aphorism that 'a program *is* its personnel, its place, its past and its prospects'.

Mechanisms

This vision of a stratified reality leads directly to the next and most characteristic tool of realist explanation, which is the notion of the *explanatory mechanism*. The terminology of a 'mechanism' is instructive and vitally important here. To this point, we have been introducing the idea informally, by steps, via a range of natural and social science examples. We reach the stage where it is necessary to formalize matters. To understand fully the importance of explanatory mechanisms, we need to understand their entire role within the realist explanatory strategy. We refrain, therefore, from offering an instant pocket definition, and instead begin by trying to capture the first (of several) crucial characteristics. One image that realists use to express the idea is through the expression of the 'underlying' mechanism. This is a useful metaphor, since it captures the idea that we often explain how things work by going beneath their surface (observable) appearance and delving into their inner (hidden) workings. We can never understand how a clock works by examining only its face and the movement of its hands; rather we examine the clockworks, and so a proper understanding requires us to master the construction of the balanced spring or the oscillation of caesium atoms.

This notion of a stratified reality is, as we have seen, a commonplace in physical science explanation, with the 'laws of nature' often being explained via microscopic processes which refer to the powers and potentialities of molecular action. With Bernoulli, realists are saying that a gas *is* a swarm of microscopic particles and the regularities we observe connecting its outward properties are generated because of the ways of acting of these molecules. When it comes to explaining *social* regularities, most social scientists would allow for the causal potential of *both* micro and macro social mechanisms.

For example, if we think of the grand-daddy of all sociological tasks, that is the explanation of suicide rates, we see that social constitution is a matter for both individual action and social constraint. Durkheim (1951), whilst accepting that the decision to commit suicide was, of course, a matter of the individual's misery, desperation, isolation and so on, was able to show that such dispositions are socially structured and thus vary with the social cohesion and social support which different communities, localities, organizations, family groupings and so on are able to bring to marginalized members. He demonstrated that the supremely 'individual' act of suicide is in fact 'socially' structured and so produced the famous research cataloguing differences in suicide rates: higher in (individualistic) Protestant communities than in (collectivist) Catholic communities; higher for widowers in their competitive (public) male networks than widows in their communal (private) female networks; higher for the childless in their (restricted) family roles than for parents with their (extended) family ties; higher on (insouciant) weekends than (well-structured) weekdays; and so on.

Social mechanisms are thus about people's *choices* and the *capacities* they derive from group membership. We find the same combination of *agency* and *structure* employed generally across sociological explanation and we thus suppose that the evaluation of social programs will deploy identical explanatory forms, reaching 'down' to the layers of individual *reasoning* (what is the desirability of the ideas promoted by a program?) and 'up' to the collective *resources* on offer (does the program provide the means for subjects to change their minds?). It is through the notion of program *mechanisms* that we take the step from asking whether a program works to understanding *what it is about a program* which makes it work. So far, we have developed three key identifiers of a 'mechanism'. Thus we would expect 'program mechanisms' (i) to reflect the embeddedness of the program within the stratified nature of social reality; (ii) to take the form of propositions which will provide an account of how both macro and micro processes constitute the program; (iii) to demonstrate how program outputs follow from the stakeholders' choices (reasoning) and their capacity (resources) to put these into practice.

Chapter 4 will explore hypothesis making along these lines in depth, but for now we can provide a brief illustration by thinking across from suicide research to those rates which tend to be of interest to program evaluators such as crime rates. If we think of the police 'contact program' (mis-)examined in the previous chapter, the realist investigator would begin by thinking about the mechanisms through which it might work. Identifying mechanisms involves the attempt to develop propositions about what it is within the program which triggers a reaction from its subjects. These hypothesized processes attempt to mirror how programs actually work, and they always work in a 'weaving process' which binds resources and reasoning together. One such mechanism within the contact program might be an 'empowerment' process. Thus if we think of the patrols as providing a new resource in that community, this capacity could work its way into people's reasoning by developing mutual trust, so that the newly empowered members of the community increase their own surveillance, crime reportage and self-protection. A recognition of these new choices and increased community resources might in turn induce the potential criminal to think again and recalculate the risk of operating in that neighbourhood. Alternatively, the increased contact capacity might fire off a 'reassurance' mechanism in which the simple presence of the 'bobby on the beat', combined perhaps with messages about 'lightning not striking twice', might work their way into the reasoning of residents to build confidence, which might in turn weave its way to increase neighbourly activity, so further increasing assuredness. The reader will appreciate that we are merely outlining processes which are not mutually inclusive and not complete in the way the above descriptions might imply. What we hope to have demonstrated, however, is something about the nature of all mechanisms. We set out the basic features of social mechanisms, as well as the difference between these and the mechanisms used in natural science explanation, with a summary of our three examples as in Figure 3.4.

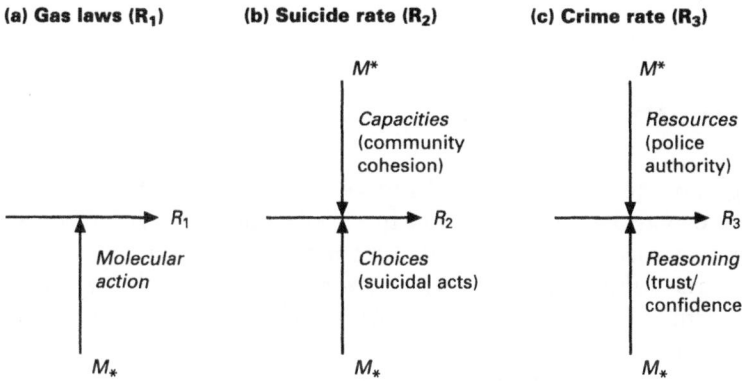

Figure 3.4 *Explanatory micro (M∗) and macro (M*) mechanisms in physics, sociology and evaluation*

This idea of calling on different layers of reality in social explanation has vital implications for the way we think about causation. When we say that the mechanism which explains a regularity is located at a different 'layer' of social reality, we employ a quite distinctive and *generative* conception of causality. Again the terminology is vital. To 'generate' is to 'make up', to 'manufacture', to 'produce', to 'form', to 'constitute'. Thus when we explain a regularity generatively, we are not coming up with variables or correlates which associate one with the other; rather we are trying to explain how the association *itself* comes about. The generative mechanisms thus actually *constitute* the regularity; they *are* the regularity. Figure 3.5 is an attempt to portray the difference between this and the notion of successionist causation. When realists say that the constant conjunction view of one event producing another (model (a)) is inadequate, they are not attempting to bring further 'intervening' variables into the picture. So the idea is not that there might be a further unforeseen event which brings about a spurious relationship between the original variables (model (b)), or that the original relationship is 'indirect' and works

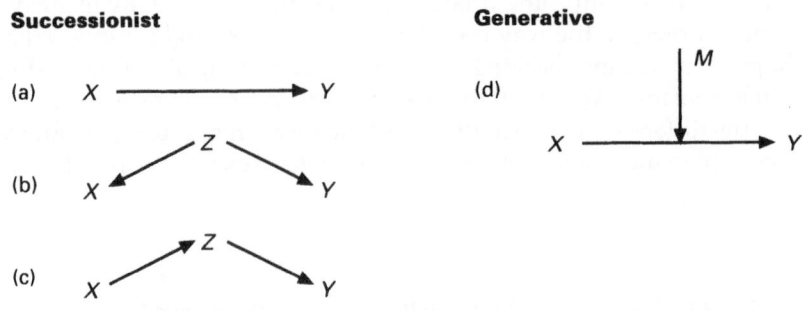

Figure 3.5   *Models of causation*

through an intervening variable (model (c)). The idea is that the mechanism is responsible for the relationship itself (model (d)). A mechanism is thus not a variable but an *account* of the make-up, behaviour and interrelationships of those processes which are responsible for the regularity. A mechanism is thus a theory – a theory which spells out the potential of human resources and reasoning.

The study of suicide rates provides a ready-made example of the differences highlighted in Figure 3.5. Suicide levels can be portrayed by assembling correlations describing the individual (that is, describing only one layer of social reality). In this perspective, explanation begins by assembling correlations (as in model (a)) showing, for instance, that marital status (X) influences suicide rate (Y). Work in the path analytic tradition tries to improve on these univariate explanations (the single are more prone to suicide than the married) by adding further individual-level variables. So, for instance, it has been claimed that the link from marital status to suicide works indirectly (as in causal model (c)) through the 'possession' of children, and so that marital status (X) influences the likelihood of having children (Z) and parental responsibilities, in turn, lessen the propensity to suicide (Y). The full successionist treatment would, of course, go on to investigate the influences of other variables – religion (U), education (V) etc. – so producing the familiar multivariate path models (Hirschi and Selvin, 1973).

The point is, however, that each separate path (XY, ZY, UY etc.) itself needs explaining in Durkheimian mode in terms of reasoning and resources, and choices and capacities, which are not expressible as properties of the individual. Thus it is a nonsense to say that one's 'marital status' or one's 'religion' causes 'suicide'. Each relationship is itself forged in a wider network of social processes. Each path or correlation is simply a descriptive outcome of how the interpersonal responsibilities, associations, loyalties forged in family and spiritual and other communities obviate, moderate, tolerate or ameliorate the individual member's propensity to suicide.

An exact parallel can be drawn across to representation of the causal action of a social intervention. Experimental evaluation is also $X{\rightarrow}Y$ fixated and reduces the business of explanation to drawing causal inferences between variables. And though it is a convenient shorthand to do so, it is also a nonsense to say that programs cause change in their subjects' behaviour. As we have seen in Chapter 2, the same goal is apparent, namely to establish model (a) relationships between programs (X) and outcome (Y). Any other process, action, idea, disposition has to be treated as a potential 'confounding variable' (Z) and experimental controls are put in place in an attempt to rule out their action. The key point is that this way of perceiving causation, whether it is achieved by statistical control (as in multivariate analysis techniques) or by the use of control groups (as in experimental techniques), overlooks a vital explanatory ingredient. To repeat, that ingredient is not a variable but a mechanism. Social interventions only and always work through the action of mechanisms, through a process of weaving resources and reasoning together. Without this being the first item on the research agenda, all subsequent work on program outcomes will remain a mystery.

Contexts

We will, in the upcoming subsection on 'change', have considerably more to say in clarifying the nature of program mechanisms. Our next task, however, is to introduce, rather more formally, mechanism's partner concept which has also been seeded rather intuitively into the proceedings thus far. This concerns the notion of *context*, which can be introduced via another standard realist proposition which runs that *the relationship between causal mechanisms and their effects is not fixed, but contingent* (cf. Sayer, 1984, p. 107). To rehearse again our favourite physical science example: gunpowder has within it the causal potential to explode, but whether it does so depends on it being in the right conditions. The same explanatory structure will write directly across into social science. For instance, we invoke the identical propositional form when we confront the well-known 'conundrum' of educational advancement. People's desires for social advancement are often channelled through the search for educational qualifications. For this strategy to work there needs to be sufficient economic growth to sustain expansion in the desired occupational sectors. If there is a continual race for social enhancement through educational qualification without an equivalent upgrade in occupational destinations, all we end up with is 'diploma inflation' and an overqualified workforce. In realist terms, it is the *contextual conditioning* of causal mechanisms which turns (or fails to turn) causal potential into a causal outcome.

Our previous illustration of the 'banking system' provides another fine example and one which is somewhat closer to the policy field. Within such a system there would be little evidence (and conceivably much denial) of any formal rule which forbade the advancement of loans to single parents, mortgages to the unskilled, and so on. However, the contextual conditions which bring about such a state of affairs are there aplenty. In order to survive as commercial concerns, banks and building societies have to make a profit on their transactions. One of the simplest ways of failing to make a profit is to have a significant rate of default on the repayment of advances. Transactions are thus judged against a perceived level of risk, which may well be judged excessive for the aforementioned groups. If one multiplies this little chain of reasoning a thousandfold, it is not difficult to see the sedimentation of a monolithic, cautionary, asset-sensitive culture. The promotion of any specific policy initiative (we loan to lone parents!) will thus involve a wrestling match with the reproduction of longer term financial convention.

All social programs wrestle with prevailing contextual conditions. Programs are always introduced *into* pre-existing social contexts and, as we shall see, these prevailing social conditions are of crucial importance when it comes to explaining the successes and failures of social programs. By social context, we do not refer simply to the spatial or geographical or institutional location into which programs are embedded. So whilst indeed programs are initiated in prisons, hospitals, schools, neighbourhoods, and car parks, it is the prior set of social rules, norms, values and interrelationships gathered in these places which sets limits on the efficacy of program mechanisms. It is thus futile for researchers to ignore and anonymize the contexts of their programs as in experimental evaluation (Chapter 2) and we have no hesitation in pointing to this lack of attention to the social conditions which pre-exist and endure through programs as one of the great omissions of evaluation research.

Programs work by introducing new ideas and / or resources into an existing set of social relationships. A crucial task of evaluation is to include (via hypothesis making and research design) investigation of the extent to which these pre-existing structures 'enable' or 'disable' the intended mechanism of change. We will leave detailed suggestions for this to the next chapter. For the time being, we can progress a little further with the contact patrol example. In the above section on mechanisms, we mentioned a couple of potential mechanisms through which they *might* work, namely 'empowerment' or 'confidence building'. It is not too difficult to imagine circumstances where these would *not* work. For instance, in terms of the latter mechanism, messages of reassurance from the community constable are likely to fall on deaf ears if the local crime rates remain static and repeat victimization continues to bite. The use of an adverse example of context is no accident here, for it highlights the fact that positive conditions in which a program *will* work might be relatively rare. Conditions which have been responsible for a crime producing mechanism might well prove inhospitable to a crime reducing one.

If the putative crime fighting mechanism really is the empowerment of a community, we might suppose that that community might need a potential source of identity and focus of leadership, a reasonably stable population, with a broad age range, no great social or ethnic divisions, an identifiable boundary and history, the existence of other community forums, and so on. It is precisely these features that the program practitioner would attempt to harden into a crime fighting resource. It is precisely such a substantive 'match' between context and mechanism which the evaluator needs to search out in understanding the success of an initiative. Programs are ideas. Ideas have their time and place. It is this conjunction that researchers must capture with the notion of context.

Regularities

We now move to the *goal* of realist explanation. No surprises in store here, for we pick up on a task which is held in common with most explanatory paradigms. That is to say that the objective of realist inquiry is to explain social 'regularities', 'rates', 'associations', 'outcomes', 'patterns'. Once again, it is appropriate to note that such an objective has been rather taken for granted in our gathering description of realist explanation and that the time has come for us to be somewhat more formal. We begin by relating explanans to explanandum according to the formula already set down: *regularity = mechanism + context*. Rendering this into prose, we are now in a position to summarize the basic logic of realist explanation in the following statement and in Figure 3.6.

Logic of realist explanation

The basic task of social inquiry is to explain interesting, puzzling, socially significant regularities (R). Explanation takes the form of positing some underlying mechanism (M) which generates the regularity and thus consists of propositions about how the interplay between structure and agency has constituted the regularity. Within realist investigation there is also investigation of how the workings of such mechanisms are contingent and conditional, and thus only fired in particular local, historical or institutional contexts (C).

The diagram in Figure 3.6, by now in its third guise, will come as no surprise. It carries two functions here. Firstly, it establishes the continuities between natural science explanation and social science explanation and program evaluation explanation. Secondly, it stresses the need for explanatory propositions to combine all three elements – M, C, and R. When Huygens explained the relationship between the length and period of a pendulum (R), he did so by demonstrating how the underlying

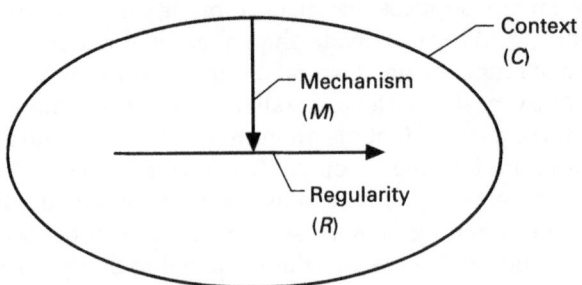

Figure 3.6   *Basic ingredients of realist social explanation*

mechanism, the gravitational and constraining forces (M), operated regularly only in the context of a cycloidal path (C).When Durkheim explained how suicide rates (R) vary across different contexts (C) such as Catholic/Protestant communities, he demonstrated how they fostered a variation in a mechanism (M), namely 'anomie', which describes differing levels of support and solidarity for the potential victim. When an evaluator tells us that a program is a success (R), s/he *should* be demonstrating what it is (M) about the program which works for whom in what conditions (C). Whilst the rates, regularities and patterns explained vary greatly in substance and complexity, it is this model of a stratified reality being composed generatively which maintains the family resemblance of realist explanation.

Change

We now come to the vexatious matter of social change. This is an issue which separates realist physical explanation from realist social explanation, and therefore requires us to distinguish more carefully between different types of regularities and outcomes which we may seek to explain. The *social* systems described in Figure 3.4 have a distinguishing characteristic which is variously described as a 'morphogenic' character (Archer, 1995) or an 'open system' nature (Bhaskar, 1979). What this means is that the balance of mechanisms, contexts and regularities which sustain social order is prone to a perpetual and self-generated reshaping. The difference between Figures 3.2 and 3.6 is that the latter is peopled, whereas in the former people exist only on the outside as experimentalists. In social systems, these people make history, though not in conditions of their own choosing. That is to say, people are often aware of the patterns and regularities into which their lives are shaped, are aware of the choices which channel their activities, and are aware too of the broader social forces that limit their opportunities. This awareness will result, in some people at least, in a desire to change the pattern. This change may or may not happen because the people desiring change may or may not have the resources to bring it about, or their efforts may be countermanded by other groups with more resources. Further unpredictability is introduced because people have imperfect knowledge of the contextual conditions which limit their actions and the proposed change mechanism itself may have unanticipated consequences. So, whilst the exact path cannot be foreseen, we know social regularities have a habit of transforming themselves. Following through this transformative nature of social systems gives social explanation a distinctly more complex task, which we can depict as Figure 3.7.

We can illustrate the idea via an example of educational change which has occurred in Britain, as well as other modern societies, in the last 30 or so years (T_1 = 1950s, T_2 = 1990s). If we compare the educational success rates of boys and girls (R_1), the traditional picture was for the former to outperform the latter. Currently the position is reversing (R_2), with girls obtaining, for instance, a 10% higher rate of 'top' GCSE passes in 1995. These rates have shifted in response to a variety of changing underlying mechanisms. For instance, at T_1 more resources would probably be directed to boys at home and at school (M_{1a}); girls would more readily opt for the short term advantage in the youth employment market (M_{1b}), in anticipation, perhaps, of a career in homemaking and childrearing. At T_2, equal opportunities policies may have balanced up school resources in the direction of girls (M_{2a}) and girls might be more likely to seek sound educational qualifications in anticipation of a career in employment as well as in homemaking and childrearing (M_{2b}). The prevailing social and cultural contexts may also be said to have shifted markedly. Thus, in the immediate post-war years, there was an employment structure (C_{1a}) which called for a workforce educated across a relatively narrow range of technical, professional (and therefore male) specialisms. The culture of female domesticity (C_{1b}) was also more or less in place to support this, and there was a mass of relatively unskilled, uneducated, male labour. T_2, however, sees a transformation to something of a 'service' economy (C_{2a}). Thus there

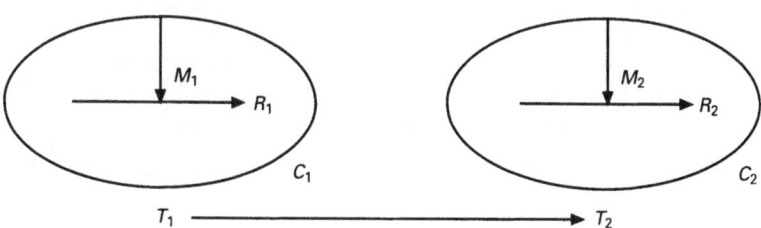

Figure 3.7 *Transformative social systems*

is a shift to educating and training a workforce for the (relatively female) commercial, sales, and administrative sectors. By this time the ideological and policy shifts in favour of equal opportunities for women (C_{2b}) have also begun to bite (if only) in the educational sectors. This paragraph is nothing more than a flimsy sketch of a major social change, the initial point being to emphasize that all social systems change, and that all social analysis (including evaluation research) involves a mastery of change.

As realist evaluators, we have to confront the business of social change, because programs and policy making are quintessentially about change. The task is made manageable since social programs actually contemplate a rather modest type of social transformation. Again, we can get to work on the idea via the rugby ball diagrams, and we depict the form of managed social change which is anticipated in most social programming as Figure 3.8. Social programming starts with the identification of a regularity (R_1) deemed to represent a social problem and faces the task of trying to shift the pattern of behaviour in question to a more acceptable level (R_2). This may involve the effort to *reduce* rates of, say, crime or recidivism or smoking, or to *increase* rates of, say, school or out-patient attendance. Herein lies the inevitable interest in change in programming, which we signify as a key concern for the evaluator by labelling as an outcome (O) the change in rates which evaluation research will try to discern and explain. Whilst we realize, of course, that policing terminology in such matters is difficult, we henceforth reserve the terms 'regularity' and 'rate' for describing the behaviours under scrutiny before (T_1) and after (T_2) the intervention. The terms 'outcome' and 'outcome pattern' will be used to describe the *change* in rates ($R_2 - R_1$) over time, and it is such outcomes which constitute the explanatory goal of evaluation research.

Coming to the matter of *explaining* the outcomes, the realist evaluator has, of course, to acknowledge the set of mechanisms (M_1) which sustained the initial problem. Thus evaluation research will concern itself with the capacities and choices which led the burglar to crime and the capacities and choices which led to the failure of a neighbourhood to

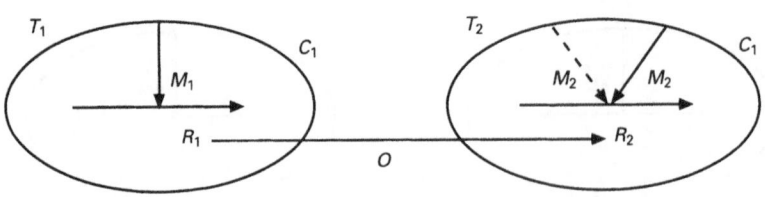

Figure 3.8 *Basic ingredients of successful programmed social change*

combat the burglary. The key explanatory resource, however, is to figure out the potential for change of the program mechanisms (M_2). As we have emphasized several times, it is not programs that 'work' but their ability to break into the existing chains of resources and reasoning which led to the 'problem'. Adopting this focus gives us realism's axiom 1 for dealing with change, which we also 'box' for emphasis.

Axiom 1

Research has to answer the questions: what are the mechanisms for change triggered by a program and how do they counteract the existing social processes?

We have described already the broad features of the realist understanding of such program mechanisms. They are 'analytical' and so involve breaking down the program into a series of potential sub-processes. They are 'stratified' in that they involve both macro and micro processes. They are 'propositional' and 'processual' in that they involve the interplay between social resources and participants' reasoning. To these features we now need to add the requirement that evaluation is particularly interested in 'change' mechanisms. Part of the explanatory requirement is thus to acknowledge that they follow in the wake of a series of established mechanisms and thereby demonstrate that they are capable of over-turning/counteracting/transforming these embedded processes. We depict this task in Figure 3.8 in which the mechanisms (M_1) which sustain the initial problem are dashed (literally and diagrammatically) with the arrival of the program mechanisms (M_2).

In research terms this means that we must disentangle what will inevitably be a *range* of mechanisms which sustained the original problem as well as the *range* of mechanisms fired within the program, and seek for a 'match'. For instance, if we consider the simplest potential mechanism for burglary reduction, namely 'target hardening' (that is, fitting stronger and more visible locks to windows and doors), we need to establish precisely how the new resource enters the potential burglar's reasoning. It may well be, for instance, that this alters the 'vulnerability' equation in which easy identification of easy entry and exit points are keys to choosing an easy target. Such a solution, however, could leave untouched other vulnerability mechanisms (such as the availability of highly prized spoils, or the low potential for being observed with a sheltered entry and exit). In short, progress in programming and research depends on being able to demonstrate which *problem mechanism* has been overcome by which *blocking mechanism*.

Turning now to the matter of context, we acknowledge a self-imposed limitation on the nature of change envisaged in most social programming and a corresponding limitation in the explanatory ambitions of realist evaluation. Social programs are all about 'social engineering', a phrase which is often used with the key proviso that what is at issue is *piecemeal* social engineering. That little epithet carries with it all sorts of ideological connotations. At this point in the proceedings, we seek only to clarify the main explanatory implication, which is that in most social programs there is no significant expectation that the prevailing contextual conditions will be transformed. A social program, unlike a social movement, does not premise or promise change on the overthrow of the existing cultural order and social organization. We have represented this assumption in Figure 3.8 by depicting change as occurring *within* broadly the same contextual conditions C_1.

Contextual conditions are, nevertheless, crucial to realist explanation and the above qualifications clarify the questions the evaluator will need to ask. We know that programs sometimes succeed and sometimes fail, and thus we cannot fail to research the issue of the *salience* of the program context for the operation of the change mechanism(s). We are asking whether these new mechanisms will 'gel' or will 'fire' given the social relations and cultural preferences which predate and permeate a program. The crucial question is therefore about the *different* contexts, C_1, C_2, C_3 and so on, in which a program may be located. We can depict the idea illustrating an instance of program failure in Figure 3.9, in which the program mechanisms (M_2) fail to fire (and are hence dashed) because they are introduced into an inhospitable context (C_2), which continues to sustain the 'problem mechanisms' (M_1).

We will suggest some appropriate research strategies for investigating contextual constraints in the next chapter. For the time being, we can illustrate the idea via a few gross and somewhat dated stereotypes about British neighbourhoods and how they might cater for a neighbourhood watch scheme. Such initiatives might operate with quite different mechanisms. One mechanism for change might be the 'eyes and ears' approach in which the watch scheme is effective thanks to increased natural surveillance. A somewhat different mechanism might be the increased 'social bonding and intelligence gathering' acquired through the rigorous orga-

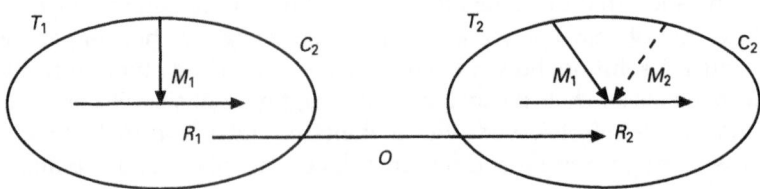

Figure 3.9   *Program failure due to inappropriate contextualization*

nization of a watch network. It is not too difficult to imagine that the former approach would work better amongst the twitching curtains of the terraced street rather than in the privet-clad privacy of suburbia. The latter mechanism, however, might be better fostered in a locality imbued with a boardroom rather than a bar-room culture. With the promise to the reader of finding some rather more refined examples to come, we summarize (and 'box') this notion of contextual constraint as axiom 2 on change in realist evaluation.

Axiom 2

Research has to answer the questions: what are the social and cultural conditions necessary for change mechanisms to operate and how are they distributed within and between program contexts?

In Chapter 1, we indicated a wish for our realistic approach to be seen as a family member of the 'theory-driven' perspectives on evaluation. At the time, we indicated that the approach was bedevilled by a family argument about the exact scope and content of the theory required. We have now delivered our answer (in three boxes). Successful empirical work is conditional on producing hypotheses which, in general, follow the overall logic of realist explanation and, in particular, posit a theory of change in the form of the mechanism question (axiom 1) and the context question (axiom 2), as above.

Evaluators will always construct their explanations around the three crucial ingredients of any initiative: context (C), mechanism (M) and outcome (O). There will always be contextual variation within and between programs, a corresponding variation in the effectiveness of causal mechanisms triggered, and a consequential variation in patterns of outcomes, giving realist research the task of modelling the different ways in which the Ms, Cs and Os come together. Now, 'when researchers study cases in terms of their different combinations of similarities and differences, they study configurations' (Ragin, 1994). Accordingly, we term those propositions which combine this trio of explanatory components *context–mechanism–outcome pattern configurations* or *CMO* configurations. These play an important part in the remainder of the book. The task of a realist evaluation is to find ways of identifying, articulating, testing and refining conjectured *CMO* configurations.

We take up this challenge in the next chapter and demonstrate a full range of realist evaluation designs for the purpose of testing hypotheses manufactured to the above formula. For the present, some consolidation of the argument is in order. The idea of hypothesis making in terms of mechanisms, contexts and outcomes will be new to most evaluators. Whilst we have adopted a sprinkling of illustrations in making our case for realism, it is high time we took on a developed example.

Realism in the car park

We choose as our example of realist theory in action a programming area which is seemingly mundane and mechanical. We want to look at car parks. More specifically, we wish to examine the problem of car park crime and attempts to reduce it through the installation of closed-circuit television (CCTV). Such programs, in fact, share a key characteristic with all social initiatives. There is nothing about police patrols which intrinsically reduces fear of crime. There is nothing about educational programs which intrinsically reduces offender reconviction. So too, there is nothing about CCTV in car parks which intrinsically inhibits car crime. Whilst it may appear to offer a technical solution, CCTV certainly does not create a physical barrier making cars impenetrable. A moment's thought has us realize, therefore, that the cameras must work by instigating a chain of reasoning and reaction. Realist evaluation is all about turning this moment's thought into a comprehensive theory of the mechanisms through which CCTV may enter the potential criminal's mind, and the contexts needed if these powers are to be realized. We begin with mechanisms.

(a) *The 'caught in the act' mechanism.* CCTV could reduce car crime by making it more likely that *present offenders* will be observed on screen, detected instantly and then arrested, removed, punished and deterred.

(b) *The 'you've been framed' mechanism.* CCTV could reduce car crime by deterring *potential offenders* who will not wish to risk investigation, apprehension and conviction by the evidence captured on videotape.

(c) *The 'nosy parker' mechanism.* The presence of CCTV may lead to increases in usage of car parks, because drivers feel less at risk of victimization. Increased usage could then enhance natural surveillance which may deter potential offenders, who feel they are at increased risk of apprehension in the course of criminal behaviour.

(d) *The 'effective deployment' mechanism.* CCTV may facilitate the effective deployment of security staff or police officers towards areas where suspicious behaviour is occurring. They then act as a visible presence which might deter potential offenders. They may also apprehend actual offenders red-handed and disable their criminal behaviour.

(e) *The 'publicity' mechanism.* CCTV, and signs indicating that it is in operation, could symbolize efforts to take crime seriously and to reduce it. The potential offender may be led to avoid the increased risk they believe to be associated with committing car crimes in car parks and so be deterred.

(f) *The 'time for crime' mechanism.* Those car crimes which can be completed in a very short space of time may decline less than those which take more time, as offenders calculate the time taken for police or security officers to come or the probability that panning cameras will focus in on them.

(g) *The 'memory jogging' mechanism.* CCTV and notices indicating that it is in operation may remind drivers that their cars are vulnerable, and they may thereby be prompted to take greater care to lock them, to operate any security devices, and to remove easily stolen items from view.

(h) *The 'appeal to the cautious' mechanism.* It might be that cautious drivers, who are sensitive to the possibility that their cars may be vulnerable and are habitual users of various security devices, use and fill the car parks that have CCTV and thereby drive out those who are more careless, whose vulnerable cars are stolen from elsewhere.

It is clearly possible that more than one of these mechanisms for change may operate simultaneously. Which (if any) mechanisms are fired turns on the context in which CCTV is installed, and this may vary widely. Consider the following:

(i) *The 'criminal clustering' context.* A given rate of car crime may result from widely differing prevalences of offending. For example if there are 1,000 incidents per annum, this may be by anything from a single (very busy) offender to as many as 1,000 offenders, or still more if they operate in groups. A mechanism leading to disablement of the offender (as in (a) above) holds potential promise according to the offender–offence ratio.

(ii) *The 'style of usage' context.* A long stay car park may have an enormous influx of vehicles between eight and eight-thirty in the morning when it becomes full up. It may then empty between five and six in the evening. If the dominant CCTV fired mechanism turns out to be increased confidence and usage (as in (h) or (c) above) then this will have little impact because the pattern of usage is already high with little movement, dictated by working hours not fear of crime. If, however, the car park is little used, but has a very high per user car crime rate, then the increased usage mechanism may lead to an overall increase in numbers of crimes but a decreased rate per use.

(iii) *The 'lie of the land' context.* Cars parked in the CCTV blind spots in car parks will be more vulnerable if the mechanism is increased chances of apprehension through evidence on videotape (as in (b) above), but not if it is through changed attributes or security behaviour of customers (as in (g) or (h) above).

(iv) *The 'alternative targets' context.* The local patterns of motivation of offenders, together with the availability of alternative targets of car crime, furnish aspects of the wider context for displacement to car crimes elsewhere, whatever crime reduction mechanisms may be fired by CCTV in the specific context of a given car park.

(v)   *The 'resources' context.* In an isolated car park with no security presence and the police at some distance away, the deployment of security staff or police as a mobile and flexible resource to deter car crime (as in (d) above) is not possible.

(vi)   *The 'surveillance culture' context.* As the usage of CCTV surveillance spreads through all walks of life and features in extensive media portrayal of 'modern policing', the efficacy of the publicity given to CCTV in car parks (as in (e) above) may be enhanced or muted, according to the overall reputation of such surveillance.

We do not pretend that this listing of potential contexts and mechanisms is mutually exclusive or totally inclusive. What we trust it reveals instantly, however, is that a bit of lateral thinking in the realm of hypothesis making requires that we trudge well off the beaten tracks in the search for supporting empirical evidence. Despite the somewhat *ad hoc* character of our lists (there being no existing sociology of the car park), we nevertheless thus make the strong claim that an investigation framed around these ideas will yield far more of worth than one driven by the quasi-experimental starting point of comparing car crime rates before and after CCTV installation. These hypotheses frame the requisite data and research strategies, and thus call upon a range of evidence entirely different from the standard comparisons. A series of studies would be required to sift, sort and adjudicate which of the various mechanism/context permutations was active, a task we can summarize with the following highly abbreviated list of investigative tacks.

1   As well as seeking for reductions in crime rate, following CCTV installation, it would be important to check on *convictions* attributable to CCTV, for this would reveal whether direct detection or taped evidence (as in (a) and (b) above) were actually capable of generating the outcome. Further evidence on these detection mechanisms could be compiled by actually inspecting the *technical capabilities* of systems in respect of whether their resolution power could identify individuals or in respect of how quickly they were capable of homing in to an offence. Tilley (1993a) reports on highly limited performance in respect of both conviction and technique, inclining him to the belief that the remaining, indirect, risk perception mechanisms are more crucial.

2   Before-and-after data, again not just on changing rate but on changes in *type* of crime and of *criminal opportunities*, may be a crucial next step but, as far as we are aware, one that has not been utilized with respect to these programs. A survey ascertaining changes in number of cars left locked and in the extent to which attractive goods were left on display would allow some test of the 'appeal to the cautious' and 'memory jogging' mechanisms (h) and (g). This could be complemented with data

on the changing pattern of thefts from cars, including the sorts of items stolen, and where they were in the car, to test the 'time for crime' mechanism (f). Without the prior theory, it is by no means obvious that actually examining unmolested parked cars would constitute an important part of the evaluation process.

3 Another important body of evidence would concern the *location* within the car park of crimes committed. If these had some spatial concentration, it would demonstrate that the potential thief had a (perhaps sophisticated) understanding of camera angles, panning times, blind spots, escape routes, response times etc. Thinking through the local geography of the outcomes would allow us to test aspects of the 'lie of the land' context (iii) as well as features of the aforementioned mechanisms (b), (d), (f), (g). These would in turn produce good process-evaluation data for the refinement of CCTV installations.

4 Data on the *temporal* patterning of crime, cross-referenced perhaps to information on the amount of *capacity* in use at any time, would be the obvious material to test the influence of the 'style of usage' context (ii). As well as informing us on whether the potential offender feared natural surveillance more or less than CCTV surveillance, a more elaborate investigation of outcomes across a range of types of car parks (long stay, short stay, commuter, rail, shopper, works etc.) will provide some evidence of the pattern of perceived risks associated with different sites, as well as intelligence on the most beneficial CCTV locations.

5 Hard evidence on the 'publicity' mechanism (e) and 'surveillance culture' context (vi) is probably the most difficult (and we suspect, the most important) to ascertain. A start on this could be made by pursuing some (experimental-type!) variations in the publicity attendant on the arrival of the CCTV cameras to see if the specifics of the message made a discernible difference to outcomes. A periodic reworking/refreshing of publicity could also be undertaken in order to detect whether the car crime rate over time was responsive. As with all of the risk perception mechanisms, potentially the most valuable data may well come from the potential risk takers themselves. In this respect, we hit a standard catch-22 of criminological research: the greater the success of a publicity deterrent, the greater the difficulty in the construction of a sample of the very respondents one needs (the deterred).

We reach the point in our brief catalogue of research potential where practical issues begin to bite, for the solutions to which we reserve the remainder of the book. There is, however, another whole phase of research development which at least deserves a mention in this penultimate paragraph. Ultimately realist evaluation would be *mechanism-and context-driven* rather than program-led. To follow through the same example, we could anticipate a broadening of the scope of inquiry to include investigation of the usage of CCTV in other areas of crime control, and even other forms of surveillance altogether. There is no reason to suppose that an entirely different set of mechanisms and contexts condition the effectiveness of stadium cameras or store detectives. Whilst the terrain may differ, we are confident that *transferable lessons* could eventually be learned about, say, the lie of the land (as context) in the multi-storey, in the football stadium and in the high street (on the last, see Brown, 1995).

We leave our example with a restatement of what we trust is the main transferable lesson of this chapter. Without a theory of why CCTV may be effective, and a theory of the conditions which promote this potential, research into its usage is blind. And thus it is in all evaluation.

4

HOW TO DESIGN A REALISTIC EVALUATION

Michael Scriven's *Evaluation Thesaurus* avers that:

> [Theories are] a luxury for the evaluator, since they are not even essential for explanations, and explanations are not essential for 99% of all evaluations. It is a gross though frequent blunder to suppose that 'one needs a theory in order to evaluate teaching'. One does not need to know anything about electronics to evaluate electronic typewriters . . . such knowledge often *adversely* affects a summative evaluation. (1991, p. 360)

This may well have been written to be deliberately provocative. It may well have been intended to relate to a different subset of evaluations from those made of programs, which is the subject of this book. As stated it is, nevertheless, dangerously misleading and symptomatic of much that prevents evaluation from informing improvements to policy and practice. This chapter seeks to reverse the ordinance and to show that empirical work in program evaluation can only be as good as the theory which underpins it.

Even in the field of electronic typewriters, Scriven's injunction, which he takes there to be self-evidently correct, is wrong. Scriven's problem is that he assumes that the theory which would be used would be drawn from electronics. Not so. The theory needed relates to the mechanisms through which the introduction of electronic typewriters may generate improvements in outcome in the contexts in which they are placed. An electronic typewriter is not merely some *sui generis* object. It functions through the use made of it by people. And that usage will depend in part on the technical features of the machine, but also on the type of work undertaken, and on the skills of those who will operate it and the environment in which they work. As the CCTV example discussed in Chapter 3 shows, the technical adequacy of a piece of technology is not necessarily or always crucial to its causal powers in a given context. The theory needed for evaluating electronic typewriters, as for CCTV, will relate to human choices and capacities. The very patient reader might like to linger here and work though a list of the potential mechanisms and contexts which might govern the impact of the introduction of electronic typewriters (of varying kinds and as opposed to other forms of writing). This working through amounts to laying the bones for a realistic research design.

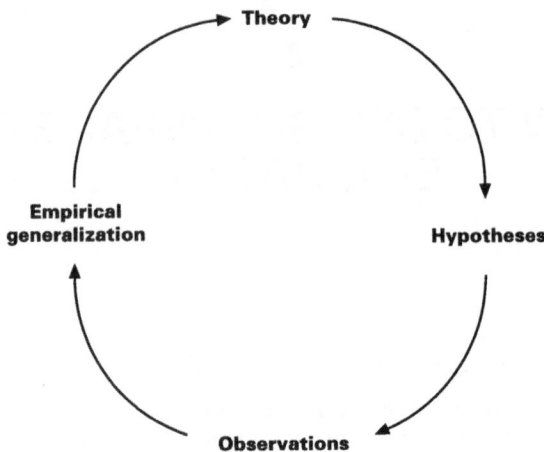

Figure 4.1   *The wheel of science (after Wallace, 1971)*

Research design is the topic of this chapter, being the obvious first element of the 'how to' section of the book. Our introduction of the language of mechanisms, contexts and outcomes is obviously intended as a challenge to much of the received wisdom on the basic principles of evaluation. When it comes to research methods and strategies, our realist injunctions do not constitute a plea for complete and permanent revolution. Thus, in broad terms, research designs for realistic evaluation studies actually follow exactly the same basic logic of inquiry as that underpinning any other area of social science. For that matter, the logic of inquiry in the natural sciences is no different either. In all cases the 'wheel of science' is followed (Wallace, 1971). Figure 4.1 shows what is involved.

Theories are framed in abstract terms and are concerned with the identification and explanation of regularities. Specific *hypotheses* are derived from these theories and state where and when regularities should be found. These hypotheses are tested through *observations* of various kinds. Observations inform *generalizations*. These generalizations may or may not conform to those expected from a theory. If they do not, this suggests either that there was some critical weakness in the research design intended to test the theory or that the theory itself is in need of revision. We are not proposing any major revisions to this textbook description of the overall research cycle, which will already be familiar to many readers.

What is distinctive about a realist design is, therefore, a matter of content rather than form, which we attempt to depict in Figure 4.2 – the realist evaluation cycle. The key difference in the diagrams lies at our point of departure and at the very starting point of the wheel of science. Realism has a unique way of understanding the constituents of theory. These should be familiar from Chapter 3: theories must be framed in terms of propositions about how mechanisms are fired in contexts to produce outcomes. All else in the circumnavigation of inquiry follows from this. Thus we are led next to a style of hypothesis making, again amply foreshadowed in previous chapters, in which programs are broken down so that we can identify what it is about the measure which might produce change, which individuals, subgroups and locations might benefit most readily from the program, and which social and cultural resources are necessary to sustain the changes.

The evaluation circuit then turns to observations and to the methods of data collection and analysis needed to test such hypotheses. Again, we cast ourselves as solid members of the modern, vociferous majority in this respect, for we are whole-heartedly *pluralists* when it comes to the choice of method. Thus, as we shall attempt to illustrate in the examples to follow, it is quite possible to carry out realistic evaluation using: strategies, quantitative and qualitative; timescales, contemporaneous or historical; viewpoints, cross-sectional or longitudinal; samples, large or small; goals, action-oriented or audit-centred; and so on and so forth. This, by the way, means not that we are simply pluralists for pluralism's sake, but that the choice of method has to be carefully tailored to the exact form of hypotheses developed earlier in the cycle.

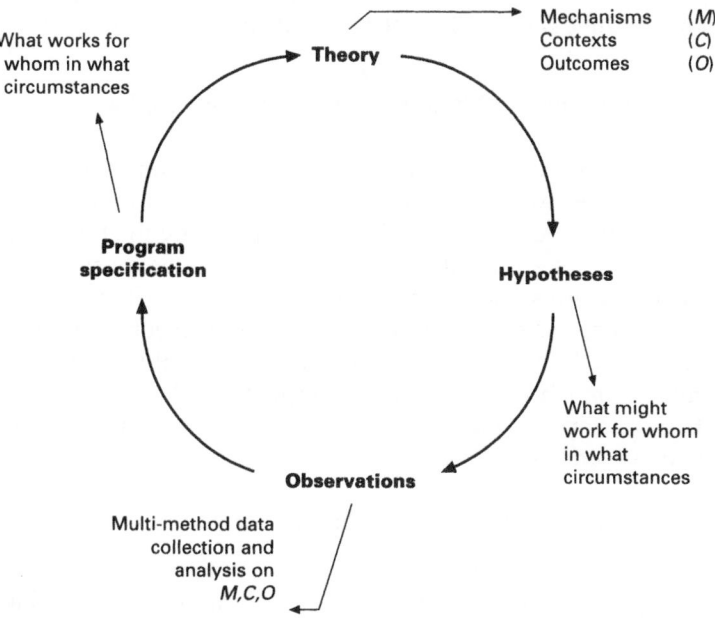

Figure 4.2   *The realist evaluation cycle*

The next loop of our cycle does depart in some respects from Wallace's wheel, in as much as we seek a goal of 'specification' rather than unqualified or unconditional 'generalization'. This is partly a question of our location in the domain of applied research with its ensuing and decidedly concrete task of discovering what works for whom in a set of *given* circumstances. The modification is also made because scientific realism casts doubt on the very possibility of the sort of universal statement that the term 'generalization' seems to imply. We have discussed some of the irresistible forces for social change in the previous chapter, and this reinforces our view that evaluation and social science generally only ever come to temporary resting places, and that 'findings' take the form of specifying those 'regularities' or 'outcome patterns' which the present state of our understanding of 'mechanisms' and 'contexts' is able to sustain.

Note finally that our circuit too goes full cycle, with the knowledge obtained from any particular inquiry feeding back into further theoretical development, which might include revising accounts of the interplay of mechanisms, contexts and outcomes, so that subtle twists in program beneficiaries are hypothesized, which lead to further observations, employing different methods, so gradually laying down outcome typologies in which the successes and failures of whole program families are explained. Chapter 5 will have more to say about how cumulation is achieved through a series of studies. For now, we inspect the initial laps more closely by looking at three rather different realist research designs.

Realistic evaluation: an introduction to three exemplars

The three studies we discuss in some detail have been selected because they illustrate very well successful realistic evaluation practice in rather different circumstances, and show how it can employ the full panoply of research techniques and strategies. Only the third was conceived fully in scientific realist terms. The first two adopt the approach implicitly, and the second even contains some redundant quasi-experimentation. As with all empirical research these inquiries have their practical imperfections and limitations, so much so that we were tempted to call them 'good efforts' rather than 'exemplars', but in the end convention ruled and so we present our exemplary efforts as follows.

An exemplar of a best case evaluation study: testing theory

The first study relates to the effectiveness of a quite simple and frequently used crime prevention measure: property marking. This issue had already been subject to some previous evaluation research. There was already some fairly well-developed theory relating directly to the issue at hand. This permitted the possibility of setting up an experiment creating the ideal contextual conditions for property marking to trigger crime preventive mechanisms. The researcher did just this. Her research design is the closest of those we discuss to the laboratory experiment of the natural scientist, in which the conditions for the regularity are constructed by the investigator. The site of the project was chosen to exemplify what were theoretically the best contextual conditions for property marking to trigger its conjectured mechanisms. The introduction of property marking was orchestrated and overseen by the evaluation researcher, who ensured that what was done was recorded to see that it accorded with the theory. Measurements were planned and targeted at the precise outcome patterns which were expected supposing that the conjectured mechanisms had been triggered. Finally the evaluation researcher considered the implications of her findings for the theory. The relatively advanced stage in the development of the theory, as well as its nature, mean that quantitative methods were available and appropriate to the evaluation study.

An exemplar of an exploratory case study evaluation: theory formation and development

The second case study is an evaluation of the crime prevention effectiveness of an innovative and quite wide-ranging and complex housing management program on two housing estates in Britain. This program's specific concern is not with crime prevention *per se*, though it was speculated that its measures might reduce crime. A rudimentary theory explaining how causal mechanisms might be triggered to bring this about was formulated. The program had not previously been the focus for evaluation research in terms of this type of effect. The evaluation team was not in a position to manipulate an experiment to create conditions for previously identified potential mechanisms to be triggered by the measures introduced, as had been the case with property marking. They were not in this sense setting up a test for a theory. They were simply observing a program and crime experience changes, using a mixture of quantitative and qualitative techniques, armed only with a very rudimentary theory but also with eyes open for other possibilities. From this they built a realistic theory making sense of the ways in which actions taken, in the differing contexts of the program's estates, triggered various mechanisms to generate complex outcome patterns.

An exemplar of a large data-set evaluation study: theory formulation and development

The third study aims to evaluate the impact of a long standing higher education program, delivered in prison, on the recidivism of participating inmates. This time, quite deliberately, a scientific realist approach was taken throughout the project. It was assumed from the outset that the program would 'work' for different inmates in diverse ways. There was indeed a characteristic diversity in the inmate students' social and criminal backgrounds and the program itself was multiform in its settings, sessions and subject matters. Moreover, whilst the case for 'adult education' has been made many times, available theory on its rehabilitative potential was negligible. Research thus began with a period of theory development, derived from qualitative investigation, in which educators were interviewed to elicit realistic theories on program mechanisms ('what it was about the programme which might generate change in a prisoner') and program contexts ('with which sorts of inmates in which conditions the initiative might be successful'). These 'folk theories' were then used to interrogate a range of data in a range of ways. We will concentrate in our description in this chapter on a large scale survey, using prison and educational records of twenty years' duration, which tracked more than 600 men through their prison, educational and post-release experience. The practitioners' hypotheses identified a great many subgroups of prisoners who were thought to have experienced particularly favourable combinations of program mechanisms and background contexts. Data on their *actual* reconvictions (outcomes) after release were compared with their *expected* reconviction rates (calculated from Correctional Services of Canada prediction scales) in order to test out the 'what works best for whom' conjectures. The design then involved a further phase of qualitative work which attempted to tease out in more detail the participants' reflections on how the different mechanisms and contexts of the program had influenced them.

These three evaluation designs are presented in Table 4.1. This highlights in a systematic way some key similarities and differences.

Table 4.1 *A matrix of realist designs*

Topic	Anticipated impact	Unit of analysis	Research strategy	Theory development	Opportunity for experimental control	Techniques	Result
Property marking	Immediate	Community	Realist experiment	High	High	Quantitative contemporaneous	Theory tested
Housing management	Medium term	Community	Exploratory case study	Low	Low	Quantitative/ qualitative contemporaneous	Theory developed
Prison education	Long term	Individual	Realist sample survey	Low	None	Multiple retrospective	Theory developed

Exemplar 1: property marking

Property marking as a way of reducing vulnerability to theft has a very, very long history. Laycock (1985), whose evaluation of a British project is discussed here, notes that property marking goes back 25,000 years to palaeolithic times when bone tools were evidently personalized. More recently there has been renewed interest. The United States has seen Operation Identification, and in Britain the introduction of postcoding, which provides brief, unique address identifiers, created an added stimulus. The popularity of property marking stimulated obvious interest in the evaluation of its effectiveness as a crime fighting measure.

By the time of Laycock's research, property marking had already been the subject of several evaluation studies. She reviews an earlier evaluation of Operation Identification in cities in the United States by Heller et al. (1975), which had identified four putative mechanisms through which property marking might have an impact on domestic burglary, each of which would produce differing expected outcomes. These conjectured mechanism–outcome configurations can be summarized thus:

(i)   Property marking might increase the difficulty in *disposing* of stolen goods (outcome), since it would be more obvious to prospective purchasers that the items had been stolen (mechanism).

(ii) Property marking might increase the *detection* of offences and conviction of offenders (outcomes), since their possession of stolen property would more easily be established (mechanism), and this fact would constitute compelling prosecution evidence in court (mechanism).

(iii) Property marking might lead to increases in the rate at which stolen property is *returned* to its rightful owners (outcome), since on recovery of stolen goods the address of the owner would be known to the police (mechanism).

(iv) Property marking might *deter* burglars (outcome) because of anticipated added difficulty in disposing of the goods and/or greater risks of prosecution (mechanisms). This deterrence might operate only for those who participate in a property marking scheme (outcome). It might also operate more broadly for all in a city in which property marking was being implemented (outcome).

The results of Heller et al.'s study were evidently that:

(a)   Property marking did not seriously hinder disposal of stolen goods.
(b)   Apprehension and conviction of burglars were not increased.
(c)   Operation Identification cities did not experience city-wide reductions in burglary rates.
(d)   Participants in property marking had significantly lower burglary rates, with reductions ranging between 25% in St Louis and 33% in Seattle.

It might be concluded from this that *part* of conjectured mechanism–outcome configuration (iv) is supported by the evidence but not the rest. That is to say, anticipated added difficulty of disposal and greater risk of apprehension operate to reduce burglary risk in regard to those actually property marked within the overall scheme, but not city-wide. As ever, evidence for this remains inconclusive, and a subsequent evaluation study in a large (3,500 households) residential area in Sweden (Knuttsen, 1984) found no reduction in burglary amongst scheme participants. Moreover, interviews with burglars found that most paid little attention to signs that property marking had been undertaken. This was not consistent with the one 'successful' mechanism–outcome pattern configuration found in the United States.

What is conspicuously absent from these studies is, of course, explicit attention to the significance of 'context'. They also fail to address an important perennial preoccupation of crime prevention initiatives, the displacement of crimes from those to whom crime prevention measures have been applied to those who have not had them. Laycock does consider context in her research design: she adds a *C* to the previous *MO* configurations. She also pays attention to the displacement mechanisms, and the circumstances in which they might be triggered.

The logic of Laycock's research design was to find the best context in which property marking would trigger the conjectured crime prevention mechanisms. At the same time she strove to find the worst context for triggering crime displacement. Failure to generate positive expected outcomes in such a scenario would suggest that there were no grounds for continuing with the practice at all. As she puts it:

> The conditions for the launch of this scheme were to be optimal on the grounds that if there were no reduction in burglary rates under such conditions then there was little point in pursuing property marking nationwide. (1985, p. 3)

Laycock thus tried to set up circumstances which would give property marking its best chance of achieving burglary reduction without displacement. She set her study in South Wales in three fairly distinct small villages, comprising 700 to 800 houses in each and 2,234 in all. These villages were strung across the floor of a valley and were surrounded by largely uninhabited hills. This geographical context minimized the prospects for displacement beyond the experimental area. Burglaries took place at a higher rate in the (poorer) central village. If there was displacement from this, it was most likely to be to one or both of the other villages. Laycock tried to effect a very high rate of property marking in the three villages to minimize opportunities for displacement to those not taking part, and also to obtain a sufficiently large sample for statistical analysis which could reveal real outcomes robustly. To encourage participation in the scheme, the Chief Constable sent a letter to all households shortly before the project informing them of what was to happen. There was a major launch with press and television coverage. All households were visited by police officers and police volunteers over a four-day period including the weekend, to maximize the chances of finding someone at home. Residents had the scheme explained and were provided with property marking pens and window stickers (decals for American readers). A week later householders were visited again by police personnel to give help with marking if it was needed and to check who had marked their property and who was displaying their sticker. Three months later the Chief Constable wrote again, reinforcing the aims of the scheme. Six months after the start of the scheme, a further visit was made by the police to check on participants' continued involvement and on the display of the window stickers; and additional stickers were provided where necessary. Across the three villages participation rates varied from 70% to 75%, much higher than those achieved in previous studies.

Instead of looking simply at changes in overall crime rates, Laycock directed her outcome measurements towards precise theoretically expected effects, paying particular attention to those where burglary reduction would most strongly be predicted. Since it appeared from the American research that the reduction of burglary rates was greatest amongst scheme participants in an area, measuring effects on burglary rates amongst them (as compared with those for non-participants) constituted a key concern in the evaluation. In addition, given the finding that it was the *perception of the risks created by property marking*, rather than any *effect it had on actual crime clear-ups*, which was responsible for the observed falls amongst participants, the difference in rates of burglary amongst those displaying window stickers was also central. Also since cash cannot readily be marked there was a particular focus on an expected greater rate of reduction in loss of markable goods.

In the twelve months before the scheme there were 128 burglaries involving 115 homes in the three villages. In the year after there were 74 burglaries involving 68 homes. This represents a higher reduction rate than that found by Heller et al. (1975) in any of their Operation Identification cities in the United States. Amongst those displaying stickers the reduction in numbers of incidents was from 91 to 35, and amongst those not doing so there was a slight increase from 37 to 39. The reductions were statistically significant. The increase was not. The overall burglary rate fell from 5.1% to 3.0%, with falls from 1.5% to 0.98% in the better-off villages and from 13.0% to 5.1% in the worse-off higher-crime village. There was thus no evidence for displacement. Consistent with Heller et al.'s findings, there was no evidence either that stolen goods were returned or that detections increased. In the high-burglary-rate village there were statistically significant falls in burglary not only for markable goods but also for cash, which typically involved loss from prepayment meters. The figures are shown in Table 4.2.

Laycock uses her findings as the basis for further realistic conjectures

Table 4.2   *Markable goods and meter break burglaries before and after property marking in high-crime village (from Laycock, 1985)*

Type of burglary	Participation	Year before	Year after
Markable property	In scheme	21	11
	Out of scheme	12	11
Meter breaks	In scheme	30	9
	Out of scheme	8	14

concerning mechanisms triggered by property marking in the context of the scheme. First, it might be the window sticker rather than property marking *per se* which triggered the crime reducing mechanism, and that what the label was saying was, in effect, 'burglar beware – you are at more risk in this household than in others, because the residents are doing what they can to increase the risk to you.' Second, previous research had estimated that as many as 80% of meter breaks had been by the householders themselves, so-called 'own goals'. These residents, by becoming involved in the scheme, inadvertently debarred themselves from claiming they had been victims of burglary by buying into a burglary prevention scheme! Third, the high take-up rate limited the scope for displacement, since there was a heavily reduced supply of easy targets, and since many of those not participating already used other crime prevention devices. Fourth, what the crime prevention scheme as a whole did was to persuade the (predominantly local) burglars that they were at high risk as a result of the property marking, since they too would be visited as part of the scheme and persuaded of the crime preventive powers of property marking: the effects of property marking are due to a self-fulfilling prophesy. Laycock's realistic theory of what was achieved through the introduction of property marking in the South Wales scheme is summarized in Table 4.3. This shows how a variety of mechanisms are triggered in the local context to generate a range of outcome patterns.

Laycock's evaluation is a theory-driven, 'best case' study, using quantitative methods. She thus states explicitly that the conditions created are not those that allow mechanical generalization to any form of property marking anywhere, but comprise those that allow some theory testing:

> The demonstration project described in this paper was set up in a carefully chosen area. There is difficulty therefore, in generalising the results of the study to other less ideal areas. But the study can be justified on the grounds that if property marking had not reduced burglary here then it is doubtful whether it could do so anywhere. (1985, p. 11)

Laycock stresses, thus, that the high-density property marking in the relatively isolated villages in the midst of very extensive local publicity created

Table 4.3 *Laycock's initial realist property marking theory*

Context	+	New mechanism	=	Outcome pattern
Small isolated area, with local burglars	+	Persuasive publicity that risks of apprehension increase	=	Reduction of burglary rates of those where risks deemed heightened
Small isolated area, with local burglars	+	Reduced perceived supply of acceptable, accessible alternative burglary targets	=	Little or no displacement
Small isolated area, with local burglars	+	Perception that householders are trying to increase the risk to burglars	=	Burglary reduction in relation to property outside scheme scope (notably cash from meters)
Small isolated area, with local burglars	+	Participation in and tacit commitment to a burglary reduction scheme	=	Reduced 'own goal' meter breaks

a particular context for the mechanism triggering potential of the measures introduced. She also begins with theory and ends with more refined theory. She has taken us round the realist evaluation cycle.

There is an interesting and instructive postscript to Laycock's evaluation. She made use of a 'natural experiment' following her original study. Thus, in this instance she did not actually do anything. Laycock conjectures that persuasive publicity to local burglars that a measure is making crime more difficult is what acts as a deterrent. She speculates that their (mistaken) reasoning was that burglary rates had fallen because burglary had become more risky, and if it was more risky it was less worth doing. She also conjectures that the effects of changes in risk perceptions fade over time.

To test this theory she observed the outcome of a 'natural' event (Laycock, 1992). Following the original property marking experiment, the results were published in June 1985. The popular reports of the findings were (as ever) rather crude. Instead of Laycock's subtle theory and research, what was prominently related locally on television and in the newspapers was the conclusion that property marking had substantially reduced the burglary rate. Laycock continued patiently to trace the burglary rates. What she found was that the rate of burglary fell dramatically after the news report. This occurred without any new crime prevention initiative. Moreover, Laycock also noted that in the course of the year after the initial property marking the rates had dipped significantly and had, especially in the high-crime village, been returning to their previous levels. Table 4.4 shows these further realist refinements to her original property marking evaluation.

Finally, it is worth noting, as Laycock herself does, how misleading a less

Table 4.4 *Laycock's refinements to her realist property marking theory*

Context	+	New mechanism	=	Outcome pattern
Small isolated area, with local burglars	+	Familiarization with new measures and recognition of unchanged risks	=	Gradual return to previous burglary rates
Small isolated area, with local burglars	+	Refreshment of perceptions of scheme efficacy via publicity	=	Renewed fall in burglary rate

than detailed look at the data could be. In the year before the scheme there were 128 burglaries, in the year following implementation of the scheme there were 74, and in the year after that there were only 66. At first sight it might seem that effectiveness is increasing. It is only theoretically informed examination of the monthly figures which shows this reading to be implausible and that there are more complex causal mechanisms being triggered in the scheme context.

What is useful for the policy maker from Laycock's study is that she shows that it is not property marking *per se* that reduces burglary, but mechanisms triggered through its introduction. Moreover these mechanisms will not always be triggered, but only in particular contexts. In addition, these same mechanisms may be triggered by other measures also, depending on features of context. All this helps both in determining where and how property marking itself might be implemented with reasonable expectations for burglary reduction (at least for a while), and in reflecting on how other measures might be called on in this and other contexts to trigger similar burglary prevention mechanisms. All this clearly has the potential for devising more efficient, effective and economical means of achieving policy objectives.

Laycock's study is analogous to natural science experiments where, as we showed in the previous chapter, realists have demonstrated that the scientist *creates conditions for the triggering of conjectured mechanisms.* Not all evaluations can mimic what natural science does. In many cases evaluators are asked to look at a program over which they exert no control. We now turn to an example of this.

Exemplar 2: the Priority Estates Project

A very large number of program evaluations, probably most, have a similar starting point to that of the Priority Estates Project: a program is in place or planned; evaluation may be required as a condition for a grant or be deemed desirable by policy makers; and an evaluator is contracted directly to undertake the work. Foster and Hope's study of the Priority Estates Project (PEP) is an example of how this can be done broadly in accordance with realistic principles (Hope and Foster, 1992; Foster and Hope, 1993). It also reveals the payoff from adopting this approach.

Because the evaluators were presented here with a ready-made program, there could be none of the close involvement in its conception and development which was present in Laycock's study. The evaluators were not, thus, concerned with the deliberate injection of realistic thought into the program. The evaluators were not program directors. Instead their relationship to the program components and actions was initially that of learners. The evaluation team began by trying to discern and reconstruct a realistic theory of the program context, mechanisms and expected crime-related outcome patterns.

Foster and Hope were not concerned with evaluating all aspects of PEP. Their focus was specifically on its impact on crime. PEP is sponsored by a British government department – the Department of the Environment – and it works with local authorities and tenants in 'difficult' public housing estates. PEP facilitates the implementation of changes in the way local housing services are delivered and managed, and the involvement of tenants in running the estates. According to Foster and Hope (1993) the following ten elements constitute the key elements of a program:

1   A local estate-based housing office.
2   A local repairs team.
3   Local lettings – a local list of applicants, local procedures for signing on and allocating tenants within an agreed priority scheme.
4   Local control of rent collection and arrears.
5   Residents' caretaking, cleaning and open space maintenance, with local supervision.
6   Resident liaison with management, usually a residents' forum acting as an advisory and consultative group.
7   Small scale capital improvements and refurbishments.
8   Well-trained staff with delegated authority.
9   The project manager as the key figure accountable for estate management.
10   A locally controlled budget for management and maintenance.

Foster and Hope (1993) note that crime prevention is 'not a specific task of PEP'. They draw on existing criminological research to try to make sense of the emergence of high crime patterns within public housing estates. They acknowledge the complexity of this, stressing that each individual estate may have its own attributes and its own internal development. They say that:

> in order to unravel the inter-relationship between the various possible causal factors, explanations may also be needed of the internal dynamics of community change on estates – in other words a chart of the 'crime career' of particular estates over time. (1993 p. 10)

They identify, though, four main generic ways in which PEP measures might trigger new mechanisms to inhibit high-crime generating processes within some areas of public housing (1993, p. vi):

1 Levels of security and degrees of defensibility of space create varying but modifiable degrees of opportunity for crime. Thus, crime may be reduced by 'creating better dwelling security' and more 'defensible space', effected through PEP inspired physical improvements.
2 Physical neglect provides significant cues to criminals that the neighbourhood is not cared for and hence no one is likely to intervene and stop them offending. Thus, crime may be reduced 'by halting the spiral of deterioration, tackling vandalism, caretaking, cleaning up the estate, thereby reducing "signs of disorder" and fear of crime, and signifying the estate is well-cared-for'. Again, these changes can be implemented through PEP interventions.
3 An estate in which residents do not have a stake lacks people interested in creating and maintaining its security, as those who can do so leave. It is then left to offenders and those unable or unconcerned to regulate their behaviour. This in turn fosters the formation of networks of mutually supportive local criminals. Crime may be reduced, thus, 'by investing in the estate so that residents will develop a positive view and thus a greater stake in their community, and a greater expectation of law-abiding behaviour'.
4 Lack of effective formal and informal social control is conducive to crime and is frequently weak in run-down housing estates with disorganized families, attenuated or hostile neighbourhood relationships, and lack of shared commitment to behavioural norms. Hence, crime might be reduced 'by increasing informal community control over crime both through increased surveillance and supervision by residents and housing officials and facilitating the development of a set of norms and expectations against offending on the estate'. Through involvement of the community in estate management PEP may plausibly effect this change.

In addition, Foster and Hope point out ways in which changes in social mix, which may derive from developments external to or interacting with PEP interventions, can introduce new causal mechanisms effecting alterations in observed outcome patterns (cf. Bottoms and Wiles, 1986; Bottoms et al., 1989).

Foster and Hope examine two estates, in London and Hull, where efforts to implement PEP are made. They adopt a 'community study' (Bell and Newby, 1972) approach to their investigation of the 'experimental' estates, examining internal spatial and social differentiation, using both quantitative and qualitative techniques. Through surveys they assemble detailed before-and-after data about crime and fear of crime patterns, and through ethnographic work they look in detail at the process through which PEP is implemented and at the experiences of estate residents. They look both at the overall effects of the PEP program and, by carefully monitoring the context and implementation of PEP measures, examine and explain variations in changes in rates of crime and the distribution of victimization within the PEP estates. They are able to conjecture which mechanisms have been triggered in the local contexts to produce quite complex outcome patterns.

Foster and Hope also include control estates, where before-and-after surveys were conducted, but where there was no ethnography. They thus represent their study as a quasi-experimental one, comparing changes between the experimental and control estates. However, as argued in Chapter 2 this cannot add anything instructive, and indeed it does not do so. Interestingly, the authors implicitly recognize as much where they refer to the need to unravel the internal dynamics of the 'crime careers of particular estates'. They acknowledge that individual estates have their own 'criminal careers' which need to be charted in detail (Foster and Hope, 1993, p. 10). It is just this realist unravelling that they accomplish with distinction in their examination of the experimental estates, showing how indeed their experimental estates did follow internal localized paths, and it is this that we focus on here.

Briefly, Foster and Hope find that on the London experimental estate the non-co-operation of key personnel effectively undermined the implementation of key parts of the PEP. Indeed frictions caused by this led to the withdrawal of PEP for a while. Morale and tenant involvement flagged and never fully recovered. On the experimental estate in Hull, PEP was implemented more fully and more enthusiastically, and we deal with it in more detail here.

Foster and Hope describe the context furnished for the program in Hull. The target estate comprised 1,083 dwellings, forming an indistinct part of a much larger 1960s development of about 3,500 units on the outskirts of the city. The estate was laid out on 'Radburn' principles, that is vehicles were segregated from pedestrians and access to dwellings was via pathways and feeder roads. There were 514 houses built of precast concrete, jammed together with little private space and no front gardens. The remaining dwellings were divided between three clustered nine- or ten-storey blocks of flats, a further block isolated from the remaining dwellings, and a few three-storey town houses. Nearly all the open space was public. There was, thus, little defensible space, and plenty of escape routes for offenders.

The estate had been built for slum clearance families, many from a notorious area which gave the estate a stigma from the start. It had 'few communal facilities, high levels of unemployment, fuel debts, social service caseloads, juvenile offenders and a city-wide reputation as a sink estate in low demand' (Hope and Foster, 1992, p. 491). The 'before' survey of 578 respondents had found mixed views of the estate, with 86% believing the estate had a bad reputation, 63% believing that it had got worse over the past two years, and 54% saying they would move if they had the choice, but curiously with 62% also stating they were very satisfied with the estate. Nearly all residents were white, and most were in the poorest socio-economic category, with only a quarter in full-time or part-time work. A quarter of the population were under sixteen years of age. Whilst 41% had lived on it for more than thirteen years, 38% had lived on the estate for less than four. There was overall a sense of helplessness and hopelessness amongst many on the estate. Some were ashamed to live on it. Despite all this Foster and Hope note a 'bedrock of neighbourliness' with 51% 'talking to or friendly with' two or more neighbours and 62% 'keeping an eye on their neighbours' property' when they were out.

Overall victimization rates stood at 98 household offences per 100 households per annum, over twice the British overall rate found in the British Crime Survey, and a third higher than the highest community-type rate found in the BCS. Anxiety about crime was also widespread. Most had witnessed incivilities such as children swearing in the street (84%), children damaging property (50%), or people drinking in the streets (57%). Some tenants had tried and failed to control unruly behaviour. Many were fearful of threatening youths. There was little confidence in police effectiveness.

In short, the context conformed pretty well to that suggested in the theoretical model: ready opportunities for crime because of the physical layout; common signs of disorder; generally poor opinions of the estate; and fairly weak formal and informal surveillance and social control. There were plausible mechanisms for crime in abundance and high-crime-level regularities to match.

Changes were introduced which might alter the existing mechanisms. Efforts were made to involve tenants in the management of the estate. A great deal of physical improvement to the environment was undertaken following extensive tenant consultation. Thus, for example, for the houses fencing, front gardens, and blocked pathways created more defensible space. CCTV was added to the existing door entry systems in the tower blocks. The key elements of PEP were implemented.

What Hope and Foster do in the course of their evaluation is to tease out a series of refinements to their starting theory. This involved coming to understand in some detail the variations within the estate, the variations in the implemented program, and the intrusion of external causal forces. The ethnographic component of the research marshalled local wisdom on active social networks within the estate. One informant is quoted, for example, as saying:

> You've got different groups within groups: we've got the adolescent group causing mayhem . . . they're out of control and they've got so many associates of criminals on the estate with them. The drunks are another . . . and we've got a

couple of ex-cons . . . released from prison recently . . . that have teamed up and they're doing other jobs on the estate too. (Foster and Hope, 1993, p.76)

With regard to the particular estate context into which PEP was introduced, Foster and Hope also identify two groups with little contact with one another. The first comprised well-established tenants, who had lived in the estate a long time, were coping despite poverty or unemployment, were involved in community organizations and controlled their children quite strictly. The second included those who were more transient, more vulnerable, less able to cope, and with more financial difficulties and more contact with social services, law enforcement and other statutory agencies. The former group, amongst whom there was more trust and more willingness to look out for each other's property, suffered less crime than the latter. Foster and Hope note the presence of a few families where the children were beyond parental control and were causing a lot of trouble, and one in particular was widely deemed to be involved in high rates of offending. This family had then drawn others, in particular juveniles, into their pattern of behaviour, creating a criminal network. Amongst vulnerable families Foster and Hope note those headed by women who were often keen to leave, and with intermittent support from boyfriends who were often in trouble with the police. There were others forming a collaborative subculture which sustained routine widespread property offending to which children were recruited, and from which it was difficult to part.

By looking at processes in the estate in detail, Foster and Hope disaggregate a 'PEP program' into a quite detailed series of *CMO* configurations. They point out that by the end of their study period only about a third of the houses had had defensible space improvements. They identify five separate areas on the estate. We concentrate here, however, on their analysis of the PEP effect on burglary rates on three of them. Area A was a part of the estate comprising housing where physical improvements had been introduced. Area B was broadly similar to A, except that the housing had not been improved by the time the evaluation was complete. Area C comprised three tower blocks.

Resident context changes

The improved area A, which had been similar to area B before PEP, developed a lower turnover and thereby became relatively better off as it received fewer of the less stable estate newcomers than the unimproved area B. The proportion who had been resident in area A for less than three years went down from 33% to 13%, and in area B went up very slightly from 22% to 24%. The three tower blocks (area C) had housed a substantial proportion of the elderly (42%) before PEP. However, partly because of allocation of the elderly to smaller blocks (area E), and partly through allocation of area C units to young, homeless, single people (few other suitable tenants wanting to live there, and possibly some deliberate targeting), the age distribution of area C altered. In the course of the study the proportion of young tenants (age 16–30) in the three tower blocks reached 42%, and those who had been resident less than three years went up from 24% to 44%. Many of the incoming young people had few material or personal resources to manage independent living.

Mechanisms introduced

In area A defensible space had been created through environmental improvements, and opportunities for burglary reduced. Residents confirmed in interview an increased sense of territoriality just outside the home. A local resident admitting a dozen or more burglaries in the area also commented that the fencing made it more difficult to look inside to see if there was anything worth stealing. In area B there was also an increase in territoriality, explained by the community development aspects of PEP, which was indicated through measurements of numbers of friends on the estate and involvement in voluntary activities, and this helped keep the burglary rate down. In area C, there was little social control over the new, young, unstable residents. They also attracted other disaffected young people on the estate, creating a distinct new subculture. This became tied into the adult offender groups, and a significant crime network emerged, with the poor and vulnerable on the estate furnishing a thriving underground market for stolen goods as well as ready targets.

Outcome patterns

The crime pattern outcomes, revealed by the before-and-after surveys, included falls in burglary prevalence rates (from 26% to 12%) in area A, stability (14% to 13%) in area B and a large rise (from 4% to 26%) in area C. Areas A and B each had 41% and area C had 9% of all the burglaries on the estate before PEP. At the time of the 'after' survey area A had only 16% of them, area B had 44% of them and area C now had 33% of them. Thus there was a substantial absolute increase in area C, a substantial absolute fall in area A, and stability in area B. In terms of overall distribution, unsurprisingly a bigger share came to be found in area C, a smaller share in area A and a fairly constant share in area B. In area C, not only had burglary increased dramatically but so too had vandalism, graffiti and damage, with the remaining (mostly elderly) co-residents complaining about the conditions.

In short, the developments in area C triggered increasing criminality, whereas developments in areas A and B had to differing extents increased social control, more so in area A where the physical improvements had been implemented in addition to the management changes. We simplify in overtly realist terms Foster and Hope's findings in Table 4.5.

The developments in areas A and B broadly corroborate Foster and Hope's reconstructed realist PEP crime reduction theory. Developments in

Table 4.5   *A realist summary of Foster and Hope's study of the effects of PEP on crime in the Hull experimental estate*

Context	+	New mechanisms	=	Outcome pattern
Area A Poor-quality, hard-to-let housing; traditional housing department; lack of tenant involvement in estate management	+	Improved housing and increased involvement in management create increased commitment to the estate, more stability, and opportunities and motivation for social control and collective responsibility	=	Reduced burglary prevalence
Area B Poor-quality, hard-to-let housing; traditional housing department; lack of tenant involvement in estate management	+	Increased involvement in management creates conditions for increased territoriality, but unattractive housing maintains high turnover, retaining vulnerable families	=	Stable burglary prevalence concentrated on the more vulnerable
Area C Three tower blocks, occupied mainly by the elderly; traditional housing department; lack of tenant involvement in estate management	+	Concentration of elderly tenants into smaller blocks and natural wastage creates vacancies taken up by young, formerly homeless single people inexperienced in independent living. They become the dominant group. They have little capacity or inclination for informal social control, and are attracted to a hospitable estate subterranean subculture	=	Increased burglary prevalence concentrated amongst the more vulnerable; high levels of vandalism and incivility
Overall Traditionally managed, low-quality housing on hard-to-let estate with subterranean criminal subculture and some difficult families	+	Variations in changes wrought by PEP and tenant allocation trigger varying mechanisms in differing parts of the estate, leading to more social control in some areas, and creating/reinforcing criminality in others	=	Mixed patterns of increasing burglary, stable burglary and decreasing burglary according to area

area C highlight the countervailing causal mechanisms triggered through changing tenant patterns effected through (non-PEP) dwelling-unit allocation practices. Overall, the evaluation reveals that exploratory case studies require detailed attention to the contextual specifics and disaggregation of *CMO* configurations.

Burglary prevalence rates (numbers victimized once or more per 100 households) reduced slightly from 10.3% to 9.6% and incidence rates (numbers of incidents per 100 households) dropped from 13.5% to 12.7%.

These burglary figures suggest little change. Comparison with the control estate would have told a different story. Here there was increase from 6.1% to 15.4% in prevalence and from 8.8% to 18.1% in incidence, but we know such comparisons are spurious. What Foster and Hope do in their evaluation is to show how understanding the impact of PEP requires the development of a complex model showing how the measures introduced in the (changing) context of the estate triggered a variety of mechanisms to generate a fine textured outcome pattern. The subtlety of the analysis incidentally shows the inappropriateness of gross comparisons with 'control' estates, vindicating their own comments about the need to trace estate crime careers in detail. Their accounts of developments in the London experimental estate (Foster and Hope, 1993; Foster, 1995) are equally subtle and would yield the same kind of conclusion.

Foster and Hope's summary of their findings from the Hull estate brings out well the realistic character of their evaluation. They say:

> In this particular configuration of events, environmental design modifications and improvements in management quality (including tenant involvement) interacted with changes in tenant turnover and allocation to the estate. Their combined effect was to alter the internal 'culture' of the estate to produce an intensification *both* of social control and criminality which found expression in differences between parts of the estate and various groups of tenants. This supports the view that the various causal influences on crime on a 'problem' estate tend to interact with one another. This is likely to occur because their effect is mediated by the internal culture of the estate community.

> The events on the Hull experimental estate illustrate the crucial importance of population change in affecting the community dynamics of a neighbourhood and hence the crime it experiences. In the public housing sector, population change is shaped by the mechanisms which allocate particular kinds of tenant to specific estates. Nothing that had been achieved on the experimental estate by the end of the study period had managed to halt the turnover of tenants on the estate as a whole [or the] increasing number of the young poor [concentrated] in an already stressed environment.

> A plausible interpretation of the events on the Hull experimental estate is that the environmental improvements in area A reduced the number of vacancies there because the new defensible environment was valued by its residents. Therefore, of the incoming residents – who were relatively poorer and less likely to be in two-parent family units – those with children were allocated to the unimproved area of houses (Area B) and those without were housed in the tower blocks (Area C). Social cohesion and 'empowerment' increased amongst the residents of area B as a result of PEP's efforts to involve them in the improvement of services and estate management – and the anticipation of the benefits of defensible space to come – but the newly arrived single parents who were housed there stood out as especially vulnerable to crime. Despite the improvements to the security of the tower blocks, and the better management of the estate as a whole, the newcomers to area C – that is, the young predominantly childless poor – replaced many of the previous, elderly residents and attracted crime to themselves, both as perpetrators and victims, concentrating crime in their part of the estate. (1993, pp. 81–82)

Foster and Hope begin by constructing a theory about how PEP may trigger crime reducing mechanisms. They end up with a more refined theory. Using a variety of data, they show that the detailed changes within the estate cannot be explained through the PEP theory alone. The complex outcome pattern instead follows from an array of processes, some to do with PEP, some not. To make sense of the (characteristically) complex outcome pattern, attention had to be paid to the particular context within which the program was implemented. PEP, coupled with other non-program interventions, triggered a series of mechanisms effecting the outcomes. The research design, articulating theory, collecting data relevant to it, close scrutiny of community life in the estate, and assiduous monitoring of the implementation process, permitted the realistic evaluation of this diverse program.

Exemplar 3: prison education

We take as our third exemplar some *work in progress*, and thus lay open for inspection the design one of us (Pawson) has implemented, with others, to examine the impact of the Simon Fraser University Prison Education Program on the rehabilitation of inmates serving in British Columbian penitentiaries. The program itself was unique, not least because it lasted over twenty years. The idea, to put it simply, was to install a *campus in a prison*, with several centres being established in federal (men's) prisons in the province in which inmates could undertake a whole series of (preparatory, humanities and social sciences) university courses over a number of semesters and thus earn themselves credits over a number of years towards a Simon Fraser degree. We describe here a vast program which had been delivered to over 1,000 men by scores of teachers and co-ordinators (and which also, rather confusingly, is referred to as PEP).

The realist starting notion behind the design is that the Simon Fraser program does not 'work' in reducing recidivism in some undifferentiated way. Perhaps the most compelling point to be made in respect of this is that for most participants on the program (teachers and students), rehabilitation was not on the agenda as a direct and manifest goal. The guiding impulse was always an educational one, namely to encourage as many men as possible, as far as possible, through a mainstream university education program. Having said this, the evaluation begins with the rather different assumption that 'non-therapeutic' objectives can *in some cases* have 'therapeutic' outcomes. Putting it like this is no outrageous arrogance, but in fact a simple matter of anecdotal common sense. Every co-ordinator on the program was able to point to some individual – Joe Bloggs – who, having been on the course, forsook a criminal career in preference for a lifestyle rooted in activities discovered whilst on the program. It should be added at once that such tales are frequently followed by accounts of other prisoners who have been academic 'stars' but from the moment of release have sought exactly the kind of trouble which has ensured an early return to the prison.

Repeatedly, in this book, we have insisted on the injunction to stop thinking of programs as some kind of unitary happening which either does or doesn't work. There is little such inclination in this case, the researchers having to face not singularity but daunting *complexity*. The prison initiative, in many ways, exemplifies the extremes of ambition in social programming. The program itself is *long term*: attending this, or any other, university course involves hundreds, thousands, millions of different events and experiences. Although the course is, of course, taught in groups, lectures, seminars etc., the rehabilitative effect applies to the *individual* prisoner as he makes (or fails to make) his way in life after prison. Thus, unlike our two previous examples of community programs in which the locality is, in the first instance, *chosen* by practitioners, here we have over 1,000 different program subjects *choosing* to come on the course for hundreds of different reasons, very few of them with eyes explicitly on a rehabilitation prize. And then there is the rather unique goal of such programs – 'rehabilitation' itself being as long term as a long term objective could be. The remedial process under research thus actually begins *well before* the offender enters prison, since it is the prisoner's beliefs, volitions, peer groups and social circumstances, in all their grim and unfortunate variety, which will have acted to justify his criminal actions. The course itself may lead to a new set of skills, social networks and preferences, but this itself is not rehabilitation. Judgements on that continue to be made *well after* the life of the program, requiring that any new non-criminal choices and identities be sustained in (and often 'in spite of') a variety of post-release circumstances, not the least of which is the general public hostility facing the 'ex-con'.

Summarizing, and at the risk of waxing too lyrical, we might say we are dealing here with one of life's richer, darker and longer tapestries. Rather more prosaically, we might spare a thought for researchers trying to come up with a strategy to track a process of such complexity and duration. From a design point of view, therefore, this investigation starts with a situation which is surprisingly common in evaluation research – the possession of no singular theory about how the program works to produce the desired outcome. For the realist, this at least gives us a clear message about the principal task – namely to get on with it and generate some hypotheses about the potential *CMO* configurations which might underlie educational rehabilitation. As with our previous cases, the researchers were able to assemble key hypotheses by drawing on the folk wisdom of practitioners as well as the formal knowledge of the academy.

We begin our reconstruction here by considering some potential mechanisms. What is it about education which can provoke a prisoner into reckoning that a way of life they once considered justified, is justified no longer? The adult education literature is not short of suggestions on this question. The weapons available are the rather genteel ones of reasoning, thought and reflection. Notions of 'behaviour modification', of 'thought control', of 'deficiency repair', of 'curing the sick mind' were not really what this group of researcher/educationalists had in mind. Since coming on and staying on such a course is a voluntary action, they supposed that the rehabilitation process works through the medium of reasoning, of choice, of figuring things out in a different way. In a highly simplified way one can summarize some of the potential reintegrative mechanisms identified in the literature as follows:

1 Education might be a spur to *self-realization*. Following a particular course might lead to inmates developing knowledge, skills and confidence which realize their potential (for the first time).
2 Education might lead to *economic potential*. Education of whatever sort can be considered to have a 'training' element which could act as a launch pad for providing different sorts of opportunities towards a new career.
3 Education might promote *social acceptability*. Education is a profoundly social activity and the behaviour and skills learned therein might become routine ways of acting which will allow an inmate to function in a wider range of settings.
4 Education might lead to *moral* or *civic responsibility*. Certain curricula will involve discussion of law making, rule keeping, justice, rights and responsibilities, right and wrong. These might filter in and become part of the general mind-set of the (ex) offender.
5 Education might lead to *cognitive change*. Education is, perhaps above all, about developing the reasoning process. In confronting a whole new range of ideas, perspectives, and philosophies, the inmate's own power of reasoning and self-reflection might be deepened, encouraging a new outlook on old problems.

These processes of change are paraphrased here not because they are exhaustive and efficacious or even particularly wise and worthy. Indeed, as everyone knows, they can be woefully far-fetched in many prison contexts where there are a whole range of contravening forces in operation. As with any social initiative, offenders only spend a small proportion of their time on the program and thus experience simultaneously the reinforcement mechanisms that these 'schools for crime' have to offer. The list above represents the background thinking to broad changes which may be associated with education, and the first task of evaluation is to try to marry these more formal statements of program mechanisms with the practitioner's accounts of how they see the routine activity of classroom life triggering changes in the resources and reasoning of inmates.

Before we get down to these particular brass tacks, it is necessary to introduce the other major axis that impinges on this particular research design, namely the matter of how *context* conditions the potential for rehabilitation. In Palmer's (1975) terms we are now discussing 'for which types of offender, in what conditions and in what type of setting do programs work'. Although this is a missing element in many 'corrections' evaluations, a moment's thought about the classroom will jolt us into realizing its importance. The best educational course in the world (of any type) needs to have reasonably appropriate students to make the best of it. Accordingly, it is a common experience of all prison teachers that their courses attract a 'certain type of prisoner'. All teachers would add furthermore that one has to be in the right institutional context in order to sustain the kind of priorities mentioned above. A substantial part of the research therefore can be considered to be about trying to specify those matches between course mechanisms and prisoners' circumstances which are particularly conducive to rehabilitation.

Once again, it is the case that the researchers do not have to begin the search for the answers to those 'who', 'when' and 'where' questions from scratch. The academic literature is full of ideas on 'targets' for rehabilitation:

1 Adult educational theories frequently focus on the 'disadvantaged', not only for political reasons, but on the supposition that such groups may pick up on and benefit more readily from mechanisms previously described. Placing effort here might provide more change than in prisoners who have experienced, and shunned, some social and educational advantage.

2 Then there is the context provided by the type of offence itself, since we cannot assume, of course, that education is a universal panacea counteracting all criminal tendencies. There is a whole variety of theories of the 'criminogenic factors' which influence the pursuit of crime. To use a negative example, it may be hypothesized that some of these, such as sex-related crimes, may describe contexts which generic educational programs cannot reach.

3 Prisoner typologies are the stuff of many ethnographies which remind us that prison culture is not singular. Cohen and Taylor's (1972) rogues' gallery provides a useful example, and makes the following (fairly self-explanatory) subdivisions: confrontationalists, symbiotic types, prison thieves, private sinners, and situational criminals. This catalogue brings a gleam of recognition to most prison educators' eyes, suggesting distinctions about who would prosper on and after the course.

4 Prison organization itself is a response to the different characters and circumstances of the inmates. Thus we have young offenders' institutions, open prisons, dispersal prisons, training prisons, federal prisons, local jails and so forth, as well as different security classifications for inmates within each establishment. Inmates are thus likely to find themselves in very different regimes, the precise 'ethos' of the establishment limiting the chances of success of any rehabilitation mechanism.

Table 4.6   *Phases of the prison program evaluation*

Phase 1	Phase 2	Phase 3
Inspection of academic literature and focusing on practitioners' 'folk theories' on why and for whom the program might work	Outcome analysis internal to the program of the particular contexts and mechanisms associated with success as predicted in phase 1	Investigation of subjects' interpretation of program to seek for a sense of self-recognition of processes described in phase 2

Readers will appreciate that these are highly abbreviated lists of some of the more obvious contexts and mechanisms which can be conjectured to govern the success of an offender education program. We list them baldly here as a brief reminder that most of them are not even countenanced within the equivalent quasi-experimental designs in the corrections programs we examined in Chapter 2. In addition, we need to demonstrate how these crucial concerns can be propelled into the heart of a realist design which is illustrated in Table 4.6. This particular design employs the full range of qualitative and quantitative methods. It is therefore a long story which we will break for the sake of clarity, leaving the encounters with the program subjects (phase 3) for separate discussion in Chapter 6.

The starting point is to acknowledge that outcomes of complex programs, such as the one described here, bear the mark of countless contexts and mechanisms. We are not suggesting that evaluators buy into all available hypotheses and that all potential *CMO* configurations be put to the test in each investigation. There is a need to focus on which combinations of circumstances provide the most compelling possibilities for change. The best source of knowledge of the inner workings of a program lies, very often, with practitioners who have 'seen it all before'. In this instance (being a 'university' program) many of the investigators had been practitioners on the program. In general, realist investigation will not only rely on rather broad hypotheses culled from the background literature, as above, but will also incorporate the 'folk wisdom' of practitioners.

Phase 1

Phase 1 was completed, in the present case, with series of informal, *qualitative* interviews in which investigators asked practitioners (each other!) to search their memory for cases, illustrations and commonalities in respect of 'what was it about the course which seemed to have the most impact in changing the men' and 'what type of inmate is most likely to turn away from crime as a result of being in the program'. These inquiries released a flood of anecdotes, and the tales from the classroom are remarkable not only for their insight but in terms of the explanatory form which is employed. These 'folk' theories turn out to be 'realist' theories and invariably identify those *contexts* and *mechanisms* which are conducive to the *outcome* of rehabilitation. Consider the following 'mediocrity' hypothesis which we take from the lips of one of the Simon Fraser co-ordinators:

> The men who are more likely to be changed are best described as mediocre. You shouldn't look for high-flyers. They are likely to be from a deprived background with a poor and maybe non-existent school record. They will be mediocre criminals too. They'll have gone on from petty crime, street crime to drugs or armed robbery or something. Then when they come onto the program they're mediocre or worse. They just survive the first semester but then gradually build up getting Cs and Bs. So by the end, they've actually come a long, long way and that's what changes 'em. It is not so much a case of 'rehabilitation' as 'habilitation'.

It is worth inspecting closely what is being claimed here. It is a 'type' of offender and a 'type' of involvement with the program which is said to be crucial. This example is presented here, of course, as a particularly rich and broad hypothesis deploying half a dozen or more distinctions to identify the efficacious processes and backgrounds. This pooling of practitioners' knowledge has given rise to scores of equivalent, if somewhat more specific, hypotheses which the researchers tried to set down with some care in advance of the formal data collection. Space restrictions require cutting a long story short and so simply naming some of these conjectures will, it is hoped, give a fair indication of the range of contexts and mechanisms under investigation: the 'engagement' hypothesis, the 'improvers' hypothesis, 'the high-flyer' hypothesis, the 'self-esteem' hypothesis, the 'protection' hypothesis, the 'breadth of learning' hypothesis, the 'second chance' hypothesis, the 'professional criminal' hypothesis, the 'drug dependency' hypothesis, the 'sexual deviance' hypothesis, the 'power' hypothesis and so on.

These qualitative preliminaries had the purpose of anchoring the next formal stages of evaluation. Thus phase 1 of the inquiry ended with the task of creating a 'variable book' which seeks to operationalize these hunches and hypotheses in order to identify, with more precision, those combinations of types of offender and types of course involvement which mark the best chances of rehabilitation. Over 50 variables were created, giving us no chance to describe the details of their construction and coding, but for the sake of illustration let us mention three examples. The variable AGEPEP (age of entry into the prison education program) was the first candidate, following the evidence of the practitioners' eyes that it was the 'calming down' set in their late 20s to early 40s who had the motivation, patience and fortitude to survive the course. The variable EDUCENTRY (grade, level, certification upon entry to prison) sustains a number of hypotheses including the idea that even modest university-level success for people with no post-secondary experience has a greater impact on self-esteem than for those having some educational capital. Note also that via these hypotheses the men are differentiated closely (and somewhat more unusually) in terms of their different *pathways* through the course itself.

Thus the variable GPADIFF (difference of grade point average across the first and second half of the course) enables the researchers to pin-point the actual degree of 'improvement' or 'decline' of performance, and so chimes with the 'greater struggle provides greater rewards' element of the 'mediocrity' hypothesis above.

Phase 2

The mixture of theorizing and qualitative investigation described so far was all preparatory to the main body of the investigation. The heart of the evaluation was an 'outcome' inquiry. Realist evaluation, as we have been at pains to point out, transforms the 'does it work?' question so that it is rendered as 'what is it about the program that works for whom?' This gave the outcome analysis the task of building up a quantitative picture, in terms of the over 50 variables deployed, of which types of inmate and which types of course experience were associated with lower recidivism. Recall here the longevity of the course, which required of the researchers the slog of compiling the data matrix by scouring twenty years' worth of inmates' prison, program and probation files. This itself is a mighty tale which rivals any other account of wrestling with 'official data', but suffice it to say here that the researchers ended with profiles on almost 700 men, a virtually complete record of all inmates who had at least two semesters' involvement with the course.

Outcome analysis, quite properly, is besotted (if sometimes bewildered) with measuring 'success' properly. The key device in operationalizing success in this instance was the use of a *predictor scale*. The scale in question is known as the statistical information on recidivism (SIR) scale. It was derived by Nuffield (1982) for Correctional Services of Canada via the collection of data on the criminal histories, demographic characteristics and social background factors of prisoners, and the relating of these to reconviction rates. She went on to perform a statistical analysis in order to deduce those factors which best predict recidivism, and a well-established set of predictor variables was identified which includes items like 'marital status', 'number of dependants', 'number of previous incarcerations', 'offence type', 'age at first conviction' and so on. These findings form the basis of the administration of the SIR scale itself, which consists of a simple checklist of information to be obtained from inmates which allows them to be assigned into five risk categories. These range from the 'very good' risk group in which (only!) one in five offenders are reconvicted to the 'poor' risk group in which two in three reoffend.

Such information is now part of the normal case management documentation prepared for each prisoner and finds increasing usage in parole, release, and sentencing decisions. The surprising thing about such prediction scales is that they have found little use in one of the major roles for which they were originally designed – namely program evaluation

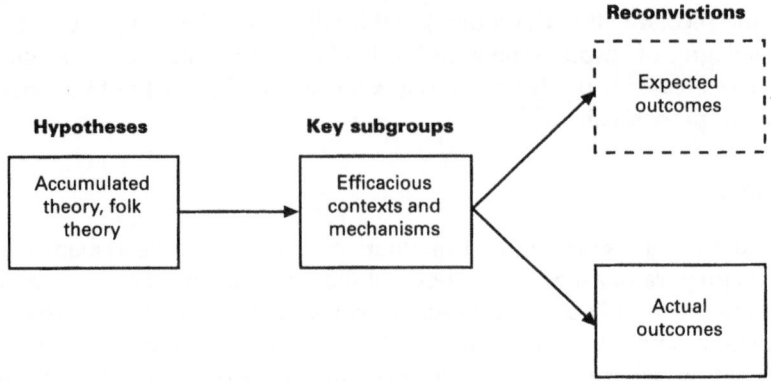

Figure 4.3 *Outcome analysis: prediction scales*

(Gottfredson and Tonry, 1987). The basic calculation could not be simpler and is illustrated in Figure 4.3. Classification and prediction methods can provide estimates of the *expected* performance for any group of subjects and these expected outcomes can be compared with the *actual* performance of the group in the program under investigation. Thus the core methodology for evaluating prison education program outcomes involved locating all inmates falling into a subgroup exemplifying the explanatory hypotheses illustrated earlier and testing to see if actual reconviction rates for that group are lower (or higher) than that predicted by SIR. In short, we can say that the method captures the ultimate evaluation question – *did they beat history or repeat history?*

Such a method allows for an 'overall' evaluation of the program, and this result is pleasing enough for the practitioners. Thus the SIR prediction was that 58% of the total sample would remain out of prison for three years following release. In actuality the percentage was 75%, representing a relative improvement of 29% – something of a triumph in this toughest area of social programming. This result, of course, tells us absolutely nothing about *why* the course worked and the real interest of the method lies in *internal variation*, in which we learn of the relative success rates of subgroups of prisoners from different backgrounds and with different experiences of the course. Which particular subgroups – the 'mediocre', the 'improvers', the 'engaged', the 'second chancers' etc. – turn out to be the real 'SIR beaters'?

This phase of the research is in progress, so we confine ourselves to a brief example by considering the fate of one pair of theories – the 'high-engagement' hypothesis and the 'mediocrity' hypothesis. The former is part of the background to most theories of educational growth and trades on the notion that 'the more extensive and prolonged the engagement the greater the grip on the inmate's person' (Schnur, 1948). The latter was uncovered in our trawl though the practitioners' ideas, as above. Whilst none of the teachers argued that turning up for the odd semester was of any use, many claimed that a modest engagement with modest success had the greatest impact on inmates.

Alas, debate on the efficacy of prison programs rarely goes deeper than this. The problem with both claims in the preceding paragraph is that outcomes are being explained in terms of some partial theories about educational mechanisms, with never a thought for context. The realist always begins by attempting to trade talk of panaceas for *CMO* configurations; both speculations may be correct *but* for different inmates in different circumstances. And, in the Simon Fraser data, we have a ready-made way of extricating the possible configurations which are illustrated in Table 4.7. Various different measures of *engagement* were constructed, three of which are illustrated in the table. Inmate / students can be differentiated in terms of their *grade point average* (GPA), the *number of credits earned*, and (using tutors' assessments of classroom performance from their educational records) a more subjective measure of *educational intensity*. Each measure was subdivided to construct a simple, self-evident hierarchy of engagement as illustrated.

The notion of 'context' is introduced by going back to the hypothesis drawing-board and thinking through subgroups for whom the different levels of engagement might be apposite. We have already seen the development of the *mediocrity* hypothesis in this respect in the direct quotation from the practitioner given earlier. This guided the researchers to think about a group with a string of early convictions and who entered prison with very low educational qualifications. The counter hypothesis, *high engagement*, was pursued in terms of inmates with the worst criminal records and with long immersion in prison culture. The significance of such contextual thinking is demonstrated by performing a *CMO* analysis on these different *subsamples* of students.

From the total sample 'working groups' were established with the aim of trying to reflect these background circumstances. Thus working group 1 consisted of subjects with *three or more convictions who entered prison with a school education of grade 10 or below.*. Working group 2 were defined as subjects who had *served most or all of their sentences in maximum security*. This allows us to perform separate SIR comparisons for inmates with a highly specific set of background characteristics and experiences with the course. For instance, we see from the GPA for working group 1 in Table 4.7 that subjects with three or more convictions with low educational entry and who only gained D grades on the prison programs were forecast to remain out of prison at a rate of 47%. They actually did so at a rate of 63%, representing a rate of improvement of 32%.

So what is the fate of the 'mediocrity' hypothesis and the 'high-engagement' hypothesis? Both indeed are borne out *in the appropriate context*.

Table 4.7 *Contextualizing the 'high-engagement' and 'mediocrity'*
hypotheses

	Predicted success (SIR score)	Actual success (3+ years out)	Relative improvement
Working group 1			
GPA:			
below average (D)	47%	63%	32%
average (C)	*42%*	*65%*	*55%*
above average (B, A)	46%	68%	49%
Intensity:			
below average	46%	59%	27%
average intensity	*45%*	*69%*	*54%*
intense	42%	65%	52%
very intense	47%	67%	20%
Credits earned:			
0–15	45%	64%	43%
16–30	45%	67%	48%
31–45	*45%*	*74%*	*64%*
46–60	35%	46%	31%
60+	48%	71%	49%
Working group 2			
GPA:			
below average (D)	49%	50%	02%
average (C)	47%	60%	28%
above average (B, A)	*51%*	*74%*	*46%*
Intensity			
below average	49%	44%	–09%
average intensity	50%	64%	27%
intense	48%	69%	43%
very intense	*42%*	*78%*	*87%*
Credits earned:			
0–15	47%	55%	17%
16–30	53%	67%	25%
31–45	46%	69%	49%
46–60	*41%*	*64%*	*55%*
60+	52%	75%	45%

The rows in bold type in Table 4.7 represent the levels of engagement which prompt the highest levels of relative improvement. It can be seen at once that the watchword for working group 1 is 'find a place in the mainstream': they fare best with modest levels of GPA, class performance and credits earned. On the other hand, for maximum security inmates, maximum allegiance to education appears to be required for it to be converted into rehabilitative potential. We thus see in these opening shots of data analysis the development of neophyte theories which we can summarize in the customary grid as Table 4.8.

Table 4.8   *Contrasting CMO configurations within the prison program*

Context	+	New mechanism	=	Outcome
Prisoners with little or no previous education with a growing string of convictions – representing a 'disadvantaged' background	+	Modest levels of engagement and success with the program trigger 'habilitation' process in which the inmate experiences self-realization and social acceptability (for the first time)	=	Lowest levels of reconviction as compared with statistical norm for such inmates
Prisoners serving majority of sentence in maximum security penitentiaries – representing a 'criminal' background	+	High levels of engagement and success with the program trigger 'rehabilitation' process in which the inmate experiences changes in powers of self-reflection and reasoning	=	Lowest levels of reconviction as compared with statistical norm for such inmates

As a *nota bene* here, it should be made clear that this summary grid 'hardens' the interpretation of the illustrated findings somewhat more than is actually warranted. We labelled this piece of research as promoting 'theory development' and it is this process which is described here. The working groups simply pick out two subsamples of prisoners according to a handful of differences in their backgrounds and course achievements. These groups obviously share a whole range of other similarities and differences and these data do not allow us to see what is actually driving the outcome patterns. In particular, we know that 'rehabilitation' is an act of choice and that the particular reasoning process at work in these groups cannot, of course, be seen in the data and at this stage can only be inferred. As with all realist explanations, we acknowledge the presence of relatively 'unseen' mechanisms during various stages of theory development. In Chapter 6, we move to phase 3 of this research and examine how the evaluator can best construct data on the program participants' cognizance of change.

For now, the general methodological lessons of these outcome comparisons must be driven home. The key point of design, and the one we uphold for imitation, is that the subgroup analysis is able to demonstrate *prodigious differences in levels of success achieved within the program.* Within this group of prisoner students, as within all programs, there will be many, many different groups of winners and losers. Identifying these subgroups for whom the program succeeds (or indeed fails) gives us a window on why the initiative works. The research strategy works by dint of some prior theoretical work which enables researchers to get an approximate fix on the likely successes and failures. Sometimes the relative performances will confirm expectations, sometimes they will lead to a readjustment of the 'folk theories'. The point is that the data analysis involves looking at, not two, but *hundreds* of subgroups in an attempt to build a whole mosaic of outcome patterns (Duguid et al., 1996, 1997). Outcomes only follow when particular mechanisms have been triggered in particular contexts, and they will only reveal themselves when investigation has traced them through the same pathway.

Conclusion

In this chapter, we have tried to demonstrate something of the versatility of realist research designs. These studies have only two things in common. The first is that they all belong to the criminal justice field, albeit at the opposite ends of the 'prevention' and 'cure' spectrum. Thereafter, the resemblance crumbles as we contemplate programs – small and large, short term and long term, individually oriented and community based. The research methods employed involve a kaleidoscopic usage of the social science toolbox in ranging from ethnography to experimental manipulation, from the usage of official data to street-corner observation, and from the gathering of folk wisdom to the crunching of a vast data matrix.

What really holds them together is the usage of a realistic evaluation strategy. What is common is the refusal to treat the program under research as a 'black box'. Continuing the metaphor, we might say that they all constitute efforts to lighten the box, and that by the end they do allow us to discern at least some quite distinct shades of grey about crime prevention and offender rehabilitation initiatives. Thus in terms of an overall research 'logic', we can say confidently that they are identical in their exploration of the three guiding themes of realist research strategy:

1 They increase specificity of our understanding of the mechanisms through which a program accomplishes change.
2 They increase specificity of our understanding of the contextual conditions necessary for triggering program mechanisms.
3 They increase specificity of outcome pattern predictions according to context and mechanism triggered.

Herein lies the family resemblance. Whether they get there by the creation of a new program or by the autopsy of a dead one, by hard data or by intuitive guesswork, and indeed via the conventional research mix of luck and judgement, they all exemplify the task of *CMO* configuration focusing.

5
HOW TO MAKE EVALUATIONS CUMULATE

Sadly, most evaluation studies seem to be one-off affairs. They neither look back and build on previous findings, nor look forward to future evaluations. All sorts of explanations (and culprits) have been identified for this state of affairs. Policy makers and practitioners are charged with not being sufficiently interested in evaluation to include it within the core program funding, with the result that evaluators merely get to peck around the edges of most initiatives. Yet again, evaluators can easily be seen as jack-of-all-trades consultants, too ready to apply formulaic methods to all problems, too ready to declare themselves instant experts at evaluating anything, with the result that they can end up understanding nothing. For whatever reason, the goal of creating cumulative bodies of evaluation research remains elusive and the task of this chapter is to create a realist template in order to show how such an objective can be attained.

Such progress is as important for policy makers as it is for scientists, a point never more clearly put than in the following quotation from Cook et al.:

> The practical value of social science depends upon its ability to deliver useful knowledge about the causes of social problems and the effectiveness of policies and programs designed to alleviate them. The immense diversity of social life, however, and the great welter of factors underlying any social phenomenon make it difficult, if not impossible, to derive conclusive knowledge from any single study, no matter how well designed or intelligently analyzed. The causal processes that appear so essential at one time or place may prove less important in another. The program that works well with one group under certain conditions may be less effective with another group when the circumstances are a bit different.
>
> These basic facts of social life render the success of social science crucially dependent upon its ability to accumulate results across the many studies of a given social process or program. The accumulation of results and the gradual convergence on information of higher quality is one hallmark of progress in any science, but it is particularly key in social science, where there may be no single, uniform answers to a given question, but rather a family of answers, related by principles that emerge only over the course of much research. (1992, p. vii)

In short, if a cardinal purpose of evaluations is to feed into improvements in policy and practice, they too need to be oriented to cumulation. If evaluations are going to be informative they must be informed. In order to devise policies more effectively to achieve objectives and to make improvements in value for money, part of the remit of evaluation must be to take on the task of continual program refinement, which requires going back and back again to puzzle over present findings about the effectiveness of current practices, and then forward to attend to new puzzles which emerge from these deliberations.

This chapter is in three sections, the first of which develops a basic model of 'realist forms of cumulation'. It will come as no surprise to learn that our model of realistic cumulation involves making progress in understanding across *the realistic explanatory triad*. Thus cumulation is a matter of deepening, specifying, focusing and formalising our understanding of program *mechanisms, contexts and outcome patterns*. We stress that cumulation is a matter of increasing understanding of how these elements are connected. We use the term 'configuration' to express the combination of ideas in $C + M = O$ propositions and develop the notion that cumulation in realistic evaluation is a matter of traversing between general theory (*abstract configurations*) and empirical case studies (*focused configurations*).

Our second point about cumulation is captured by the reminder that scientists do not perform experiments to the exclusion of all other forms of research. They exist outside the laboratory in libraries, lecture theatres, conferences, conventions, seminars, the World Wide Web (and coffee bars) and are driven back inside by the challenge of the conjectures and findings of other scientists encountered in these travels. A clear parallel beckons. By now we have made it quite clear that one-off evaluations can only test a restricted range of the potential explanations of program impacts. Running a series of evaluations will obviously improve explanatory purchase but still cannot be expected always to do all the work. Realist cumulation will thus often involve *weaving the results of other forms of empirical research into the evaluation cycle*.

Another familiar message also awaits. For cumulation to occur, we need *improvements in theory*. Cumulation is not a matter of achieving a series of studies with reliable, replicable, and universal applicability. The social world (bless it) will always conspire to throw up changes, differences, and apparent anomalies from trial to trial in any field of programming. Theory is the bridgehead between the goals of generalization and specification in evaluation research. Cumulation in evaluation research is thus about producing *middle-range* theory, of a kind abstract enough to underpin the development of a range of program types yet concrete enough to withstand testing in the details of program implementation.

The second and major section of the chapter is devoted to a single case study in replication and cumulation. Since we are discussing the accumulation deriving from a complex series of studies, the learning curve is often somewhat steep and invariably long, so unfortunately we cannot present more than one exemplar: it would simply take too much space to do so. We hope that the reader will be satisfied to see how snowballs can be made to grow through a fairly detailed account of this instance.

Crime prevention is amongst the biggest growth areas in UK evaluation, and thus provides good examples of how and how not to attempt to combine the wisdom achieved from many, many single studies. Our account starts with the hugely esteemed and famously successful Kirkholt burglary reduction project. We follow a false trail to cumulation via attempts to *replicate* the project. This is then contrasted with the progressive problem shift constituted by a program of work investigating the phenomenon of 'repeat victimization', which formed one element of the Kirkholt findings. What we have in this case is a series of follow-up studies, self-consciously linked and progressively refining an understanding of the mechanisms, contexts and outcome patterns associated with repeat victimization and efforts to reduce it. Realist theory development is both the product and the spur to each sequential wave of studies.

The final section of the chapter will draw together the vital lessons on how evaluations need to be conceived, managed and written up in order to maximize the scope for cumulation. We summarize the series of practical steps through which evaluations might be reshaped in order to prioritize cumulation. We (belatedly) draw into the discussion a distinction between the deliberate accomplishment of cumulation through a series of *planned*, interrelated studies, as opposed to the *post hoc* gathering of wisdom which might be gleaned from combing through a set of *existing* studies. The success of the latter approach, often termed 'meta-evaluation', is shown to depend entirely on the same set of realist principles of cumulation, though the ability to weave the three strands of mechanisms, contexts and outcome patterns in and out of this particular approach is shown to suffer rather more limitations.

The final section of the chapter also briefly draws attention to the ineluctable limitations to cumulation. It will be shown that it is in principle as well as in practice impossible to reach a complete statement of all the permutations of mechanisms and contexts upon which invariable outcome patterns depend. Nevertheless, the realist account can furnish us with a more accurate account of these limitations to convey to the policy maker, and show us that there is indeed good reason to engage in a form of inquiry that never ends.

Realistic cumulation

We begin by acknowledging the different hopes and aspirations regarding 'cumulation' which exist across the different schools of evaluation. We duck the challenge of describing and refereeing yet another campaign of the paradigm wars, since our immediate objective is to draw out a basic tension between the goals of 'specification' and 'generalization', the ramifications of which generate a surprising point of agreement across the squabbling schools.

To illustrate, let us begin with the 'constructivist' schools and recall a proposition already quoted from Guba and Lincoln (1989, p. 49) to the effect that all situations are unique and that problems or solutions cannot be generalized from one context to another. They have a point. To be sure, no two 'offender education programs' are ever going to be exactly alike and any particular one being examined may involve some practitioners acting out their own choices in their own way which can influence the whole balance of proceedings. No two communities hosting a 'community policing program' will ever be the same and the very one under scrutiny may well have key participants who are predisposed to the initiative in such a way as to influence its whole balance. So it is with any program, and this sheer, glorious ubiquity and diversity of people in programs sets the face of the constructivist paradigm against the goal of 'generalization'. This vision of 'the devil in the program detail' commits it, by contrast, to evaluation as the deeper and deeper 'specification' of the constructions held by the multiplicity of stakeholders in any particular program (until, that is, time, patience or funding runs out).

Experimentalists are different. Their approach to evaluation is founded on the existence of program uniformities. They have a point. Not everything is transient and irregular; we manage to get by day-to-day, quite unmagically, because of a recognizable order about the social world; indeed, when it comes to programs, the commonest experience of most practitioners when visiting other projects in their speciality is to come away with a strong sense of recognition. The experimental approach is thus deeply committed to the task of demonstrating the causal regularity that program X causes outcome Y. This task is accomplished by dealing first of all with 'internal validity' and ruling out other influences $(Z_1, \ldots, Z_N)$ which may have been responsible for Y by statistical or experimental control (see Chapter 2). Generalization is achieved by an extension of this logic to notions of 'external validity', in which the program is replicated in other circumstances so that we can check that the uniformity holds good in the presence of an even more heterogeneous set of potential confounding variables $(Z_M, \ldots, Z_\infty)$. The conundrum here is that in order to generalize, one needs to specify and control every single potential confounding influence (including this one – '∞') before one gets to the law! The existential import is a generalized belief in empirical generalizations, even though no one has yet to claim the discovery of a program whose outcomes fit this description. The practical consequence is that experimental evaluation becomes a quest for the deeper and deeper specification of control conditions (until, that is, time, patience or funding runs out).

The debate about cumulation frequently runs around these circles, with the high hopes for generalization being dashed by the dull hand of specification. Our argument here is that this perpetual play-off of *specification versus generalization* misses the cumulation prize. Both accounts are assuming that cumulation will take the form of the discovery of an empirical generalization, in which we move from the statement 'this program led to this outcome' to the universal statement 'these programs always lead to these outcomes.' Constructivists assume that this journey is impossible and therefore give up on cumulation. Experimentalists perceive the task as fraught with difficulty, plead patience and await cumulation stoically. Realists know that science does not arrive at laws inductively and, therefore, search for cumulation beyond the thicket of specification.

We can unravel the problem here by making clear two crucial and contrasting goals of evaluation, which might be deemed as the quest for the 'continual betterment of practice' as opposed to the goal of the 'secure transferability of knowledge'. In realist terms, the former goal works through a process of *CMO* configuration focusing. For instance, once we have learned that property marking inhibits burglary (*O*) through a process of good publicity (*M*) in close communities (*C*), the task is to fine-tune these interrelationships. Indeed one might say that the issue is to *personify* the configuration, and the betterment of practice would undoubtedly turn on a tale of Sgt Evans's gift for gossip amongst residents of the Glendower estate and the fact that he made sure that the denizens of the Garry Owen Drinking Club knew full well that receiving a marked video recorder was tantamount to taking it on with a 'not for sale' sign.

Driving further and further into such issues, we will end up in what we might call the 'descriptive particulars' of any individual program. Important as they are for our first goal, it should also be stressed that such wisdom can only inhibit comparison. It cannot be cashed in cumulatively. In order to generalize, in order to create transferable lessons about programs, we need to get away from such day-to-day specifics. Generalization is not a matter of understanding the *typicality* of a program in terms of its routine conduct. Rather the process of generalization is essentially one of *abstraction*. We move from one case to another, not because *they* are descriptively similar, but because *we* have ideas that can encompass them both.

The distinction we are alluding to here has been drawn many times in the methodological literature in social science, as in Znaniecki's (1934) contrast between 'enumerative' and 'analytical' induction, Mitchell's (1983) division between 'statistical' and 'logical' generalization, and Sayer's (1984) distinction between 'quantitative generalization' and 'qualitative abstraction'. The archetypal case of the former in each of these pairs is 'population sampling'. This works through a process of understanding how *representative* a particular sample is of the population from which it is drawn, in order to be able to make generalizations back to that population. This is a totally inappropriate way to conceptualize how we learn lessons from program evaluations because a program, of course, is not simply a sample of subjects drawn from a finite population. Rather it is one 'case' of an unspecifiable number of past, present and future programs. And it is one case amongst many, moreover, not just of 'subjects' but of a vast array of other 'stakeholders'. Neither should we contemplate generalizing across to a 'broader population' because the program is also defined institutionally in terms of 'treatments', 'localities', 'funding levels', 'political climates', 'policy frameworks', 'implementation plans' and so on *ad infinitum*. The very notion of the 'representativeness' or 'typicality' of a case gets utterly lost as the descriptive baselines increase. We give an example of how this mushrooming complexity inhibits comparison in the next section, and move on to the alternatives as contemplated in the above dualisms.

What proponents of 'analytic induction', 'logical generalization' and 'abstraction' have in mind by way of cumulating knowledge is a process in which we move from one specific empirical case to a general theory and back to another case and so on. What are transferable between cases are not lumps of data but sets of ideas. The process works through the development of a body of theory which provides an *organizing framework* which 'abstracts' from a program a set of essential conditions which make sense of one case after another. Many (perhaps most) researchers would ascribe to the importance of toing and froing between the empirical and the theoretical as the route to progressive understanding and transferable knowledge. Alas, such a prescription is itself unclear, because the usage of the term 'theory' has been contested throughout the history of social science. The history of that particular concept has been told many times and we might summarize the work of three of the great summarizers (Merton, 1968; Boudon, 1980; Sayer, 1984) by saying that 'theory' has been taken to mean:

1 methodology
2 general orientations
3 analysis of concepts
4 *ad hoc* or *ex post factum* interpretations
5 empirical generalizations
6 derivations and codifications
7 axiomatic systems
8 hypotheses
9 explanations
10 paradigms
11 conceptual frameworks
12 causal propositions
13 middle-range theory.

This is no place to struggle through the pros and cons of each meaning, but what we can do is extract those elements which reflect those usages which are crucial to the realist project. Figure 5.1 is our attempt to map the process of the accumulation of knowledge in evaluation research. The idea of reducing to the single diagram what in practice will consist of the efforts of perhaps scores of researchers over dozens of years is a trifle ambitious, so we begin with a 'key' which will guide us through the simplifications. The arrowed lines to the right represent movement up and down the ladder of abstraction. So at the top of the diagram, (a) to (c), we have the efforts of the 'theorists', beginning at the very top with the most abstract

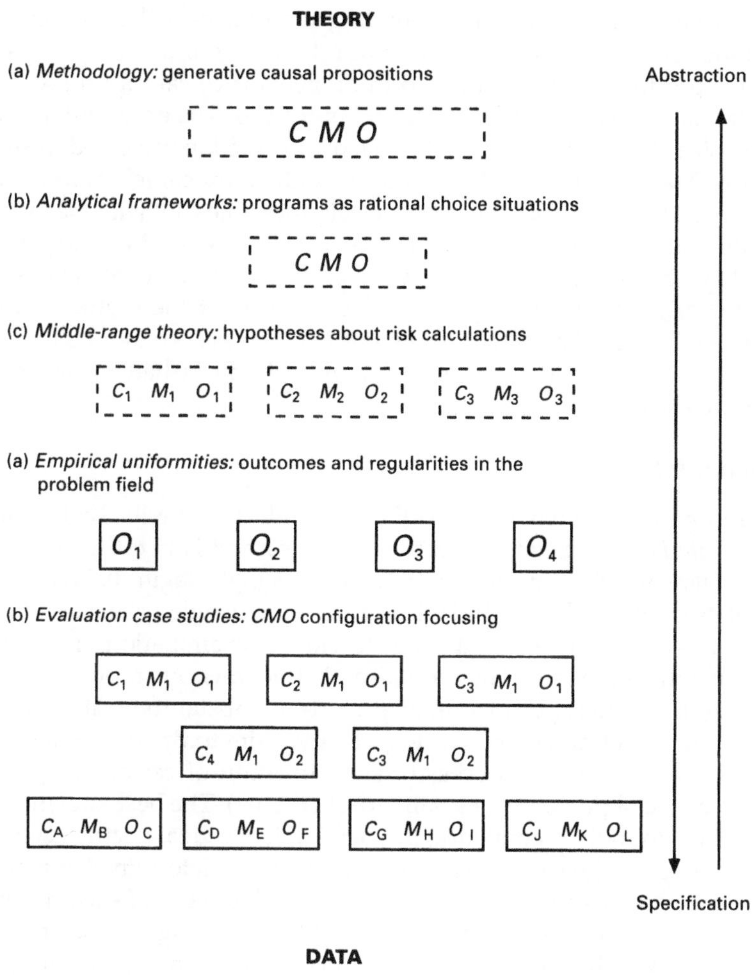

THEORY

(a) *Methodology:* generative causal propositions

Abstraction

$$\boxed{C \; M \; O}$$

(b) *Analytical frameworks:* programs as rational choice situations

$$\boxed{C \; M \; O}$$

(c) *Middle-range theory:* hypotheses about risk calculations

$$\boxed{C_1 \; M_1 \; O_1} \quad \boxed{C_2 \; M_2 \; O_2} \quad \boxed{C_3 \; M_3 \; O_3}$$

(a) *Empirical uniformities:* outcomes and regularities in the problem field

$$\boxed{O_1} \quad \boxed{O_2} \quad \boxed{O_3} \quad \boxed{O_4}$$

(b) *Evaluation case studies: CMO* configuration focusing

$$\boxed{C_1 \; M_1 \; O_1} \quad \boxed{C_2 \; M_1 \; O_1} \quad \boxed{C_3 \; M_1 \; O_1}$$

$$\boxed{C_4 \; M_1 \; O_2} \quad \boxed{C_3 \; M_1 \; O_2}$$

$$\boxed{C_A \; M_B \; O_C} \quad \boxed{C_D \; M_E \; O_F} \quad \boxed{C_G \; M_H \; O_I} \quad \boxed{C_J \; M_K \; O_L}$$

Specification

DATA

Figure 5.1 *The elements of realist cumulation*

contributions which try to capture essential ideas and structures of all social programs. We then move down the layers to the relatively more concrete and substantive, the leap into empirical investigation being signified by the change to Greek symbols (α) and (β). At each of the levels, we try to signify the nature of the contribution made to producing transferable, cumulative knowledge. That contribution, without exception, consists in filling out our knowledge of *CMO* configurations, with the variation in the contribution of the various functions being signified by an array of different boxes, symbols and subscripts as will be explained in the text.

Element (a)

The first element of realist theory building almost goes without saying, and combines elements of 1 and 12 from our 'typology of theory' in insisting that we produce theories in the form of 'generative causal propositions' which relate mechanisms, contexts and outcomes. The only fresh point to emphasize about this concerns the role of 'abstraction' involved in such a process. The power of the 'mechanism, context, outcome' framework to represent *any program* or indeed *any* social process lies not with the fact that the ideas are 'typical' or 'representative' of *all* processes but with the fact that they *simplify* all processes down to an essential core of attributes. The *CMO* configuration can thus be said to operate at the highest level of abstraction in social research – sometimes known as a 'contentless abstraction' (a feature we denote in Figure 5.1 with a large dashed box indicating unlimited scope!)

Element (b)

The second key element of realist theory building is inevitably the *conceptual orientation* or *analytic framework* as in items 2 and 11 in the above listing. This is also described usefully as a 'way of seeing' (Ragin, 1994) or, in the plural, 'schemata' (Sayer, 1984). These are more detailed sketches of ideas that a researcher develops in order to aid the examination of a specific 'class of phenomenon'. They are also abstractions but represent a step towards the concrete, since they provide a substantive rather than a methodological framework. Once again, they aim to provide general representations through a process of simplification of certain very broad classes of social processes (a smaller dashed box!). The best known example of an analytic framework in social science deals with economic transactions and gives us the notion of price being determined as a matter of the meeting of supply and demand. It is with the use of such schemata that the ability to generalize begins to build. They bring a sense of uniformity to outwardly different transactions such as, in this instance, the purchase of a car, a corporation or a cream cake.

In the case of social programs we have bumped time and again through the book into the motif of 'constrained choice', the idea that programs engage in trying to change the balance of choices open to their subjects. What we are suggesting here is that evaluation should thus draw recurrently on the venerable analytic frameworks which have tried to explain how we humans make choices. Rather than pile in with the specifics of the choices confronted in actual programs (will Sgt Evans persuade the recalcitrant Morgans to go to the bother of marking all their property?), cumulation in evaluation is actually made by abstracting out from this particular scene to the general principles of the drama as reconstructed in 'rational choice' theory. This argues that one can make sense of broad swathes of social behaviour by understanding that human action is based

on a calculation of the costs and benefits which accrue from different decisions. For instance, if one looks at the growing non-membership of trade
unions, the failure of many people to vote in elections, the creation of traf-
fic jams to the coast on a sunny bank holiday, and the decreasing
occupational value of a given level of education, each can be explained
using the same structure (Boudon, 1974). Instead of looking at the details
of how decisions are made in each of these cases, rational choice theory
shows how the regularities are generated through formally similar mechanisms within saliently similar contexts. In each case the individual is
faced with the choice of acting co-operatively with the rest or pursuing
short term utility maximization (Olson, 1965). In circumstances (C) in
which individuals are *without knowledge* of what others will decide, there
are no good grounds (M) for self-denial. But the consequence of no one
denying themselves short term advantage is that all suffer a worse outcome (O) than that which could be achieved through some small
self-sacrifice. Because the theory works through a process of simplification
which extracts the *necessary* conditions involved in the choice (utility maximization in the absence of knowledge of the choices of others) rather than
the *contingent* relationship (the bloody-mindedness of the Morgans), we
have an abstract *CMO* configuration with the promise of general utility. Sgt
Evans's task, for instance, is to explain the perils of short term utility maximization and to make abundantly clear the choices of others (he, of course,
might use different words).

Element (c)

The third mode of theory required in realist cumulation drives us to the
boundary of theory and data, and allows us to grapple with program ideas
in some detail. We refer of course to Merton's own speciality from the
typology of theories, namely item 13, *middle-range theory*:

> Theories that lie between the minor but necessary working hypotheses that
> evolve in abundance during day-to-day research and the all-inclusive systematic
> efforts to develop a unified theory that will explain all the observed uniformities
> of social behavior, social organization, and social change. (1968, p. 39)

What Merton had in mind here was that from a small core of ideas, it is
possible to develop a wide range of testable propositions. In realistic evaluation terms, this means that we build up families of configurations
$C_1M_1O_1$, $C_2M_2O_2$, $C_3M_3O_3$ (see the well-circumscribed dashed boxes in
Figure 5.1). We have already seen this as a familiar feature of the single-
case realist evaluation. Examples galore were given in the previous chapter
of how education mechanisms would work in different ways for different
groups of prisoners, of how crime prevention mechanisms would operate
to produce different outcomes in the different parts of a locality. The basic
idea of middle-range theory is that these propositions do not have to be
developed *de novo* on the basis of local wisdom in each investigation.

Rather they are likely to have a common thread running through them traceable to the more abstract analytic frameworks just described.

For example, a simple development of rational choice theory is the idea that decisions to commit crimes are informed by the levels of perceived risk, reward and effort involved (Clarke, 1992). This suggests that we can understand variations in crime rates across different categories by making hypotheses about the various different levels of perceived risk, effort and reward. It also suggests that crime prevention programs can be based on mechanisms designed to increase that perception of risk and effort or reduce the perception of reward. Studies of the effects of video cameras on bus vandalism, steering-wheel locks on car crime, widened aisles in markets on theft from shopping bags, caller identification devices on obscene phone calls, and even the introduction of (non-toxic) natural gas on suicide rate are all indicative of similar mechanisms being triggered in different conducive contexts (Clarke, 1992). With this interface between theory and data, we get our first clear glimpse of how evaluation might achieve transferable lessons, the key point being that the pathway of cumulation depends on finding sets of interlinked hypotheses (for example on risk calculation) which act as a conduit between abstract concepts and real-world actions.

We now follow this path into the domain of the empirical in order to examine how the data collected can be marshalled for the task of providing a cumulative body of information on program effectiveness. Put simply, the key to the process is that data collection and analysis are not simply directed to the task of discovering whether a set of programs works and 'aggregating' the results; rather the task is to test, refine and adjudicate the middle-range theories produced at level (c). It is useful to distinguish two phases to this empirical work, as follows.

Element (α)

Here we draw attention to the myopia which can strike those who conduct research on programs, in that when one becomes an evaluator, the capacity for constructing and using data from anything other than evaluations often seems to disappear. This is somewhat short-sighted since information on the causes and extent of problems is as important as data on solutions; recall that we see programs as offering blocking mechanisms to cope with problem mechanisms (Chapter 3). Following through our example of crime reduction through risk adjustment, it is apparent that much available data on crime patterns can be important in establishing the general nature of the risk/reward problem to be cracked. Thus if we are hoping to establish a burglary reduction program with wide applicability it is useful to attempt to collect data giving an indication of how the risk calculations get made in the first place. For instance, what is the distribution of victims in terms of types of houses or neighbourhoods chosen (O_1)? What are the favoured times (of day, week or year) of victimization (O_2)? Are there any key markers of vulnerability, such as age, sex, race (O_3)? Are new or repeat victims preferred (O_4)? The attentive reader will note that we have inflicted slight damage on our preferred terminology here (from Chapter 3) in that these patterns constitute the problem 'regularity' to be tackled rather than the 'outcome' of the program which attempts to do so. They should really be labelled R_1 etc., but for the sake of maintaining a little elegance in the diagram we have kept them as Os. The key issue here, however, takes us back to Merton (1968, p. 149), and his insistence that we perceive knowledge of such *uniformities* not as the 'empirical generalizations', not as the end-product of investigation, but as its 'raw material' to be explained within the middle-range theory framework. Swathes of relevant data are available to illuminate the rational choice/risk theories of crime reduction, and the process of cumulation requires that researchers be conversant with information in the form of police records, crime surveys, official data, insurance data, auditors' reports etc.

Element (β)

We now come to the function of program evaluation as such, which we summarize under the rather ugly term of 'configuration focusing'. Each evaluation within a problem area is seen as a case study, and the function of the case is to refine our understanding of the range of *CMOs* which seem to have application in that domain. We derive, quite literally, a catalogue of answers to the question of what works for whom in what circumstances. The catalogue, of course, is not amassed in the 'add another one to the list' style as in a library, but in a manner which involves ascending and descending the route between abstraction and specification. In the following paragraphs we present a simplified, idealized outline of the process, to be followed in the next section by a messy, real example of the actuality.

Following through the example of the middle-range 'risk enhancement' thesis, we begin our depiction of the case study process by imagining that consolidation takes place and that a series of evaluations on market-aisle widening, telephone-call number tracing, and steering-wheel lock installation have successful outcomes suggesting that the 'increased risk' mechanism (M_1) is effective (O_1) at least in some instances (C_1, C_2, C_3). We depict this in Figure 5.1, with the dashed 'hypotheses' boxes replaced by solid 'data' boxes. This is merely the beginning of the case study story, however, because we know that, sooner or later, other case studies will come up with inconsistent results. The law of the 'lack of universal panaceas' is represented on the next line down of Figure 5.1, in which we depict a case of apparent program failure in which risk enhancement through the introduction of security lighting in a neighbourhood fails to impact on burglary rates $(C_4 M_1 O_2)$ and envision another trial of a steering locks scheme in which their initial positive impact rapidly fades $(C_3 M_1 O_2)$.

Instead of shouting 'foul!' and questioning the reliability and validity of one or other of these studies, the realist instinct is to go back to the theory drawing-board in order to search for a refinement in understanding of the risk enhancement mechanism which would allow us to separate and interpret the different outcomes. The chances are that the case studies will prompt a range of supplementary hypotheses. Perhaps there is a suspicion that the street lighting measure has failed because burglars figure that it does not increase the likelihood that someone will actually be able to apprehend them. Perhaps there is a suspicion that steering-wheel locks fail to deter for long because of the street wisdom that their frail mechanics reduce their risk enhancement value to about ten seconds. Rather than these being perceived as local hunches about the technical capabilities of specific measures in particular localities, transferable lessons may be learned if the ideas are cast back into the more abstract terms of the conceptual framework and middle-range theory under investigation. For instance, following the first 'failure', we might refine our risk enhancement hypothesis to say that the manifestation of risk needs to be ensured by the presence of some 'capable guardian' able to act upon that risk (Felson, 1994). Under the second 'failure', we might modify our understanding of the contexts in which risk enhancement works by differentiating crimes according to whether the 'network' of potential perpetrators is highly connected or dispersed.

Research travels to and fro in this manner until we reach the next wave of case studies, which by then (the bottom line of Figure 5.1) are testing rather complex configurations. Following our example through, we can imagine that investigation has transformed so that the case studies become a test of the 'risk enhancement, capable guardian, perpetrator network' thesis. We can imagine a series of crime reduction schemes attempting to increase the perception of risk *and* having a clear manifestation of the risk *and* being aimed at fragmented groups of potential offenders. Case studies no doubt would reveal that some work and some do not, prompting yet another lap of the abstraction/specification cycle. We represent the findings here in a highly schematic form $C_A M_B O_C$ etc. in an attempt to show that the mechanisms, contexts and outcomes under investigation by this stage are complex ($A = 1 + 2 + 3$ etc.). The cumulation process proceeds in this manner. What develops is not a 'master theory' or a mass catalogue of inconsistent results but a typology of broadly based configurations (Layder, 1993, chapter 7).

When does the process end? For the evaluation community, of course, the answer is never. It is, or should be, in a state of perpetual motion up and down the ladder of abstraction/specification. The practitioner's efforts, by contrast, are likely to be much more finite and come, at least, to a temporary resting place in the process of specification. The design of a program should not be just a matter of trial and error, folk wisdom, and self-scrutiny. Practitioners ought to be informed and carry a set of well-worn principles into a program in order to refine them to meet local conditions. The more researchers have 'been around' the configuration focusing cycle, the better are they able to interpret how a particular *CMO* configuration should operate. Eventually such understanding should be turned over for its fine-tuning in the implementation of new programs. The cycle thus 'ends' back with the specification of individual cases, the difference being that Sgt Evans should enter the fray with a much fuller job description.

The road to cumulation is a long one (even in the sanitized version presented here). We hope, however, to have at least demonstrated the potential advantages of the 'cumulation as theory development' model over the moribund search for 'cumulation as empirical generalization'. It remains to show that it works.

A case study in replication and (then) cumulation

We turn now to an exception to the general rule of isolated, generally uninformative evaluations, interspersed perhaps by the odd anomalous exemplar of realistic excellence, to show how cumulation has been achieved over a longer period of time in one particular area. This section shows how *CMO* configurations emerge in the hurly-burly of real research. It will be clear that this accomplishment has been wrought at some considerable effort and there are some distinct culs-de-sac where implicit realism was forgone, as well as impressive achievement where it was followed. The tale which follows is a somewhat messy but educated one, even where the realism shines through, and this messiness is perhaps inevitable. Often one thing will have to be done at a time; promising lines of inquiry in one area may have to be followed up for a while to the exclusion of others; emerging conjectures on recurrent contexts or mechanisms or regularities will be tested, with scant regard for developing other parts of our *CMO* triad; and so on. The point is that via a series of studies over time there is a continuous movement forward, and that no element in the triad gets lost. To echo a slogan introduced at the start of this chapter, the hallmark of realistic evaluation work is that it is informed, and this continuity of intelligence gathering is the key to cumulation. Indeed it is informed beyond the business of evaluation research *per se*. The example which follows is alive to and immersed in salient currents of more purely criminological theory and empirical research. This sensitivity to and orientation to non-evaluation research can, as we shall see, be essential to successful cumulation.

Kirkholt (one step forward)

Kirkholt is a local authority estate in Rochdale, a small town in the north of England. The Kirkholt Burglary Prevention Project (Forrester et al., 1988; 1990) is often hailed as an exemplar of crime prevention. It is looked to by practitioners and policy makers alike as a source of good practice (Burns,

1990). As so often in evaluation, our attention is attracted to the project, as was that of the policy community, by some outstanding outcome data. The recorded crime rates for the years before and after the implementation of the Kirkholt Burglary Prevention Project indicated dramatic and sustained falls in burglary. Using March to February figures, in 1986–1987 – the year before the project – there were 526 burglaries. The corresponding figures for succeeding years are given in Forrester et al. (1990). There were 223 burglaries in 1987–1988, 167 in 1988–1989, and 132 in 1989–1990. These represent a fall from approximately 25% to 6% per annum of the 2,280 households on the estate.

As so often in evaluation, an apparent triumph can also bring out the doubters and the sceptics. Kirkholt was a veritable avalanche of an initiative, bursting with ideas, measures and personnel. As such it is prey to a critique, of which we ourselves are rather fond (recall Chapter 2), to the effect that in its profusion of interventions, it is not quite clear exactly what it was about the project that created this massive impact. What is more, a report by the Safe Neighbourhoods Unit (1993) questioned whether it was the project at all which had led to the observed crime reductions, arguing that contemporaneous estate improvements undertaken by the local authority could have been responsible. Farrington (1992) in turn reanalysed the Kirkholt data, with results consistent with the original interpretation. We are met here with the customary charge and counter-charge about *internal validity*, a topic on which we have had our say in the previous chapter.

Our topic here is *external validity*, but our realist course of action begins at the same point, that is to say we need to get this program disaggregated, we need to get it analysed down a bit in order to see what worked and whether it would work elsewhere. This task would normally drive us automatically into a *CMO* analysis of the Kirkholt intervention. We refrain from this for just a few pages, since we initially want to pursue the prospects of another way of generalizing the lessons of Kirkholt, namely through replication. What follows, therefore, is simply our listing of 'attributes' of the Kirkholt project derived from published accounts. Kirkholt practitioners might give it a different gloss. The aforementioned critics might latch onto different features. Realists, of course, are well over the shock of knowing that *all* accounts are selective; the trick is to understand the ramifications, so let us proceed with our list.

The following describe major features of the Kirkholt project:

1 *'Kirkholt' was conceived and undertaken as a well-resourced demonstration project.* The evaluation of the Kirkholt project was funded by the British Home Office Crime Prevention Unit and handled by its Research and Development Section. This Home Office connection may have brought credibility. It certainly made the project relatively well provided for in terms of expertise, and may have helped draw in other resources. £298,398 was spent between 1985–1986 and 1989–1990.

2 *'Kirkholt' was about developing crime prevention measures in high-crime areas.* By the prevailing national standards Kirkholt had an extraordinarily high burglary rate. The recorded incidence rate in the year preceding the Burglary Prevention Project stood at 25% of households. This compares with a national rate for recorded burglary of 2% in 1988 and a British Crime Survey national rate of 5% for 1988.

3 *'Kirkholt' was about tackling high-crime areas which are clearly circumscribed and can thus be treated as identifiable communities.* Kirkholt comprises 2,280 dwellings. It is a relatively self-contained estate, clearly bounded by a motorway and major roads. Anyone entering or leaving the estate would know that they were doing so. It is also culturally fairly homogeneous, comprising almost exclusively members of the white working class.

4 *'Kirkholt' was about the removal of highly attractive targets (coin meters), which had made the area a popular one with burglars since such 'money boxes' could confidently be expected.* In the year leading up to the project 49% of the burglaries included theft from coin meters for electricity or gas, and 27% involved loss of meter cash only. It is not clear what percentage of households had these meters. Part of the scheme, however, included their removal.

5 *'Kirkholt' was about carefully diagnosing a particular crime problem (burglary in an estate) and tailoring responses to it.* Prior to the project the nature of the crime problems of Kirkholt was examined through interviews with 76 burglars, 237 victims, and 136 neighbours of victims. An analysis of police crime report forms was also made. This work then informed the planned suite of interventions.

6 *'Kirkholt' was about developing an effective interagency response to crime.* Manchester University, the local police, the probation service and the local authority worked together closely during the project. They also drew in many other agencies. The geographical location of the project offices alongside the local housing offices facilitated a close working relationship. The police and probation services led the project in succession and when not leading the project members of each of these agencies had time set aside to work on it.

7 *'Kirkholt' was about harnessing the community to protect itself from crime (through cocooning).* Kirkholt is not the sort of area which has traditionally provided fertile ground for the establishment of neighbourhood watch schemes (Husain, 1988; Laycock and Tilley, 1995). The formation of mini neighbourhood watch schemes (termed 'cocoons') was very actively encouraged and much work was put into their maintenance. To begin with they comprised only six or so dwellings but grew to 20–25.

8 *'Kirkholt' was about focusing on multiple victimization and reducing it.* Crime prevention resources were allocated to victims, who were found to be four times as likely to be revictimized as those on the estate who

had not been victimized. Target hardening, adapted to the specific risks revealed by research and the judgements of trained police officers, was allocated on this basis. Cocoons were fostered by bringing together the victimized and their neighbours.

9 *'Kirkholt' was about clarity of initial research, clarity of crime prevention method tailored to research findings, and clarity of leadership in implementing measures.* If the *post hoc* descriptions of Kirkholt are accurate (and there is no reason to believe they are not), the scheme was characterized by unusually clear planning, implementation, monitoring and evaluation. There was a strong academic input from Manchester University.

10 *'Kirkholt' was about burglary prevention and was offence specific.* Kirkholt was not an all-purpose crime prevention project. It turned on specific analysis of the burglary problem and the development of particular measures to reduce it.

We hold the list here. Clearly it has the potential to go on forever. Whilst this is obviously a complex initiative, we would have the same problem with any such program in the availability of an infinitely large number of descriptions of an infinitely large number of social transactions. Any of the features mentioned could be spelled out in greater detail. All of the stakeholders' views could be interrogated at much greater length. All of them could hold the key to the success of the program. Without some analytic framework, we find ourselves staring into the familiar 'black box', of which we depict a realist version in Table 5.1.

Here we have an encapsulation of the problem of cumulation. How do we translate these 'somethings' into transferable burglary reduction lessons?

Table 5.1 *Kirkholt as a black box*

Context	+	Mechanism	=	Outcome
Something about Kirkholt	+	Something about the project	=	Dramatically reduced rate of burglary

Replications (two steps back)

Because Kirkholt had apparently been such a stunning success, not surprisingly there was a good deal of interest in whether or not its lessons were generalizable. One classic way of finding out if this is the case is by *replication,* with other practitioners/researchers trying the idea out on their patch. A form of cumulation is promised through beguiling logic: it worked there, and if we find out that it works here, then we must be onto something really useful. One of the present authors was commissioned to see what became of this logic by examining a series of efforts which had been undertaken to replicate Kirkholt within a major English crime prevention program – Safer Cities (Tilley, 1996). Because the folk running Safer Cities had been to various talks by those involved in Kirkholt, and because its exciting findings had recently been published, there were lots of efforts at replication to choose from. In what follows we look at only two of them, though the same general conclusions would go for all, as can be seen in Tilley (1993b). The following descriptions of the putative replications (?R) match number for number the description given of Kirkholt.

Candidate replication 1 (?R1)

1   The project spent just over £95,000 over two and a half years, including £30,000 of government funds outside Safer Cities funding. Its expenditure was thus much less than Kirkholt's.
2   The project was not sited in a particularly high-crime area. At the start of the scheme the burglary rate was about a quarter that found when the Kirkholt project was established.
3   The area comprised some 8,000 households. Thus it was close to four times the size of Kirkholt. It had few clear boundaries separating it from adjacent areas and no clear centre.
4   There were few electricity and gas coin meters. They did not figure as targets of burglary, as they had in Kirkholt.
5   Problems were diagnosed but using different data sources from those used in Kirkholt. Police records of burglary in the area were analysed in the early months of the project. Victims were interviewed twice. Fourteen burglars were interviewed. No neighbours were interviewed.
6   This was a multi-agency project, but structured differently from Kirkholt. Here the police and probation were the central players. There was a full-time secondment from both. Neither was at any point clearly and explicitly in the lead, as had been the case in Kirkholt. The local university had limited involvement.
7   Efforts were made to establish 'neighbourhood concern groups', to mobilize community activity in crime hot-spots. These approximate neighbourhood watch schemes, though there is not the same direct and necessary contact with the police. Area coverage was patchy: at 25%, nothing like Kirkholt's 90% coverage was achieved.
8   Analysis of the recorded burglary data on ?R1 revealed that council tenants had the highest rate of revictimization, and they had first call on security upgrading work. Target hardening of council tenant and housing association victims was thus the first priority. Others judged vulnerable were also included, though owner occupier victims, unless in receipt of state benefits, were not included. As in Kirkholt there

was thus a focus on multiple victimization, though it was expressed in this slightly different way.

9   There was a fairly clear conception of the project at the start of it, but this became less so over time. There was continuing academic input as in Kirkholt.
10 Like Kirkholt, ?R1 was clearly and explicitly about burglary.

Outcomes: in the year before ?R1, 571 burglaries were recorded. This rose to 694 during the first year of the project and 991 over the second year. The rate of increase was marginally less than that in the surrounding area.

Candidate replication 2 (?R2)   This comprised a suite of initiatives aiming to respond to various crime problems on a housing estate, one element of which was concerned with household burglary.

1   This was a standard, relatively low-budget Safer Cities scheme. It had far fewer resources than Kirkholt. ?R2 cost £55,894, including £24,000 for lighting improvement, £10,280 for a BMX/skateboard track, and £21,614 for lock fitting. The lock fitting element was specifically directed at burglary prevention.
2   At the start of the project the burglary rate was 9%, about a third the rate on Kirkholt when work began there.
3   ?R2 is clearly circumscribed, with one major entry point. It comprises 835 dwellings, just over a third the size of Kirkholt. Asians make up 5% of the population.
4   There are no precise figures for burglaries involving gas and electricity coin meters, but the local supply companies had a policy for their removal.
5   There was very limited problem diagnosis at the planning stage. In 1989, prior to the project, 49 residents of ?R2 were interviewed by special constables. There were no interviews with victims or neighbours of victims. No burglars were interviewed.
6   No full-time staff were seconded to ?R2. The project was led by Safer Cities.
7   No special efforts were made to establish neighbourhood watch in any form.
8   Security upgrades were offered to all on the estate. Security work, including fitment of window locks, door locks and chains, was undertaken at 81% of the properties on the estate, those not covered including some already having adequate security and others not providing access.
9   There was no academic input into the ?R2 project.
10 Burglary was a major focus for the target hardening on ?R2.

Outcomes: in the twenty months prior to the point at which 80% of the target hardening undertaken was complete (it look four months for this) there were 111 domestic burglaries on the estate. In the following twenty months there were only 38.

Even with this foreshortened example of two 'replications', the difficulty becomes clear. Outcomes vary widely and do not seem to follow from 'the program' in any clear manner. We are merely piling one 'black box' on top of another. In view of the range of attributes listed here (and recall they are necessarily selective) the very act of deciding what constitutes a real replication is clearly a major problem. Are all the features listed necessary? Are others which are omitted crucial? Are some elements more important than others? Can individual aspects be abstracted? Is it the particular collection of specific crime prevention measures which must be adopted, or is it the procedures for identifying those that are appropriate in the circumstances? In short, which attributes are incidental and which are essential?

Each of the described projects has certain similarities and certain differences from Kirkholt. Neither is an exact replication. Indeed, no such thing would be possible. No project could occupy the same space and time, take place in identical conditions, or follow just the same course. Strict replication, if by that we mean exact copying, is clearly impossible. Popper is right when he says:

> All the repetitions we experience are *approximate repetitions*; and by saying that a repetition is approximate I mean that the repetition B of an event A is not identical with A, or indistinguishable from A, but only *more or less similar* to A. But if repetition is thus based upon mere similarity, it must share one of the main characteristics of similarity; that is, its relativity. Two things which are similar are always similar *in certain respects*. (1959, pp. 420–421)

We draw an unsettling conclusion from this. If replication is based on 'mere similarity', it is utterly impossible to advance a case for cumulation. Consider, for instance, the lack of success of ?R1. It can be interpreted in two ways. It may be taken to show that the measures fail and the Kirkholt findings are called into question. Defenders of the earlier project could argue that the new results cast no doubt on the successes of Kirkholt but merely reflect the fact that ?R1 was not a strict replication. The success of ?R2 can also be read in two ways: those seeing sufficient 'similarities' will find a growing body of evidence for the success of *a* program; those with an eye on the differences will note the success of *two* rather contrasting approaches. If one simply relies on observable similarities and differences between projects, decisions about replication, replicability and generalization become no more than a matter of taste: advocates and critics can in an unfettered way pick and choose cases to suit their arguments (see Tilley 1996 for a fuller discussion of 'relativist replication').

Efforts simply to mirror Kirkholt in all its details are doomed to failure. The example testifies, in an immediate and bleak way, to the methodological point made earlier that cumulation cannot take the form of empirical

Table 5.2   *A realistic reconstruction of aspects of Kirkholt*

Context	+	Mechanism	=	Outcome pattern
A high-crime area marked by very high rates of reburglary	+	Security upgrading of previously burgled premises to increase difficulty and risk of apprehension in burgling particularly attractive properties	=	Lower rates of revictimization together with a reduction in the burglary rate overall
High numbers of prepayment meters, with a high proportion of burglaries involving cash from meters	+	Removal of cash meters reduces incentive to burgle by decreasing actual or perceived rewards	=	Reduction in percentage of burglaries involving meter breakage; reduced risk of burglary at dwellings where meters are removed; reduced burglary rate overall
A medium-sized socially homo-geneous, clearly defined estate with little through traffic	+	Cocoon home watch increases perceived risks of recognition of offenders, plus heightened levels of informal social control	=	A reduced burglary rate overall and a general reduction in crime and incivilities

generalization but must involve the development of theory. A realistic reconstruction of Kirkholt shows how we can begin to dig our way out of this apparent hole. Theory construction begins in Table 5.2 which shows in a very simple and rather speculative way how the project can be decon-structed into a series of context–mechanism–outcome pattern configurations, which explain how particular outcomes may have been produced. This analysis injects some explicit realist theory, to try to make sense of what is salient and what is not salient in Kirkholt.

These are modest beginnings, but they do illustrate how explicit attention to context and mechanism is needed to make sense of outcome patterns. What is more, they restore to the centre of attention the key characteristic of 'Kirkholt' which in fact made it an outstanding piece of crime prevention practice, namely its careful matching of measures to contexts to address sys-tematically identified regularities in the local burglary problem. Each row of Table 5.2 is, in effect, a Kirkholt 'theory'. Thus we see in the first row that the very high existing rates of reburglary (C) led the team to single out already victimized homes for target hardening (M). This follows through in terms of a specific outcome target which is to reduce revictimization (O_1) as part of the overall effort to lower burglary rates (O). What takes the realist eye is the success of this particular theory. Thus whilst we have already noted the huge overall reduction in burglary, the most remarkable datum which really emerges from the project is that *the probability of reburglary amongst those already victimized was reduced from four times the expected rate to zero in the first seven months of the project* (Forrester et al., 1988).

In the absence of explicit attention to such precise lines of *CMO* thinking, those trying to follow in Kirkholt's footsteps and those asked to evaluate those efforts were lost. To retain the momentum of Kirkholt, the key is thus *not* to replicate, for one may have to wait many a moon before one comes upon another community of 'potentially close but demoralized Lancashire lads and lasses with a penchant for own-goal meter burglaries in which the same weaker residents repeatedly fall prey to local villains who know the exact lie of the land' and so on. Real progress is obtained by further development and testing of the Kirkholt theories. Speculative and low-level as they are, the three *CMO* configurations in Table 5.2 represent the real hopes for cumulation. We follow the implicitly realist line of advance in the theory and research on repeat victimization.

Repeat victimization takes a hold

The phenomenon of repeat victimization (also sometimes called multiple victimization or revictimization) has been known to criminology for over two decades. What brought repeat victimization to prominence in British practice, policy and research terms was indeed the Kirkholt project (Forrester et al., 1988; 1990; Pease, 1992). As we have made clear, attention to repeat victimization was but one element of a complex project. It followed from the careful examination of police recorded crime data relating to burglary, which showed that revictimization was a particular problem. The accounts of the research findings, whilst stressing the importance of revictimization, did not do so to the exclusion of other aspects of the work of the project. Yet it is this which has spawned subsequent research efforts, and the cumulation achieved. Cumulation thus begins by going backwards from programs to the problem and in reverse from the cure to the causes of 'repeats'.

One of the academics at the heart of the Kirkholt project (Pease) began to sharpen our understanding of the scope and detail of the regularity with a study of burglary patterns of Saskatoon in Canada (Polvi et al., 1991). This was not an evaluation study *per se*, but a classic piece of scholarly research using available data which fed into the process of cumulation. The study found patterns of revictimization similar to those identified in the Kirkholt project. It also showed that the risk of revictimization was at its height immediately following an incident and then quickly faded as time passed. If revictimization did not occur within six months, then as Figure 5.2 shows, burglary was little more likely than for those not previously victimized, and after twelve months no more likely.

What the Saskatoon study adds to Kirkholt, in realistic terms, is represented in Table 5.3.

A series of studies and demonstration projects then followed, which

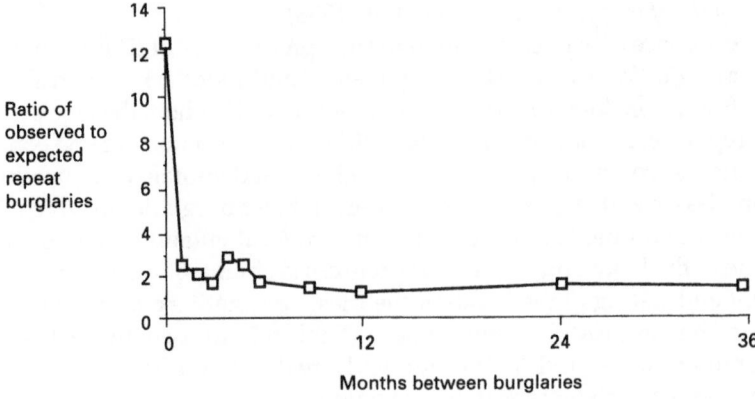

Figure 5.2   *Time course of repeat victimization (adapted from Polvi
et al., 1991)*

attended to repeat victimization across a range of crime categories.
Sampson and Phillips (1992), writing of a scheme aiming to reduce racial
attacks on an East London housing estate, describe patterns of repeat victimization similar to those found in relation to the previous work on
burglary. Those racially attacked were more at risk of subsequent racial
attacks than those who had not been. Their heightened risk was at its highest just after the initial attack and then dropped rapidly over time.
Burquest et al. (1992) examined vandalism and burglary against schools in
Merseyside. They found again that victimization was very unevenly
spread (of 33 schools, four experienced 34.1% of the incidents over twelve
months), and that its time course was similar to that found in the case of
domestic burglary (of 263 repeat incidents over a twelve-month period, 208
occurred within a month). Tilley (1993c) looked at schemes aiming to
reduce crime against small businesses. In regard to commercial burglary,
he found in Hartlepool that of 22% of businesses burgled once, 40% were

Table 5.3   *Repeat burglary regularities confirmed*

Context	+	Mechanism	=	Regularity
Something about Kirkholt and Saskatoon, and maybe anywhere	+	Somehow	=	Unexpectedly high rate of burglary revictimization, fading rapidly over time

Table 5.4   *More and more repeat victimization regularities*

Context	+	Mechanism	=	Regularity
Something about East London housing estate	+	Somehow	=	Uneven rate of racial attacks; heightened risk immediately after an incident, fading over time
Something about Merseyside	+	Somehow	=	Uneven rate of vandalism and burglary against schools; heightened risk immediately after an incident, fading over time
Something about Hartlepool	+	Somehow	=	Uneven rate of commercial burglary; heightened risk shortly after an incident
Something about Merseyside C Division	+	Somehow	=	Uneven rate of domestic violence; heightened risk shortly after an incident

burgled at least twice; of the 40% burgled at least twice, 48% were burgled at least three times; of the 48% burgled at least three times, 57% were burgled at least four times; and of the 57% burgled at least four times, 63% were burgled five or more times within a year. He also found that 119 out of 229 repeat incidents took place in the first fifth of the year. Lloyd et al. (1994) describe a scheme aiming to reduce domestic violence. They found that over a 25-month period, 7% of households reported at least one incident; of these, 42% reported a second; of those reporting two incidents, 52% reported a third; of those reporting three, 77% reported a fourth; and so on. Moreover, after a first incident, 35% of households received a second within five weeks; after a second incident, 45% suffered a third within five weeks.

A pattern was emerging! Across a wide range of personal and property crime types and in various contexts a relatively small proportion of victims experienced a relatively large proportion of all incidents, and they were most vulnerable during a 'heightened risk period' soon after victimization. Table 5.4 shows how we can represent the studies mentioned so far in realistic terms.

What we have at this stage is the discovery of a very powerful regularity about crimes and their victims. Starting from the practical effort to monitor precisely the nature of burglary patterns on a housing estate in the north of England, a remarkably consistent pattern of the changing risks of revictimization shows up across a range of offence types in varying contexts. We omit details of yet more substantial evidence supporting what is, by any social research standards, a venerable uniformity (Mayhew et al., 1993; Mirrlees-Black and Ross, 1995; Trickett et al., 1992) and move on to contemplate the idea that it might furnish a sound basis for planning crime prevention work (Farrell and Pease, 1993; Bridgeman and Sampson, 1994). As Farrell and Pease put it, findings about patterns of repeat victimization provided a basis for getting the crime prevention grease to the crime squeak. Instead of dissipating efforts across a wide range of potential targets for crime, these results suggested a way of targeting resources on those who are most vulnerable at the time when they are most at risk. Note that such an idea, whilst particularly strong at suggesting who should be targeted, has nothing to say about the content of any potential program. We intend no criticism in pointing this out, but merely remind the reader of the state of play in Table 5.4 with its forest of 'somethings' and 'somehows'. What we have at this stage is evidence of a powerful uniformity and no more.

Enter theory

In order to understand the regularity, we must turn to theory. Most of the key areas of evaluation research have appropriate bodies of general theory to call upon. In the case of criminal behaviour there are a range of 'perspectives', 'conceptual frameworks', 'paradigms' from which to choose (behavioural, biological, classical, developmental, labelling, left realist, rational choice etc.). When it comes to the matter of explaining the whys and wherefores of the criminal's choice of victim, a range of theories based on 'rational choice' principles have come to the fore. One such theory is known as 'situational crime prevention' or 'opportunity theory' (Clarke, 1992); another well-established criminological theory from the same family is 'routine activities theory'. As with all social science theories, the functions of these perspectives vary: they provide universal conceptual frameworks which can be applied across the targeted substantive field and beyond; they supply ontological frameworks positioning the individual and society; they ally the perspective to a chosen epistemology which governs the way explanations are constructed.

Realist evaluation has relatively little use for all this additional pro-, para-, and metatheory (having made up its own mind on such matters, thank you very much). What the realist evaluator needs from these perspectives, however, is middle-range, substantive theory. Social scientists used to working with these grander bodies of theories often have grander ambitions, and the realist evaluator needs to work rather hard to ransack from them propositions relating mechanisms, contexts and outcomes. We illustrate the point with routine activities theory (RAT). This is a theory whose expression and development runs along highly formal lines. According to this, three conditions must be met for a (predatory) offence to take place: there must be a 'motivated offender', a 'suitable target' and the 'absence of a capable guardian'. This elementary, indeed tautological, starting point has proved remarkably fertile in helping to make substantive

Table 5.5   *A realistic theory of widespread repeat victimization regularities*

Context	+	Mechanism	=	Regularity
Repeated co-presence of particular motivated offender and suitable victim in the absence of capable guardian	+	Offender informed that, pro-tem, risks low enough, rewards available sufficient and crime easy enough	=	High rate of repeat offences, with short term heightened vulnerability

sense of crime patterns in space and time. The changes in supply, distribution and movement of motivated offenders, suitable targets and capable guardians are shown to make intelligible alterations in large scale spatio-temporal crime pattern regularities (Cohen and Felson, 1979; Felson, 1994).

Farrell et al. (1995) make use of RAT in trying to understand repeat victimization regularities. They argue that for racial attacks, domestic violence, burglary, robbery, and the physical and sexual abuse of children, the observed patterns of repeat victimization can be explained by the routine activities context and the ways in which this makes crime a convenient option for offenders. Once offenders have committed a crime successfully then, almost by definition, we can say that they encountered a suitable victim in the absence of anyone who stepped in to stop the felony. Assuming continued motivation, they know that further success from future efforts on the *same source* can also be expected. The offender knows that the rewards are there (be they goods to be stolen or satisfaction from an assault), that the risks are low (they were not prevented from committing the crime or apprehended in the course of the offence), and that the crime is not too difficult (they can get in, they can intimidate the victim and not meet effective resistance). There is no need to accept the inconvenience and uncertainty which would be associated with efforts to trace another suitable victim. In the short term at any rate, conditions can be assumed to remain just as conducive to successful offending. We can thus represent the basic theory explaining the repeat victimization regularity according to the standard realist formula as in Table 5.5.

Typically it is the case that any general body of social theory will fetch up a range of explanations for a particular uniformity (Stinchcombe, 1968). By thinking of the risk factors involved in choosing a victim it is possible to come up with a rival explanation for the repeat victim regularity. The assumption behind our initial explanation of observed repeat victimization regularities is that the *same offender* (or a fellow criminal) is returning to the *same victim*. It is the *offence itself* which increases vulnerability to revictimization. This is known in the literature as 'event dependence' (Chenery et al., 1996; Farrell et al., 1995). Spelman (1995) has pointed out that the same observed repeat victimization regularities could also be produced by 'risk

Table 5.6 *An alternative realistic risk heterogeneity theory of widespread repeat victimization regularities*

Context	+	Mechanism	=	Regularity
Repeated co-presence of particular motivated offenders and suitable victims in the absence of capable guardians in high-crime areas	+	Offenders routinely estimate relative risks, rewards and difficulty and offend accordingly	=	High rate of repeat offences, with chronic heightened vulnerability

heterogeneity'. Some victims (persons or properties) may be chronically susceptible to crime; others may be much less susceptible; for others still, crime might be relatively infrequent. In high-crime areas housing high numbers of motivated offenders, easy access to attractive targets will be tempting to any of a wide variety of potential offenders. Looked at *in aggregate*, this state of affairs would create a pattern akin to that identified in most of the repeat victimization literature so far. There would be a tendency for repeats to appear to be concentrated after short periods since the relatively small number of those very susceptible would be frequently victimized with little time between incidents, the less vulnerable would tend to have longer periods between incidents, and so on. In this case, we have a subtly different balance of context and mechanism ingredients producing a virtually identical outcome, as shown in Table 5.6.

Same regularity – different context and mechanism. Sound familiar? We are getting closer here to the bane of the evaluator's life in which a program aimed at seemingly similar problems can emerge with quite different results. We are suggesting that this fecundity of the middle-range theory can provide the pivot by which we draw from a set of general (and thus generalizable) principles a set of specific (and maybe even contrary) lessons. In the present case, it is generally conceded that the observed problem (the repeat victim regularity) could be produced by either of, or a combination of, 'event dependence' and 'risk heterogeneity'. The explanatory issue is then that of determining the relative importance of the two theories, and these may well vary by crime, space and place.

Bringing these theories into the policy evaluation sphere involves thinking through the practice implications in regard to how to protect the most highly victimized. Programs would indeed differ markedly. If event dependence were true, we are dealing with the same offender choosing the same victim, repeatedly and regularly. Those so victimized could have the cycle broken by (a) *detection*, that is efforts to apprehend and take out of circulation those offenders who are repeatedly returning, and (b) *deflection*, that is immediately decreasing the perceived rewards and increasing the perceived risk and difficulty in successfully committing the identical

Table 5.7 *Realistic event dependence theory driven approach to preventing chronic repeat victimization*

Context	+	Blocking mechanism	=	Outcome pattern
Repeated co-presence of the same motivated offender and the same suitable victim in a absence of a capable guardian	+	(a) *Detection*: improved measures to enable apprehension of repeat offender	=	(a) Improved arrest rate of repeat offenders; reduced number of chronic repeat victims
		(b) *Deflection*: deterrent measures targeted on the vulnerable victim to increase difficulty or decrease reward for the offender		(b) Long term reduced overall rate of revictimization

Table 5.8 *Realistic risk heterogeneity theory driven approach to preventing chronic repeat victimization*

Context	+	Blocking mechanism	=	Outcome pattern
Repeated co-presence of motivated offenders and suitable victims in absence of capable guardians in chronically high-crime areas	+	*Perception*: long term decrease in discernment of high-crime-area vulnerability; separation of motivated offender group from vulnerable targets	=	Reduced long term risk to the chronically revictimized; no change in low-rate revictimization

crime. If risk heterogeneity were true, then those areas repeatedly victimized would require relatively permanent efforts to deal with the source of their vulnerability, and this might involve (c) *perception*, that is effecting more fundamental changes at the community level by attempting to shift the overall discernment of the rewards and risk levels for the high-crime areas. Exactly what interventions will trigger the required mechanisms in either case is unclear, and is not itself a task for 'theory' but will depend on the local context – the clarification of which should form the focus for further evaluation research. This is what needs to be stressed here. The formulation of the (two) realistic theories provides the task for further research (including evaluation research) which is to test them out and arbitrate between them. Table 5.7 shows in a rather simplified way what the program and evaluation might look like if driven by realistic event dependence theory on repeat victimization. Table 5.8 shows the same for risk heterogeneity theory.

Cumulation (at last)

Our progress chasing reaches a crucial turn as we take the short drive across the Pennine chain from Rochdale to Huddersfield. We return to evaluation research as such and, indeed, to evaluation work still in progress at the time of writing. What differentiates this from so many other projects is that it is clearly intended to build on previous work (Anderson et al., 1995). Program implementation and evaluation incorporate what is already known from repeat victimization research and what is suspected from routine activity theory and allied perspectives, and on this basis is able to push forward in forging better specified *CMO* configurations. The project aims to make attention to repeat commercial burglary, domestic burglary and theft of motor vehicles, which are all high-volume crimes in Britain, a routine feature of policing in Huddersfield. One reason, incidentally, for the continuity of theory and method here is that the entire pattern of development is in the hands of no more than a dozen individuals and one rather 'capable guardian'. Our account is produced on the basis of preliminary reports, briefing papers and discussions with an academic criminologist / evaluator (Pease), a research worker and program manager (Chenery), and a practitioner (Anderson).

The police officers implementing the program in Huddersfield were familiarized with research findings to date about repeat victimization, and with what had evidently been achieved in reducing it. The officers were also introduced to routine activities theory which was used as a heuristic device to help think about ways of preventing revictimization. Working groups were set up to try to think through what might be done. The first looked to ways of reducing victim suitability (deciding to treat absence of capable guardian as a feature of victim suitability) and the second to ways of reducing offender motivation. The task of the working groups was, in effect, to translate a formal theory into a substantive one.

Several features of the program development here are noteworthy. One is the promotion of a teacher–learner relationship between researcher and practitioner, a topic on which we will have more to say in the next chapter. For the purposes at hand, however, the main interest is how program implementation captures this move between the general and the particular which is crucial in developing cumulative, transferable policy lessons. We start with routine activities theory (crime = motivated offender + suitable victim – capable guardian) which provides an abstract, tautological conceptual framework of the conditions which sustain any crime and which thus can be applied to all crime. The fact that this conjunction of conditions is likely to endure after an offence explains why criminals often choose the same victim and is thus translated into a middle-range (*CMR*) theory about repeat victimization (see Table 5.5). This is then translated into a broad program (*CMO*) hypothesis suggesting that change depends on these conditions being altered in order to detect or deflect the offender (see Table 5.7). The final stage is the specification into a substantive program (*CMO*) theory in which action is targeted on the offenders, guardians and victims of Huddersfield.

Jointly, thus, Pease, Chenery and the practitioners devised a program for repeat victimization prevention, driven by the application of routine activities theory. Resources would not permit the application of the full range of measures to all victims. It was decided therefore to adopt a graduated approach where the more resource intensive measures would be applied only to the already repeatedly victimized, since they were at greatest risk of revictimization. What some have come to call the 'Olympic model' was devised, whereby one victimization would provoke 'bronze' measures, a second a 'silver' response and a third 'gold' treatment. Variations in precise outcome pattern would, of course, be expected according to which of the conditions for crime were removed and according to the method used. Table 5.9 shows what is being undertaken to address the burglary issue. It

Table 5.9   *Theoretically informed effort to reduce burglary revictimization in Huddersfield*

Context	+	New mechanism	=	Outcome pattern
Bronze Motivated offender + suitable victim – capable guardian in one previous victimization	+	(i) Victim letter for morale building (ii) Postcode pen to make stolen goods less attractive (iii) Cocoon watch to increase natural surveillance and increase risk to offender (iv) Rapid repair + security upgrade makes entry more difficult	=	Reduced rate of reburglary of those burgled once
Silver Motivated offender + suitable victim – capable guardian in two previous victimizations	+	(i) Crime prevention officer advice + police patrol: reduces apparent vulnerability to prospective offender (ii) Mock occupancy devices: entry looks more risky to burglar, who prefers low-risk empty properties (iii) Search warrant: incapacitation through targeting detection on previously convicted offenders with similar *MO* etc.	=	Reduced rate of third burglaries to those victimized twice; increased rate of reconviction of previous offenders
Gold Motivated offender + suitable victim – capable guardian in three previous victimizations	+	Silent Home Office alarm + daily police patrol + priority finger-printing: greater prospect of catching and incapacitating offender when offence in progress or subsequently	=	Increased overall arrest rate of known and unknown offenders and reduced fourth victimization

can be seen in particular that the theory *assumes* event dependence, particularly at the gold level. Here, measures trigger quite a different mechanism from the bronze and silver. They are primarily concerned with apprehension and incapacitation of the repeat return offender rather than with their deterrence or deflection. If event dependence is true (or partially true) the bronze and silver responses will deter/deflect the less confident or committed return offenders, leaving the more sophisticated (and more expensive) apprehension-oriented gold for the more determined or pig-headed returner. Clearly, the strategy as a whole should also yield outcomes of higher rates of clear-up of burglary offences, lower rates of revictimization, and lower rates of burglary overall.

It would take us too long to spell out the precise tactics involved in every nook and cranny of this initiative. The 'silent Home Office alarm', for instance, is one that transmits directly to the police control room and will activate an immediate response with the aim of catching the offender 'on the job'. Other tricks of the trade should be decipherable from the outline 'guide' above. The point we want to emphasize about the program is that it is *not* a blunderbuss initiative. What we see here is a graded response following the realist mantra of 'what works for whom in what circumstances'. What we see is thus a *CMO* configuration focusing at a fairly concrete level which comes about because the question of finding the appropriate mechanism to apply to the specific context has been driven into the 'matrix of aims' of the project (Anderson et al., 1995, p. 21). As we have seen, this pursuit of specification never stops, a fact that is reflected in another feature of the project, the '*aide-mémoire* of responses' to officers (1995, p. 38) which reminds them that they have responsibility to make recommendations and modifications to the overall design as seems appropriate in the particular contextual circumstances of the victim. This implementation leeway attacks an entirely typical feature of programs, in that there will always be unforeseen variation in groups targeted which can only be attended to by local knowledge. For instance, within the gold response category another detection device available was the 'hidden video camera'. Its actual deployment, it being a fiddly little thing to load with cassettes and thus only good for nimble fingered victims, depended on the common sense of the practitioner.

The obverse of this process of progressive theory focusing is that empirical data feed back up the ladder of abstraction. Because evidence has been forged in response to a line of theory development, it can be used to test out and adjudicate between hypotheses going well beyond the specific program. We are limited in our description here to only the preliminary data from an unfinished inquiry but they still give a good indication of the range of claims that can be interrogated. We start with an example which confirms a feature of the case studies of the previous chapter, namely that the Huddersfield project itself comprises dozens of sub-theories and thus requires the pin-pointing of dozens of distinct empirical tests. We give some indication of these by outlining some differences in the anticipated gold, silver, and bronze outcome patterns in Table 5.9. One sub-theory thus argues for a policy of detection rather than deflection in chronically revictimized homes. It is possible to test the success of this assumption with some standard before-and-after data on, for instance, those homes fitted with temporary alarms. In this instance we discover that in comparable pre-project and project periods the arrest rate following from the use of these devices in Huddersfield rose from 3.8% to 14%, whilst in the surrounding force area it declined from 8.1% to 4.3% (Anderson et al., 1995).

Feedback on the more general theory also occurs. For instance, the theoretical assumption underpinning almost the entire program is, as we have seen, routine activities theory. And in particular, given the emphasis on revictimization on a house by house basis rather than neighbourhood by neighbourhood, 'event dependence' has been supposed to operate as opposed to 'risk heterogeneity'. The Huddersfield research allowed an interesting adjudication of the two theories in that records were compiled of the pattern of revictimization in a neighbourhood immediately after a burglary. They show that, 'After burglary at a particular house, its neighbours are no more vulnerable than those in dwellings somewhat further away. In contrast, there are many more victimizations at the house already burgled.'(Anderson et al., 1995). This offers at least partial corroboration for the 'same house same offender' presupposition and supports the subsequent efforts to target the program along these lines.

Other results are even more theory-invasive. As opposed to a rather nicely nuanced pattern of burglary reduction outcomes, the strategy had little impact whatsoever on vehicle crime. Throughout the project, changes in theft of vehicles from Huddersfield merely kept pace with such changes in the force generally (Anderson et al., 1995). This was despite the implementation of an equally subtle campaign of gold, silver and bronze responses to car crime. There is no need to dwell on details of the Olympian efforts in terms of 'driveway barriers', 'Thatcham protection' and 'special number plates' in this instance, because the overall failure is perhaps a sign that we are in the wrong conceptual framework altogether. Perhaps the more impulsive joys of car crime are poorly captured within the very rational choice framework which underlies 'event dependence programming'. Or perhaps the way 'repeats' are conceptualized needs to be different. Instead of owners or individual vehicles, perhaps the salient event that is repeated is the theft of the same model or the theft from the same parking place (Pease, personal communication). If Porsche 911s are, in effect, clones to steal, then the theft of two examples constitutes repeat victimization. Particular bays in car parks likewise might define risk. There would again be event dependent regularities, preventable perhaps in different ways.

Some findings, of course, remain resolutely in the domain of local practitioner program theories. For instance, the aforementioned fine-tuning of the Huddersfield project at the discretion of the local officer will undoubtedly yield better outcomes but the lessons probably are not to be abstracted for posterity. In the police canteen at Huddersfield in January 1996, we learned from Sgt Illingworth why he had chosen to have a hidden camera installed at young Mr Boothroyd's rather than old Mrs Parkinson's. We haven't had the chance to see if he was proved correct, but no doubt the outcomes are seeping into the local wisdom driving the project.

Our search for cumulation in evaluation research has been told in terms of two journeys. The first, from Kirkholt to ?R1 and ?R2, went effectively nowhere. Efforts to replicate the original Kirkholt project were inadequate, and the inadequacies related in part to the way in which the results of Kirkholt were reported. It simply was not clear what could properly constitute a replication and there is thus no recognizable cumulation from Kirkholt to its direct intended replications. The second journey went from Kirkholt to Huddersfield. It did so via a rather different route which involved climbing up and down a ladder of abstraction whilst engaging in a process of theory development and testing. There was cumulation of understanding from one program to the next because there is refinement of a theory of repeat victimization, embryonic in the first case study and becoming more and more focused in the latter.

The repeat victimization story since Kirkholt is one of movement from (a) an isolated, black box observation of some notable outcomes, married to an innovative but insufficiently articulated program theory, to (b) recurrent regularities and outcomes, with increasingly theoretically articulated CMO configurations to interpret them. There is clear cumulation in understanding of regularities, outcome patterns, contexts and mechanisms, as well as their configurations both at a more abstract and at a more concrete level. It is equally obvious that no end point has yet been reached. The various 'tests' and 'adjudications' illustrated above are in no sense final, but lead instead to the ability to ask more and more refined questions. The relative success of the program with repeat burglary and the relative failure with repeat car crime suggests, in the case of the latter, a sequence of programs and evaluations based on preventing 'repeats' as defined by the parking bay or the vehicle marque. The findings on the 'neighbour effect' suggest attention be paid to the next most similar and familiar target in a UK context – namely *two* doors away amongst semi-detached houses. More broadly, it may well be that event dependence is a huge factor in repeat victimization and that detecting repeats is *ipso facto* a method to detect prolific offenders. It is to this link between offender profiling/targeting and repeat victimization that Pease and colleagues are now turning.

The point is that, whilst the journey never ends, it is possible to trace a line of progress both in the understanding and the evaluation of projects aiming to reduce repeat victimization. It is the existence of CMO theories which underlies this cumulative development and allows us to know what further needs to be undertaken in research and evaluation to achieve still further cumulation. The example illustrates that cumulation is possible, what is entailed in achieving cumulation, what that cumulation has amounted to, and above all that scientific realism can make sense of that cumulation.

Cumulation: some accumulated wisdom

It is difficult to see how the progress made could have been achieved without significant evaluator understanding of earlier studies. Our example shows, we think, that cumulation turns on the presence of knowledgeable evaluation researchers, capable of and choosing to orient their work to established levels of understanding, and to changes in these over time. What we have here is the antithesis of what so often happens: a series of evaluation studies undertaken by those with little interest in or knowledge of earlier findings. We attempt to summarize the lessons of the case study by setting down a few clear practical pointers for those conducting demonstration projects, those evaluating demonstration projects, those commissioning evaluation studies, and those involved in undertaking and evaluating replications:

1 The CMO/CMR theories incorporated and developed within demonstration programs by policy makers and practitioners must be spelled out explicitly in evaluations so that evidence appropriate to test and arbitrate between them can be collected.
2 Evaluators will normally need to supplement policy maker and practitioner CMR/CMO theories with others drawn from additional sources, including previous evaluations and other research.
3 Evaluation reports simply indicating whether or not there has been a change associated with the introduction of a program should not be commissioned or accepted by policy makers. They are of no value, since nothing can be learned from them about what and what not to do in the future.
4 Evaluation reports must identify not only the changes associated with the introduction of a program, but also what brought them about. That is, they must include conclusions about $CMOs$.
5 Commissioners of evaluations must recognize that rather little can be learned from one-off evaluations, however large they may be. Series of projects need to be developed explicitly if cumulation in understanding, effectiveness and efficiency are to be attained.
6 If they are not to be disappointed, policy makers and practitioners using the findings of a demonstration project must attend explicitly to the distinctive contexts in which measures triggered change mechanisms in the program which they are following.
7 Those commissioning evaluations must award contracts to those with

the knowledge and competence to orient their studies realistically to what has been learned of *CMO/CMR* configurations previously.

8 Evaluators must explicitly orient their work to a growing body of *CMO/CMR* understanding, to ensure that opportunities for cumulation are taken by later evaluators, in order that policy makers and practitioners can improve their service delivery.

These scientific realist principles obviously go for any area in which project evaluation is undertaken. The very least they do is bring home the 'negative' lesson that the same program can have quite different 'outcomes' when 'replicated' in different contexts. Had this realist truism been appreciated and followed earlier there would have been less chance of the destructive 'nothing works' conclusions of the 1970s and 1980s, and the doctrine would not have held sway for such a long time. Moreover, even if 'nothing works' no longer works as a slogan for the criminal justice system, the story of much intervention and evaluation remains one of uncertainty and inconsistency. There has not been cumulative development in theory or practice. This follows, it is argued, at least in part from weaknesses in methodology.

The prospects of retrospective cumulation

So far we have discussed cumulation through a series of interrelated studies, and have suggested how evaluation work might be orchestrated to achieve that cumulation. In practice, as we have acknowledged, more typically evaluations are undertaken as a series of one-offs with little knowledge of or interest in what has gone before, and little effort to elaborate a realist theory which can be tested by well-targeted outcome pattern measurements. This poses the question of what has actually been learned from all these prior studies and has led to efforts to reanalyse what often add up to several hundreds of evaluations in any one field in order to see what they reveal in the round. We refer, of course, to 'meta-evaluation' which in essence is the aggregation of the evidence from a number of studies into a single database which allows the results to be analysed collectively rather than individually. This is no place to begin a discussion of the techniques involved. Basically, however, they (i) allow an estimation of the 'overall treatment effect' of a broad class of initiatives in that the idiosyncrasies of any particular study tend to average out in the round, and (ii) provide an estimate of 'differential effects' by examining the variability of outcomes and seeing if they favour particular client characteristics and treatment types.

Clearly there is some affinity between the latter aim and the notions developed in this chapter, as can be seen from the following quotation on programs for juvenile offenders from Lipsey, probably the most sophisticated recent exponent of meta-evaluation:

It is no longer constructive for researchers, practitioners and policy-makers to argue about whether delinquency treatment and related rehabilitative approaches 'work' as if that were a question that could be answered with a simple 'yes' or 'no'. As a generality, treatment clearly works. We must get on with the business of developing and identifying the treatment models that will be most effective and providing them to the juveniles that they will benefit. (1995, p. 78)

On the other hand we have to admit that we find the meta-evaluation track record to date somewhat disappointing. Our reasoning comes down to the 'raw materials' of such studies, the difficulty being that the quasi-experimental evaluations ordinarily used to drive meta-evaluations are, as indicated in Chapter 2, very poorly placed to provide the vital explanatory clues. The first meta-evaluations insisted that in order to be included in any overall review, original studies must have 'true compatibility between untreated and treated groups' (Martinson, 1974) or there must be 'post-treatment follow up with control group comparison' (Gendreau and Ross, 1987). More recent meta-evaluations have a more permissive definition of what counts as a bona fide initial evaluation but are likely to take 'design quality' into account as one of the explanatory variables in treatment variance (Löesel, 1995). It should be obvious by now that we do not share the assumed design hierarchy at work here. Alas, the nearer researchers move to the supposed methodological pinnacles in terms of 'randomization', 'control' and 'statistical power', the more likely are they to fail to register attention to explanatory mechanisms and contexts. What is more, two of the other vital ingredients for cumulation highlighted here, namely the process of theory development and the usage of empirical evidence from non-evaluation sources, are almost always absent in the typical meta-evaluation. Looked at pessimistically, this inclines us to doubt whether such aggregative modes of inquiry can reveal anything other than the inconsistency and uncertainty already alluded to. More optimistically, we note that in our experience even the most outcome-fixated studies do contain *implicit* and *fragmentary* hypotheses about CMO configurations.

It is thus possible to envisage a form of 'realistic meta-evaluation' which would be directed at these broader explanatory ends. It would involve combing through evaluation studies looking for clues as to possible CMO configurations and seeking prospects for testing them *ex post facto*. To date 'realistic meta-evaluation' is a club of one in the form of an examination of neighbourhood watch in Britain co-authored by one of the present authors (Laycock and Tilley, 1995). Space precludes a full account of this here. Suffice it to say that the review ends up with a highly differentiated account of the potential causal mechanisms triggered by neighbourhood watch in varying crime and community contexts, generating widely differentiated outcome patterns. In coming to this view, though it is consistent with what is plausible in the existing evaluation research, the authors were drawn into a good deal of very highly provisional CMO configuration theory building. Perhaps not surprisingly (since they were not developed for the purpose) very few existing case studies seem to allow for a natural testing and adjudication of developing lines of theory which is at the very centre of our understanding of cumulation. It may be that retrospective evaluation reviews will provide more in the way of conglomeration than cumulation of *CMO* configurations. The jury is still out.

Limits to cumulability

Whilst cumulation is possible through a series of evaluations and whilst transferable lessons for policy and practice are there to be learned, it is important not to overstate what can be achieved. Some well-known onto-logical and epistemological limitations lie in wait for the magniloquent evaluator. The social world is an 'open system' (Bhaskar, 1979). Unlike a laboratory, where the conditions for the effective triggering of causal mech-anisms can be created, no such opportunity exists in the social world. Moreover, as stressed in Chapter 3, people within that social world are active. They create and re-create their social worlds. They are able, more-over, to act reflectively. They have a grasp of the world they live in, and behave in terms of their understandings. The capacity for reflexivity puts limits on the predictability of future conditions, for these conditions are the creation of social actors. Of course, much is re-created, and many of the conditions for action put limits on the real choices open to actors. But, for all that, actors do not reconstruct their worlds in an altogether mechanical way, and they do make choices. And because the social world is in this way open, contexts cannot be controlled and actors' decisions in situations are intrinsically unstable. In a rather grander way, Popper (1957) makes the point that future knowledge is unknown. If it were known we would know it already. Unless knowledge ceases to develop we shall always be ignorant of future knowledge (and we could never be certain that it will cease to develop). Since knowledge plays an important part in shaping our social world, that too cannot be foretold.

The social world is in continuous flux. Change is endemic. Even if broad contextual changes may occur at glacial rates, local contexts are more volatile, both from the reflexive behaviour of those within them and from 'external' impacts. Thus, even where it may be possible to specify local con-textual conditions for mechanisms to be triggered, ensuring that those circumstances are stable will seldom be possible. It is clear, thus, that local programs are chronically vulnerable to the intrusion of or invasion by more immediate external contextual conditions, overwhelming the pro-gram and the conditions for its success. Externally induced contextual changes from, for example, political, population, transportation, adminis-trative, economic, or even climatic sources can subvert (or enhance) the mechanism firing potential of a program. Contexts for action are thus intrinsically uncertain. We can never know that what 'works' today will always work since the conditions for things to work cannot ultimately be guaranteed, and the reflexive penetration of conditions for action and for choice by actors mean that their responses cannot mechanically be predicted (Giddens, 1984).

As an example, recall the explanation of repeat victimization using routine activities theory, according to which crime occurs when motivated offenders meet suitable targets in the absence of capable guardians. Whilst we found ready and profitable usage of these concepts in understanding the strategies and successes of the Huddersfield program, it is equally obvious that the same ideas can be put to use in interpreting longer term changes in the distribution of crime, some of which changes might transform or even countermand the objectives of such a local initiative. Changes in manufacture produce, for example, large numbers of new high-value, portable and anonymous goods, such as mobile phones, mini hi-fi systems, compact video cameras and lap-top computers; these are highly *suitable targets* which criminal activity can be expected to follow. Changes in family life mean more women go to work, fewer chores are done by children, young people are permitted to organize their own social lives; this means there are fewer *capable guardians* and changing patterns of opportunities. Changes in transportation mean that *motivated offenders* have a wider range of movement in areas where they may spot suitable targets without capable guardians and easily make their getaway. Changes in patterns of residential specialization tend to lead to congregations of *motivated offenders*, dramatic divergence in *suitable* and *unsuitable targets* and extremes of *capability* and *incapability* with respect to *guardianship*.

What we are faced with here is the fact that any particular program is embedded in an almost infinite range of assumptions about how the social world works. Going beyond the changes listed in the previous paragraph, we might say that program outcomes depend upon: the presence of particular forms of government, the existing legal, moral and religious climate, the extant forms of culture and communication, the existence of historical memory, the present use of language and meanings, and so on. None of this can ever be fully articulated, yet the operation of any program is ultimately contingent on it. A vast web of unspoken theory lies behind any articulated program theory and, because these unarticulated conditions for initiatives are so extensive, they are not and probably cannot be fully articulated. Programs, in short, are social accomplishments resting atop of other social accomplishments and so by their very nature are inherently fragile.

This is not defeatist talk, it is realist talk. These epistemological limits on what can be known exist for all forms of enquiry. The open system nature of investigation confronts all forms of social research. The perpetual nature of social change is a challenge to all perspectives of evaluation methodology. Such problems are not unique to scientific realism. Scientific realism, though, is able to explain in its own terms the limitations on cumulability. From the outset (Chapter 3), we have stressed the embeddedness of programs within a wider set of macro and micro social forces and acknowledged that causal impacts are not fixed but contingent. Above all we have stressed that cumulation is not a matter of discovering the immutable, timeless laws of social programming. Rather, what we seek was identified in the opening quotation from Cook et al. (1992) on the very first page of this chapter, namely a 'family of answers'. We have attempted to show how such families develop here. Any newly delivered program such as the Huddersfield project can be seen as the offspring of an abstract *CMO* configuration, which in turn has predecessors in prior programs, previous research and long standing bodies of theory. This lineage is vital in setting up the project and explaining some of its outcomes, but it can never explain its unintended consequences, or indeed all its failures. That is a task for local knowledge and *CMO* configuration focusing, the point being that the realist framework provided here then furnishes the means of passing on this further accumulation of knowledge to the next generation of initiatives.

6

HOW TO CONSTRUCT REALISTIC DATA: UTILIZING STAKEHOLDERS' KNOWLEDGE

In one way or another, in order to get their data, evaluation researchers usually end up talking to people. From the outset, evaluators have thus to come to a reasoned position on the questions of 'how to do the asking?' and 'who to ask?' Despite the domination of the use of verbal data across the social sciences, these two issues remain controversial. Methodological disputation is, of course, habitual in the human sciences, and a timeless 'polarity principle' is seemingly at work: whatever the technique, whatever the strategy, two camps of a basically opposite persuasion seem to fore-gather and glare at each other, with the result that methodological choices seem forever framed in mutual hostility.

With respect to interviewing strategy, the choice available is often por-trayed as that between 'structured' and 'unstructured' approaches. In the former a more formal style is adopted. Here the researcher is bound to a fixed set of questions, with fixed wording, and subjects are bound to closed, predetermined answer boxes. In the latter, the format is basically conver-sational. Researchers work only with a broad list of 'themes' to be explored, and subjects frame answers according to their understanding of these issues. From the beginning, in introductory 'methods' textbooks, we tend to learn about interviewing as a choice between the pros and cons of each strategy. The selection of interviewing strategy is thus presented as a matter of inclination towards standardization versus sensitivity, enumeration versus emancipation, anonymity versus ardour, and so forth.

Such polarities are often 'nested', with preferences on one such methodological choice being overlain with other epistemological and ontological bifurcations. The 'how to ask?' and the 'who gets asked?' issues become inextricably linked. Thus in the world of evaluation, the inclination towards *structured* interviewing often runs parallel with a preference for measuring *outcomes*, which often presupposes an *experimental* orientation, which in turn is said to privilege the concerns of *program managers* and *policy makers*. The inclination towards the *unstructured* interview is more recognizable in researchers who prefer to understand *process*, which often presupposes some kind of *constructivist* research strategy, which in turn involves remaining faithful to the concerns of *practitioners* and *subjects*.

The previous couple of paragraphs will be recognizable as a mini-portrait of the 'paradigm wars'. Many commentators have wished them dead, some indeed perceive them dead (Stern, 1995). Whilst we still detect a rather strong pulse (Pawson, 1996), it is clearly incumbent upon us to recognize another powerful set of methodological voices in this particular debate. These espouse pluralism. What tends to be argued is that pragmatic, get-your-hands-dirty researchers should have no truck with the supposed polarities, since in real research it is often sensible, indeed advantageous, to operate with a combination of methods. This would mean using both structured and unstructured interviewing and indeed combinations thereof, such as the 'semi-structured' interview. In the case of distinguishing the appropriate 'stakeholders' in an evaluation, the pragmatist would, of course, argue for a comprehensive vision with the aggregation of as many viewpoints as is practicable.

This chapter will examine the construction of evaluation data from a realistic perspective and attempt to throw fresh light on the 'how/who to ask?' questions. As the reader may suspect, we aim to declare a plague on the houses of both the purists and the pragmatists. It should be abundantly clear already why we have no truck with the technical absolutists. The realistic explanation of programs involves an understanding of their mechanisms, contexts and outcomes, and so requires asking questions about the reasoning and resources of those involved in the initiative, the social and cultural conditions necessary to sustain change, and the extent to which one behavioural regularity is exchanged for another (recall Chapter 3). Such propositions cover a range of information concerning both processes and outcomes, which could not be captured exclusively by a formal or by an informal interviewing style, or indeed by focusing on the concerns of an exclusive set of stakeholders.

Does this not immediately lead us to plan B, and identify us as signed-up members of the pragmatic pluralist party? Our answer is 'no', and indeed on several counts 'no!' Our initial hesitation stems from the fact that pluralism, with its 'a bit of this and a bit of that' approach, actually leads to no new thinking beyond the ill-defined compromise. The argument tends to go as follows. Structured methods are good for measuring outputs (such as crime rates or rehabilitation rates), unstructured methods are good for understanding reasoning (such as attitudes to crime or rehabilitation): our investigation needs both, so let us opt for some semi-structured, multi-method approach. We consider this ill-defined for several reasons. Firstly, it does not tell us how to blend the two bodies of information. Pluralism is disappointingly short on answers to such questions as: how should one actually construct the semi-structured question? How does one analyse the tick box information alongside narrative? How does one actually 'triangulate'? Secondly, it is woefully weak in knowing where to stop. That is to say, as information and potential stakeholders begin to multiply under pluralism, we have no clear guidelines on whose views to prioritize, on what to do if viewpoints differ, on whether we want attitudinal or behavioural information from each group, and so on.

This brings us to our identification of the problem and the thesis of the chapter. The great shortcoming in methodological thinking about data collection is in fact widespread throughout the social sciences and indeed held in common by both the paradigm warriors and the peacemakers in the paragraphs above. Both the 'dogmatic purist' *and* 'pragmatic pluralist' approaches actually share a common misconception of the purpose of the interview. The formal, structured interview, the informal, open-ended interview, the semi-structured interview, the multi-method approach to data collection are all *data-driven* strategies. The task is thus to ascertain (according to the favoured method) information which is faithful to the subject's thoughts and deeds. They are thus all constructed under the working assumption that *the subject and the subject matter of the interview are one and the same thing*. We aim to supplant this notion with the counter-proposition that data construction should be *theory-driven*. Thus on the realistic model, *the researcher's theory is the subject matter of the interview, and the subject (stakeholder) is there to confirm, to falsify and, above all, to refine that theory*.

The theory in question will, of course, be a realist theory of the mechanisms, contexts and outcomes which define how programs work. The chapter is given over to demonstrating that such a platform will provide a much clearer purchase on the issues of 'how' and 'who' to ask. The chapter is organized into four sections. We begin by retracing our steps a little in order to clarify the failings of the current orthodoxy on data collection. We then move on to extract those elements of realist explanation we believe are crucial in guiding data collection and show that the dynamo concepts – mechanisms, contexts, and outcomes – prefigure a *division and hierarchy of expertise* across the stakeholders in a program. This presents the researcher with the opportunity for a careful mapping of 'who knows what' as the organizing framework to data collection. We then present formally our model of the realistic interview, introducing its two key strategies: the *teacher–learner function* and the *conceptual focusing* function. As per usual, the final section of the chapter is devoted to examples – in this case of interviews with program subjects (prisoners) and program practitioners (crime prevention workers).

Old antagonisms

The fact that 'talk is cheap' may have propelled researchers and evaluators galore into using the interview as *the* tool for data collection. Yet these artificial, unrehearsed encounters between strangers remain an enigma.

Thus, despite interviews possibly being *the* most inspected piece of social interaction, researchers remain at loggerheads on how to harness the flow of information that emerges from these dialogues. We refer, once again, to the battle lines between 'structured' and 'unstructured' interviewing and, as a preface to attempting to transcend this distinction, we reduce a few decades of argumentation between the two to the following couple of paragraphs and diagrams.

Figure 6.1 represents the flow of information in the more formal, structured approaches. The subject's ideas and the subject matter of investigation are one and the same thing. The rationale is to provide a simple, neutral stimulus in order to tap the true 'responses' or true 'values' of individual subjects. The usage of an identical stimulus and set responses with all subjects is said to allow for proper comparison to be made across the entire field of potential viewpoints. The researcher begins with a theory of the information (variables) required from the subject; these are then operationalized into set questions and response categories; respondents answer by saying which of the categories applies to them; and finally responses are analysed to gain an overall picture of the population studied. Critics of such an approach stress that, contrary to the stated aims of the strategy, the researcher's conceptual system is *imposed* wholesale upon the flow of information. The subject's response is limited entirely to a set of

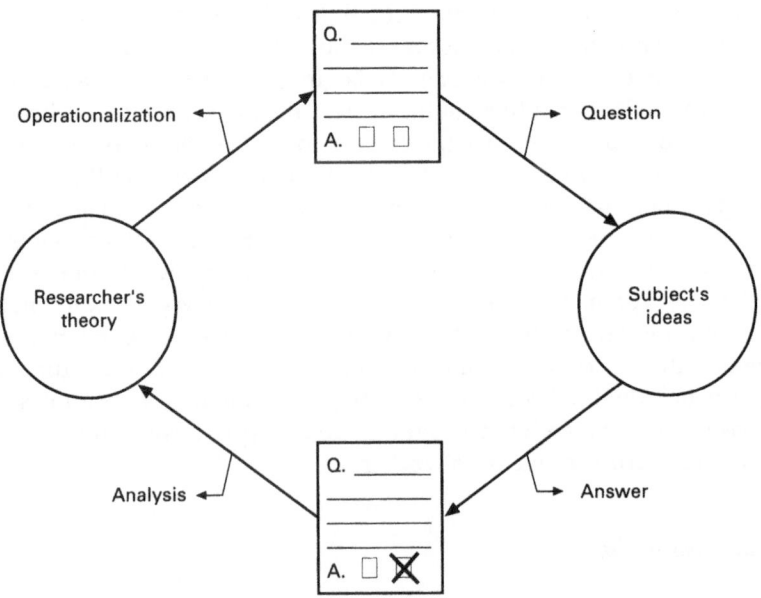

Figure 6.1   *The structured interview*

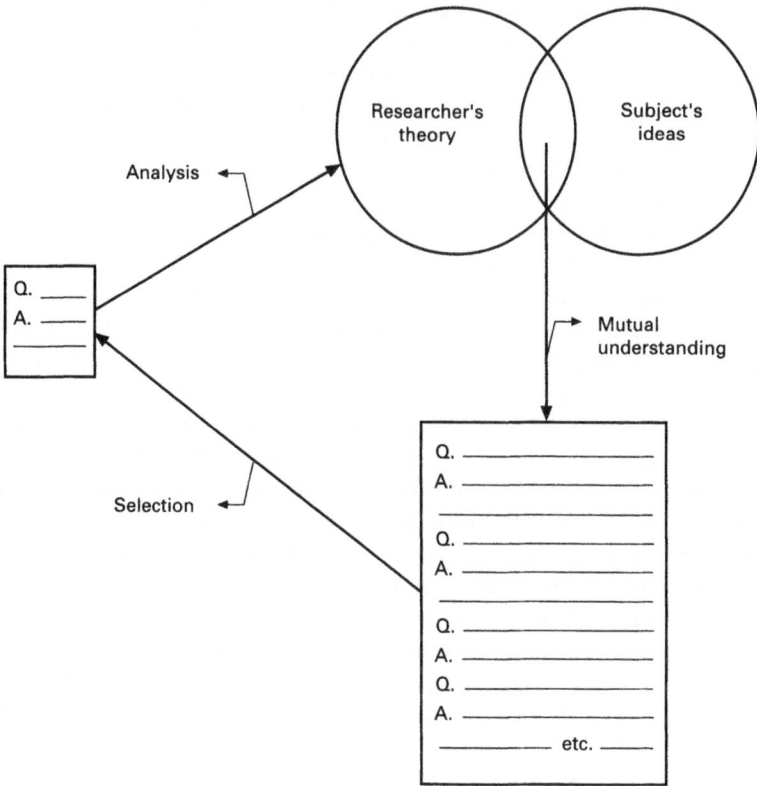

Figure 6.2 *The unstructured interview*

operational fragments. Set questions and predetermined response categories offer little opportunity to question, or even understand, the researcher's theoretical framework, with the result that the subject's own ideas may be misunderstood.

Figure 6.2 represents the flow of information in the unstructured (qualitative) interview. The subject's ideas and the subject matter of investigation are one and the same thing. Data collection has the task of creating a conversational setting in which the information provided is faithful to the frame of reference of the respondent. The investigator offers minimal steerage of the research topics within broad areas of discussion as they seem appropriate to each respondent. The idea is that mutual understanding emerges via the in-depth exchange of ideas. The researcher then selects out for report those extracts from the total dialogue which most thoroughly crystallize the perspective of the subject. Analysis then consists of a descriptive narrative of the key world-views. Critics of such an approach stress that the information collected in such a situation is diverse and discursive and thus hard to compare from respondent to respondent. Researchers are accused of *selecting* from this massive flow of information and thus fitting together small fragments of the respondents' utterances into their own preferred explanatory framework. Whilst the data are supposed to emerge in 'mutual' understanding, the researcher's theory is never clearly on view to the subject, and only shows its face after the event in the research report.

This particular opposition has proven more dogged and less prone to settlement than any other domain in the technical repertoire of social science. The reason, of course, is that the two data collection styles are emblematic of broader methodological antagonisms. 'Positivism versus phenomenology' starts here. 'Quantitative versus qualitative' takes its meaning here. It would be tedious to rehearse any further these old methodological squabbles. Realism as a philosophy of science has been deliberately constructed to stand *between* the poles of positivism and relativism. This book is committed, therefore, to the view that, whilst programs comprise the multifarious thoughts and deeds of a variety of stakeholders, evaluators can find objective ways of choosing between rival accounts. We take the view, moreover, that usage of a particular data collection strategy does not commit the researcher wholesale to a particular explanatory package, so that it is possible to be empirical without being empiricist, and so that one can examine subjectivities without being subjectivist. In short, at the practical level, realism is dedicated to some form of pluralist empirical inquiry.

The real task is to say what sort of pluralism. Here we would distinguish between pluralism as *toolkit hauling* – a commitment to more comprehensive, all-inclusive methods of inquiry, versus pluralism as *toolkit selecting*, a commitment to marrying the appropriate method to the appropriate research task. For us, too much recent methodological advice has been of the former kind. Most good evaluations end up needing to look at outcomes and processes. It is not sufficient to offer the pragmatic suggestion that such inquiry should use some 'combination' of structured and unstructured data collection methods. 'Combination' can mean all things to all researchers. It could be understood as an injunction to deliver every research issue in the form of items in a semi-structured interview or, conversely, to mount a tick-box questionnaire alongside a series of informal conversations. 'Combination' could quite as easily involve conjoining the faults instead of the virtues of the standard methods: recall from the instant summary above that both methods are accused of imposing a framework onto the information extracted. 'Combination' can invite the collection of a surfeit of different types of information – quite possibly telling tales which simply talk past each other. In short, the combination of qualitative and quantitative data should offer something more than 'weight of evidence' but also should invite a sense of explanatory 'completeness', 'synthesis' or 'closure'.

It is a similar tale when it comes to some of the pragmatic pluralist expectations about 'who' to question. It has become rather fashionable to generate long-as-your-arm lists of potential stakeholders to an evaluation in the expectation that the data collection should be democratically orga-nized to represent all views (Guba and Lincoln, 1989; Joint Committee on Standards for Educational Evaluation, 1994). Without any sense of priori-ties, without the notion that there is a division of expertise (and, therefore, inexpertise) on different aspects of a program, the call for pluralism as 'combination' is simply a further invitation for information overload.

What we are suggesting here is that pluralism for pluralism's sake offers no new suggestions for channelling information between researcher and respondent, no new strategy for collecting data, and indeed no new system for knowledge construction. What we are stuck with is just some arbitrary combination of the 'logics' depicted in Figures 6.1 and 6.2. Readers with prodigious memories will recall our frustration in attempting a diagram-matic representation of Rossi's notion of 'comprehensive evaluation' in Chapter 1. It is much the same with the pragmatic notion of data collection: one just does not know where to start.

Having leapt free of the paradigmatic chains and the clarion calls to the one true method, pluralist method finds itself bewildered with choices. The problem is that not only is 'methodolatry' (Bell and Newby, 1977) aban-doned, but a clear sense of explanatory objectives is often lost in consequence. As a result pragmatic pluralists have settled, *de facto*, for the objective that empirical research should be 'faithful to that which is being studied'. This sets the tone for a data-driven approach to inquiry and has colluded in making evaluation a fragmentary brew of case studies. This idea of 'letting the issue dictate the method' relies far too simply on the 'given-ness' of what is there. Goodness, we know enough about the theory laden-ness of observation by now to appreciate that theoretical considera-tions shape what we see. It is high time we looked again at the potential for an application of 'theory' to settle the issue by focusing and prioritizing inquiry. Only when we know what precisely it is that we are studying can we reach into the toolkit for the appropriate instrument.

Who knows what

We believe that data collection priorities are set within theory. And we repeat for emphasis the thesis of the chapter, namely that *the researcher's theory is the subject matter of the interview and the interviewee is there to confirm or falsify and, above all, to refine that theory*. To many this italicized statement will seem a curiosity, since theoretical considerations are seldom consid-ered to have such an immediate 'reach' into the world of data and the concerns of the subject. Nothing could be further from the truth.

The ingredients (mechanisms, contexts, and outcomes), propositions (mechanisms acting in contexts cause outcomes) and diagrammatic representations (rugby balls galore) of realist theory should be, by now, horribly familiar. What is new here is the idea that exactly the same building blocks can provide a fresh framework for thinking about data construction. Put into shorthand, our claim here is that realist theory provides a mightily useful launching pad of empirical inquiry, in that we develop priorities on the issue of 'what's to know?', which gives us immediate insight into the two key issues of data collection, namely 'who might know?' and 'how to ask?' The notions of 'mechanisms', 'contexts' and 'outcomes' foreshadow, of course, the complex range of evidence required by the evaluator. As we have seen through many examples to this point, understanding a program requires that evaluators are mindful of processes both macro and micro, influences from both the individual and the institution, and causal powers emanating from both reasoning and resources. Programs, in short, are complex social organizations. They thus have a division of labour, and this suggests something of great interest to the researcher, namely a potential *division of expertise*.

In this section we want to make a tentative mapping of 'who might be expected to know what about the program'. We will draw an initial distinction between the wisdom of *practitioners, subjects* and *evaluators*, leaving Chapter 8 to introduce the thoughts of another important group of stakeholders, the *policy makers*. We offer no pat formula in making suggestions with regard to the location of 'key informants' and the significance of their expertise. This will vary from program to program, as might be obvious if we compare subjects involved in a prison education program (for whom it might be their principal daily occupation) with participants in a neighbourhood watch scheme (who might not even register the existence of the scheme beyond the erection of the lamppost signs). *As a first approximation*, however, we can offer the following distinctions:

1 *Subjects* are likely to be far more sensitized to the mechanisms (*M*) in operation within a program than they are in relation to its contextual constraints (*C*) and outcome patterns (*O*). Programme mechanisms provide the reasons and resources which encourage participants to change and, as the persons on the receiving end of these processes, subjects are invariably in a good position to know whether they have been so encouraged. They are, however, likely to have a rather personal view of choices made and capacities changed within an initiative and so not be able to speak of fellow participants' encounters with program mechanisms. Similarly, their fixed position within a program will mean that their sensitivity to the influence of context will be greatly limited since the circumstances in which they encounter the program will be, for them, entirely routine. Subjects, of course, normally experience just one journey through a program and, therefore, may have little understanding of its outcome pattern which is an aggregate of thousands of such trajectories.

2 *Practitioners* translate program theories into practice and so are to be considered the great 'utility players' in the information game. They may well have adapted the initiative to try to get the best out of subjects, and so will have specific ideas on what it is within the program that works (*M*). They are also likely to have experienced successes and failures (*O*), and thus have some awareness of the people and places (*C*) for whom and in which the program works. What we cannot expect from them, however, is any systematic charting of the 'what works for whom in what circumstances' pathways (*CMO* configurations) associated with their project. The people and places they encounter are real, and the nature of the relationship with them will, literally, be a 'working' one. Working relations are highly personal and experienced practitioners work best by tailoring their efforts closely to the current personalities involved without necessarily anticipating the needs of the potential target population as a whole. Institutions are habit forming; actions become taken for granted, and may thus be chosen without an eye on the full range of program possibilities. Institutional goals tend to be immediate and local and set within moveable goal-posts. All of these factors inhibit the ability of practitioners to abstract and to typify and generalize their understanding of programs.

3 *Evaluators* draw on a quite different pool of knowledge. They carry theories into the encounter with programs. These theories may be embryonic or well developed, but (assuming that they are realistic) they start with a common explanatory blueprint. They begin with the expectation that the program will consist of a series of *CMO* configurations. Researchers will draw knowledge of the content of these 'what works for whom in what circumstances' hypotheses from their study of similar and previous programs, as well as from the more abstract propositions of social science theory. Such wisdom is likely to be stronger on form than content, and may lack the local detail of the type that practitioners and subjects can best supply. What is not lacking, however, is intelligence on where to find those details because, of course, the final element in the researcher's basic understanding of a program will be a sketch map of the division of expertise, precisely of the kind that is being spelled out on this page.

This division of expertise sets a clear task for data construction in evaluation, namely to enable a cross-fertilization between these different interpretative currents. Each of these stakeholders has something to teach the others and something to learn from the others. Before we spell out details of how to engage in 'teacher–learner' interviews, it is appropriate to remind ourselves of just how often we have already encountered this splicing together of 'knowledge profiles' by recalling a couple of characters and the lines of communication between them in evaluation studies already examined. Remember the prison education program researchers having a bit of theory development done for them when the 'mediocrity hypothesis' dropped from the lips of one of the program managers (Chapter 4)? It is worth adding that this pearl of wisdom was hard won amongst rambling anecdotal tales of how 'Earl took over the whole course if you'd let him, while Duke just sat there quiet as a mouse' (Earl was the recidivist, of course, and Duke was never seen again). In a similar manner, Foster and Hope's decision to evaluate the Priority Estates Project in terms of the social topography of town house, maisonette and tower block (Chapter 4) was, no doubt, closely informed by talk of how 'Of course, these young kids who's in here, I guarantee yer anybody under 20 living in one of these flats isn't working. Unfortunately, I'm not saying all young kids are bad, they're not, but it's out of that element that you get all the bother, not just with them but with the people who visit 'em. We had a kid move into [a particular flat]. The first day up there, there were 13 people laid on his landing just waiting for him to come home. This is what you're up against. There's too many of 'em it's physically impossible to shift 'em all . . . you're outnumbered' (Foster and Hope, 1993, p. 58, quoting caretaker for tower blocks on the Hull PEP estate). Knowledge collided in quite a different way (Chapter 5) when the Huddersfield police (on the look-out for ways of focusing effort where it counted) met Professor Pease (brimful of ideas about why repeat victimization was so prevalent).

This initial tour of the acuity of program subject, practitioner and researcher has been designed to highlight a set of different but complementary world-views. There is, however, a much more general point to be made about people's perspicacity with regard to their own choices and circumstances. This issue crops up frequently in discussions about the nature of social explanation and has come to be identified by Giddens's (1984) teeth-clenching phrase – 'the knowledgeability of the social actor'. His argument, with which we concur, is that people are always knowledgeable about the reasons for their conduct but in a way which can never carry total awareness of the entire set of structural conditions which prompt an action, or an appreciation of the full set of potential consequences of that action.

It is useful to consider the make-up of this self-understanding in terms of the basic building blocks of realist explanation. Thus we can posit of, say, prisoners that they have a rudimentary understanding of the standard outcome patterns (O) into which their lives are channelled – and thus know that the odds are stacked against going straight. They also understand something about the contribution of parts of their past culture (C) to their present predicament – and can point to the collusion in crime of family and friends (some of whom may now be wing-mates). Above all, in our experience, they will acknowledge the paramount influence of their own reasoning (M) – and so will own up cheerfully to that fact it was *their choice* to go in for a bit of thieving, then drugs and onto armed robbery and so on.

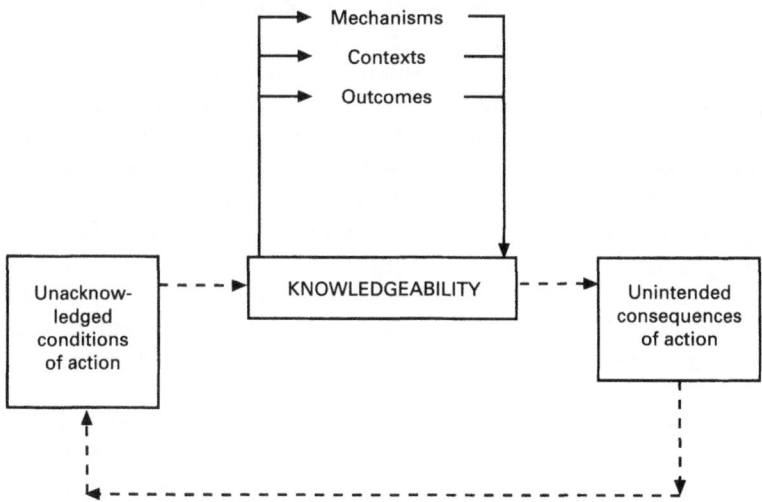

Figure 6.3   *Realism and the (partly) knowledgeable actor*

This, however, is not the whole story and if we think of the choices involved in taking part in a prison education program, there is a fringe of incompleteness in self-understanding which Giddens characterizes by the terms *unacknowledged conditions of action* and *unintended consequences of action*. For instance, prisoners may well enter the education block with a clear understanding of why it is a reasonable choice from the few opportunities available (others being industrial work, cleaning, lock-up etc.), without necessarily appreciating that certain of their background features (age, criminal history, previous education etc.) have made their candidature much more likely than that of many of their fellows. Nor will their multifarious reasons for trying education (sanctuary from the wings, escape from boredom, a good doss) necessarily correspond with the outcomes that may ensue (developing academic interests, making new friends, rehabilitation!). In attempting to construct explanation for the patterning of any activity the researcher is thus trying to develop *an understanding which includes hypotheses about their subjects' reasoning within a wider model of their causes and consequences.* This 'positioning' of the subject within social explanation is summarized in Figure 6.3, which borrows from Giddens (1984, p. 5).

This idea that all worthy citizens know where they are coming from and going to (*but not quite*) is simultaneously one of the most liberating and daunting propositions facing the social researcher. It requires us to construct not only a 'division of expertise' but a *hierarchy of expertise* with respect to the issues being investigated, and in so doing firmly places the researcher at the top of that hierarchy. Evaluation research has the task of getting a fix on the action and beliefs of each stakeholder within a wider model of their causes and consequences. This proposition, absolutely simple as it is to utter, utterly unremarkable as it looks, has huge practical implications for data collection. What it means is that whilst it is quite possible to analyse down the information required in an inquiry into its component parts (mechanisms, contexts, outcomes) and transform these into data collection instruments (questionnaire items, empathetic interviews, measures etc.) and to find informants appropriate to each item (practitioners, program subjects, auditors, demographers etc.), all of this evidence is actually feeding the investigation of much broader propositions. Thus the first test of any fragment of data is to demonstrate its salience to the theory under scrutiny.

For too long, researchers have been beguiled into worrying about the integrity of the data with respect to the data's immediate author – the research subject. The ultimate validity question, however, is *not* whether a ticked box is a true representation of a subject's attitudes, or whether some extended quotation of their words is faithful to their beliefs. The true test of data is whether they capture correctly those aspects of the subject's understanding which are relevant to the researcher's theory. This applies even in relation to those aspects of inquiry on which the subjects possess great expertise. To return to our example of those subjects with unrivalled time on their hands for self-contemplation, we can say that prisoners on education programs will know better than anyone in what ways and to what extent their reasoning and choices have been changed during the initiative. To this extent they are 'mechanism experts'. The research question being tested through them, however, will be about 'mechanism salience'. It will concern, for instance, whether such changes of mind will withstand the counter-pressures involved across a variety of post-release circumstances. And in this respect subjects will know *some* of the story. All this is tantamount to saying that researchers are '*CMO* configuration experts', because in explaining the impact of a program they will attempt to show how the partial views of all stakeholders are swept along in the broader currents depicted in Figure 6.3. On the realist model, data collection is thus charged – *not* with the descriptively infinite task of capturing the stakeholder's ideas, beliefs, hopes, aspirations about a program, but with the task of demonstrating which aspects of these beliefs are relevant to the *CMO* theory under test, so that the respondent can contribute to that test.

The realist(ic) interview

We begin our exposition of the conduct of the realist interview in Figure 6.4 with an initial model of the information flow between researcher and subject, incorporating the notions that the exchange of ideas is driven by the

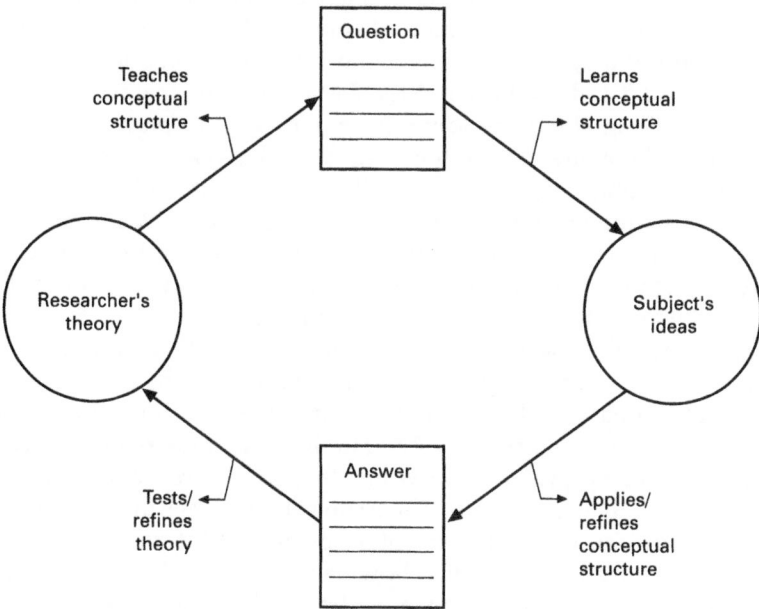

Figure 6.4   *Basic structure of the realist interview*

researcher's theory, that there is a division of expertise across the issues investigated, and that there is a hierarchy of expertise in respect to the overall workings of the program. We would, incidentally, also deem this approach 'realistic', in that we expect the respondents to be more than answering machines because they are (partly) knowledgeable, too, about several of the tricks of the interviewing trade.

By leading with theory, Figure 6.4 brings out two erstwhile hidden features of data collection, namely (i) the *teacher–learner function* and (ii) the *conceptual refinement process*. The former is depicted in terms of the 'northern' section of the information roundabout, the latter describes the return route to the 'south'. There will be greater or lesser emphasis on one or other of the two features according to which aspect of the realist theory is being explored and the state of development of that theory. Before we get onto such variations on a theme, it is appropriate to establish the main differences between this model and the current interview orthodoxy.

The information highway on our model remains the orthodox 'researcher asks the questions, subject answers them' sequence, as can be seen from the outward resemblance between Figures 6.1 and 6.4. We must not, however, be beguiled by this similarity. The most common interviewing experience is that if one puts a straight question, then most of the time one gets a straight answer. This little miracle happens routinely because researcher and subject will commonly share a taken-for-granted set of conceptual building blocks. We enter all conversations with a readiness to make sense and indeed social interaction is premised on this realm of the *accepted-as-real* (Giddens, 1984, p. 331). The assumption that we will (eventually) be talking about the same thing allows us to plunge on with a conversation knowing that for the purposes at hand a common terminology will be established, anomalies will be sorted out, and a background network of shared meanings can be called upon (Sacks, 1972). This everyday familiarity with conversational practice is in fact a double-edged sword for the researcher. It will always make an interview happen, but not always allow for the apposite data to be constructed.

This is where the *teacher–learner function* comes in. We are interested initially here in concepts which have a well-established place in the researcher's theory and for which we are collecting information in a theory testing role. In terms of more familiar interview parlance, we are discussing 'factual questions' in which the subjects reply by describing some aspect of their behaviour. The issue is to consider the nature of the flow of understanding between interviewer and interviewee or, once again in more traditional terms, how can we know that the subject is attending to the researcher's understanding of the issues in question? The traditional (structured interview) answer to this problem is to rely on precision in question wording and clarity in operationalization. Questions are asked in the simplest possible form which nevertheless remains faithful to the concept under investigation. To this end, the major effort of this school can be summarized in the oft stated goals that questions should be clear, precise, unambiguous, intelligible and *not* leading, compound, hypothetical, embarrassing, memory defeating and so on (Schuman and Presser, 1981).

The problem with the structured approach is that all these various goals and ambitions are sought variable by variable, question by question. Here we arrive at the crux of the matter. Our basic objection is that, whilst the precise turn of phrase will always be important in the conduct of an interview, operational definitions alone are rarely sufficient to orient the subject to the underlying research tack. In reducing the inquiry to variables and values on variables, they, in fact, construct meaning in a way contrary to the way theory will have been devised. Theory has a complex and deep structure which we have described in Chapter 3 and summarized with the *CMO* rugby ball. The researcher will have come to learn the meaning of any individual concept therein, through its place in the realist propositional net. So whilst interviewers should know full well the nature of the hypotheses embedded in any particular question, interviewees can remain blithely unaware, or indeed be deliberately kept in the dark, in respect of these purposes and meanings. For instance in a local crime prevention evaluation, respondents are often asked to respond, before and after the initiative, to the same bald set of questions about their behaviour towards neighbours, police, security and so forth, without any direct reference being made to the way the initiative impacted on their behaviour.

Usually it is the case that much of this 'collateral information' on the ideas of the researcher is smuggled in rather implicitly across the pages of the questionnaire. What we are suggesting here is that the researcher/interviewer should play a much more active role in *teaching* the overall conceptual structure of the investigation to the subject. In practice this involves paying far more attention to 'explanatory passages', to 'sectional' and 'linking' narratives, to 'flow paths' and answer 'sequences', to 'repeated' and 'checking questions' (for details see Pawson, 1989, Chapter 10). The researcher's theory will have been constructed in terms of 'what bit of a program works best for which subjects in what circumstances' and its meaning is best conveyed to the respondent in this manner.

As every interviewer knows, respondents always want to know far more than is conveyed in the formal structure of the questions and already routinely trawl for such snippets of collateral information about an inquiry. So, as well as providing straight answers to straight questions, subjects also ponder (mostly in silence): 'who is this person?', 'what is she after?', 'why am I being asked?', 'what should I be saying?', 'what have others said?', and indeed, 'will I be asked the same question again when the initiative is over?' The realist model has a unique tack on such 'hypothesis seeking' behaviour. The aim is not to try to *minimize* it (as in the structured approach), or to try to *avoid* it (as in the unstructured approach), but to *channel* it. We can summarize this first key objective of the realist interview by saying that the battery of questions posed and explanatory cues offered should be understood as putting the subject in a position which allows them to think (still in silence, incidentally):

'Yes, I understand the general theoretical ground you are exploring, this makes your concepts clear to me, and applying them to me gives the following answer . . .'

A further adaptation of the standard interviewing techniques is needed in respect of those aspects of realist explanation to which interviewees have privileged access, namely their own thought processes. In conventional terms, the interviewer's choice here is basically between questions posed as attitude scales and conversational prompts designed to encourage the respondents to explicate their own 'definition of a situation'. In realist terms, this is where the *conceptual refinement function* comes in. Such a process is intended to describe the logic of collecting data in respect of program mechanisms (M) and, in particular, to supply a formula for investigating how subjects make choices in relation to a program. The process is depicted in terms of the return leg to the outward formal question in Figure 6.4. This is the moment in the interview in which the respondents get the opportunity to have their own say (decidedly out loud) about the choices on offer within a program.

The key point is that on the conceptual refinement strategy, respondents deliver their thoughts on their own thinking in the context of, and (perhaps) as a correction to, the researcher's own theory. To explain: the overall structure of the researcher's questions will in general terms mark out the area in which the subjects will make decisions, as well as highlighting what some of the crucial choices and preferences might be. The subjects' task is to agree, disagree and categorize themselves in relation to the preferences and attitudes as construed in such questions *but also* to refine their conceptual base. In short, we are postulating a formula for 'attitude' questions (more properly, items in the cognitive and affective domains generally) in which respondents are offered a formal description of their own thinking *followed by* an opportunity to explain and clarify that thinking.

Again it is useful to try to explain these aims in relation to shortcomings of some of the standard interviewing tools. The first difficulty will be well known to anyone who has confronted some of the standard batteries of attitude scales and personality inventories. The task is usually along the lines of strongly agreeing, agreeing, don't knowing, disagreeing, strongly disagreeing in relation to a statement like, 'I can control my problems only if I have outside support' (aficionados will recognize an item from the 'locus of control' scale). Such questions often have respondents screaming inwardly for *context*, under the argument that their answer might be somewhat different if the 'problem' in question is a broken car or a broken heart. Perversely, the same reaction is also quite evident in unstructured interviews in which respondents are invited to tackle a subject from their 'own perspective'. Veterans of this approach will recognize the tension involved in being asked to talk about *oneself* whilst clearly being the subject of *someone else's* inquiry. Little cries for contextual help are continually evoked in terms of, 'am I along the right lines here?', 'you wouldn't want to know about that, would you?', or indeed, 'is this the kind of stuff you want?'

The basic idea of the conceptual refinement function is to avoid such difficulties by carefully contextualizing the domain in which subjects reflect on their own thinking. This state of affairs is the real condition for *mutual understanding* to emerge. To repeat, realist explanations offer hypotheses about their subjects' reasoning *within* a wider model of their causes and consequences, and the attraction of this particular interviewing strategy is that it reflects a practical division of labour which is best able to put these pieces together. The key once again is the placement of subjects in relation to the lines of investigation, and we attempt to summarize their position with a rather different thought bubble created in the respondent's mind:

> 'This is how you have depicted the potential structure of my think-
> ing, but in my experience of those circumstances, it happened like
> this. . . .'

Into action and into words

Examples are overdue at this point and are about to be delivered. Firstly,
we should point out that the above model of the realist interview is not
meant to imply the existence of some singular and unique technique which
captures the idea. The previous sections present a set of priorities, some
key functions, and above all a 'logic' for the interview. The 'I'll show you
my theory if you'll show me yours' strategy has echoes in a number of
existing methods. Two that come instantly to mind are *vignettes* (in which
the stimulus stories are constructed to smuggle in the key theoretical para-
meters under investigation, upon which the respondent is asked to reflect)
and *pilot interviews* (which say – answer these questions and please also tell
me what you think of them). The actual form of the interview will thus
depend on the precise stage of theory development or testing which
inquiry has reached. As a sample of this range, we present two examples.
In the first, we have a partially developed theory of how a program works
and the task of the interview is to refine that theory by teasing out more
detail from the participants on how their reasoning was influenced. In the
second, we discuss the development of the program itself, and so the task
is to extract from the diverse, rough and ready ideas of practitioners a set
of reasoned priorities with respect to which mechanisms should be fired in
which contexts to produce the anticipated outcomes.

Dons and cons

Our first illustration comes from some interviewing that one of us
(Pawson) did on a small scale prison education project at HMP Full Sutton,
UK. This research also acted as an exploratory exercise aimed at devising
a robust method for obtaining inmates' interpretations of educational initiatives and so acted as a pilot for the Canadian prison program
evaluations described in Chapter 4. Readers awaiting the completion of an
account of phase 3 of the design of the Simon Fraser evaluation will find
the method described here.

Towards the end of the studies of the first cohort of men through the Full
Sutton course, Pawson made an attempt to draw an overall picture of the
men's accounts about how (if at all) the course had changed their attitudes, reasoning, outlook etc. There were, of course, no standard
questionnaires, personality inventories or attitude scales ready-made for

such a specific purpose, so one had to be invented. A diverse set of data collection instruments was piloted but by far the most progress was obtained with a modification of a 'discussion document' produced by a prison service regional education officer which took as its task to list and elaborate upon the potential 'aims and objectives' of the prison education service. The adaptation took the form of rewriting each statement of aspiration contained in the document, so that it became a sort of attitude rating questionnaire to which the prisoners could agree/disagree and so forth.

As a research instrument, this could certainly be improved upon. It omits some entire categories of potential change and in the Canadian version of the study there is a much more comprehensive attack on this problem. However, the example does have the basic methodological features alluded to here. The original document was written by an 'insider' with an eye on encouraging penal educators to look beyond getting offenders' bums on classroom seats and their names on examination certificates. Thus it relates the classroom experience to broader concerns about prison and after, and indicates some potential pathways to rehabilitation. It contains (and this is the important bit) the accumulated wisdom of practitioners on a range of personal developments which might be associated with educational programs in prisons. In short, and using the language developed earlier, we can say that the items represent the then current stage of the researcher's theories and the immediate task in interviewing was to 'teach' this conceptual structure. This was done by making clear to the respondents that *they* were being asked to reflect upon and respond to a series of statements which *others* had made about the education of offenders. A little sub-plot here is that given its origins, which were made known to subjects, there was a 'whiff' of the Home Office about the construction of the items. This added a little spice when it came to getting the men to complete and comment upon the questionnaire.

The actual form of questionnaire was as in Figure 6.5. The students were presented with a list of statements representing possible goals of a prison education course and they were asked to respond to each item according to how the statement applied to their experience of the Full Sutton course. They were required to place answers in one of four categories as shown.

Rather a lot can be learned by the simple device of *ordering* the responses from those features which the men found most consistent with their own experience down to those which they considered inapplicable. As ever in data analysis, it is the patterns of response we are seeking to uncover and this can be aided by the device of superimposing some breaks and boundaries within this rank order. In Figure 6.6, we distinguish those objectives which collectively met with (i) considerable to modest agreement, (ii) moderate to slight agreement and (iii) slight to no agreement. We also insert a mid-point axis (score 2.5) which can help us see the general balance of sentiments.

This applies to me . . .

to a considerable extent	1
to a moderate extent	2
to a slight extent	3
not at all	4

There follows a list of the statements and for each we record the mean response score using the scale as above.

The course:

Mean response

(a) helps inmates to accept themselves and their feelings more fully   `3.4`

(b) helps inmates to become more self-confident and self-directing   `2.4`

(c) helps inmates to become more acceptable persons to society   `3.1`

(d) helps inmates to accept more realistic goals for themselves   `2.5`

(e) helps to change the moral outlook of the inmates   `3.1`

(f) helps inmates to become more flexible in their opinions   `2.0`

(g) helps inmates to behave in a mature fashion   `2.8`

(h) helps inmates to change their maladjustive behaviours   `2.8`

(i) helps inmates to become more acceptant of others and of other points of view   `2.2`

(j) helps inmates to reject their criminal past   `4.0`

(k) helps inmates to assume responsibility for their own lives   `3.4`

(l) helps inmates improve their power of concentration and persistence   `1.8`

(m) helps inmates to discern previously undiscovered talents   `2.0`

(n) helps inmates to correct their personality characteristics in constructive ways   `2.8`

(o) helps inmates to experience success   `2.2`

(p) helps to provide a basis on which inmates can build a new life   `2.6`

(q) helps inmates to achieve control over their actions and choices   `2.6`

Figure 6.5   *Questionnaire as conceptual structure*

1–2

Considerable to moderate agreement:

'improve powers of concentration and persistence'
'become more flexible in opinions'
'discern previously undiscovered talents'

2–3

Moderate to slight agreement:

'experience success'
'acceptant of others and other points of view'
'self-confident and self-directing'
'accept more realistic goals' ————————————— (2.5)
'behave in a more mature fashion'
'correct personality characteristics in constructive ways'
'change their maladjustive behaviours'

3–4

Slight to no agreement:

'more acceptable persons to society'
'change moral outlook'
'accept themselves and their feeling more fully'
'assume responsibility for their own lives'
'reject their criminal past'

Figure 6.6   *Data outcome pattern*

It is possible to make some rough and ready sense of the above configuration by seeking to uncover the 'themes' which underlie the difference
between those aspirations with which the men concur and those of which
they are sceptical. It can be seen readily enough that the items with which
the men concur concern the improvement in 'mental powers', 'learning
skills', 'flexibility of viewpoints' and so on. In short, the connecting thread
here is a recognition of personal change along a dimension that perhaps
speaks for itself – namely *academic-related change*. The roots of scepticism
about the transformative capacity of education seem more diverse. There
would seem to be (at least) two distinctive features which underlie doubt.
The first is when the items refer to *public acceptability*. The thinking here,
presumably, is that all prisoners know they are no longer free agents,
expect a tough reception on release and do not expect things will be dramatically different, with or without a diploma. The second dimension
which the inmates declare untouched by their presence in the academy can
be thought of as items pertaining to *personal character*, especially those
statements getting at their inner self and most specifically, of course, the
only item on which there was unanimity, namely item (j) and its insinua-
tion that education allows them to reject their criminal past.

What we have to this point is an unremarkable, not to say undistin-
guished, piece of attitudinal scaling which produces, incidentally, some

rather unwelcome results – there being only the faintest whiff of 'rehabilitation' in all these data. Orthodox methodological thinking divides habitually at this point. The quantitative instinct would be to get more formal: the pilot items could be beefed up, a proper factor analysis could be attempted, and a rather larger sample could be constructed (have we mentioned that the above data are culled from seven inmates?) The qualitative instinct would be to ditch the lot as arbitrary number-crunching and to go for personal involvement as the high road to understanding personal change.

It is possible to escape these weary old methodological strait-jackets by considering more closely the men's reasoning in response to being presented with this battery of propositions. Pawson can still recall vividly, two years on, the Full Sutton students' outward reaction to this exercise. They moaned, they groaned; a couple of them were on the point of refusing to complete the task at all (until threatened with the alternative of yet more lectures on the founding fathers of sociology!). The roots of this discomfort were exactly the same as most people feel when they are asked to complete such exercises, but in this case magnified several times. That is to say, attitudinal statements are normally regarded as irritating simplifications and only with some generosity can one reduce the richness of life's experiences down to the pre-set categories. In this particular instance, some of the simplifications were regarded as more than mere irritations: they were seen as positively insulting (in certain respects which we will come to in a moment).

The methodological point that shines through this, however, is that the questions perform a much more significant function than as the specific *stimuli* to respective *responses*. Neither are they an *invitation* for respondents to muse on whatever aspects of their experience are central to them. Taken as a piece, these formal questions set a clear agenda which represents a body of theory, offering up the researcher's potential explanations for a closely circumscribed set of actions. Their key role, therefore, should be to involve the respondent in a closer articulation and clarification of these theories. This can be done (and was done in this instance) by the simple device of getting the respondents to explain *why* they have plumped for the particular responses to the particular items. This is a commonplace enough tactic in semi-structured interviewing, but one that is never understood in the way which we are presenting it here, namely as a superb vehicle for the 'here's my theory, what's yours?' strategy of data collection. What is induced by this process is a great deal of conceptual hair-splitting and this is precisely the kind of data which lead to better focused explanation.

Let us look more closely at a couple of examples of this process at work. Question (j) about inmates rejecting their criminal pasts because of contact with education got short shrift, yet the subsequent account of *why* the statement is disregarded prompts the inmates into a much more subtle level of reflection on their own reasoning. The following extracts give the accounts of four men on why they registered 'not at all' in answer to this question. As always, transcripts fail to give the underlying 'mood' of the answer, which might be summarized helpfully here as 'furious', 'imperious', 'cool', 'cooler', respectively.

> But to *reject* your criminal past, I'm not rejecting it. I'm not rejecting what I've done, but you don't reject it do you, you . . . you take and you . . . you step on from there and you try and learn from it. You don't go, well you don't know. It's a part of . . . its a part of you.

> I know why overall I've scored so low it's because it's I . . . I . . . I do have this thing umm . . . about personal responsibility, you know I . . . I acknowledge that I'm in prison through my own fault, and umm . . . if I'm going to stop coming into prison it will be down to my own motivation.

> I mean it's [the question] assuming that it [the course] is gonna change somebody's whole outlook on life and behaviour and everything. I don't relate to it, don't relate to it at all. I mean I can see that the more educated you are the more you can get away I suppose. But I don't connect with it at all.

> In my case, when I commit a crime I know I'm doing wrong and I know if I'm going to get caught, I'll go to prison. So it's not as though I'm *rejecting* it.

A similar theme emerges in relation to the question of whether education can help inmates to accept 'themselves and their feelings more fully' (question (a)):

> I feel that I accepted myself and my feelings before I came onto the course, before I knew of the existence of the course.

> I fully accepted my feelings a long time before I came here.

> I agree that this course and education still could really help those people who don't really understand yourself [themselves]. Firstly I understand myself and I don't really see that [the course] leading me in to that direction. Really [this] is one thing I have to discover myself.

What even these few clarifications reveal is a tension in most of these prisoners' beliefs about education. It is recognized as 'improving' and yet they want to take credit for the improvement. They 'learn' but not as empty buckets filled with knowledge against their better judgement. It is recognized that education can lead to self-understanding but only because prison conditions are already conducive to intense self-reflection, since they provide many hours, days and years of opportunity for the same.

This tension was perhaps best expressed by 'Brendan McNally', the prisoner who was most hostile to this particular phase of the research because he felt the questions were 'patronizing' and were full of 'civil service rhetoric'. He set out to swat down their 'preconceived ideas' with an almost complete series of scores at level 4 (statements apply 'not at all') in his written responses. Under follow-up questioning, he relents a little and finds that he was 'making a nonsense of some of his own scoring.' Basically he backtracks:

> I will go down the road of agreeing, because, err . . . I feel that education is a civ-ilizing process . . . it could well prove a contributing factor in the adjustment to acceptable behaviour. Change is something that comes within but you would be taking on board education . . . it's a catalyst . . . more than a catalyst, as I've said before, it's a civilizing process.

Here is another man choosing his words carefully and, being an educated sort, he does indeed know his 'catalysts' from his 'contributing factors'. Actually, the most telling phrase he uses here is probably 'taking on board education' and this is an image which comes through most strongly in all of the men's discussion. *If we take as the starting point that many prisoners rou-tinely engage in self-scrutiny and choice making then what a rigorous period of education can perhaps provide is a means of extending, deepening and affirming such processes.* Or to put this back into prison parlance:

> It's not the course that's changed you as such, it's you've developed an interest inside you, you know.

> By and large you've got your own . . . you've got your own way of working . . . and you can work in a number of directions . . . you're sort of given advice on which way to go and that, but at the end of the day it's your choice.

The sprinkling of metaphors in the above on 'interests inside you', 'taking on board education', 'step on from there' contains important messages about the importance and nature of cognitive change as a potential mech-anism for rehabilitation. The upshots of such reasoning are being explored in the research to come. Here we should return to the general method-ological significance of this tale. We readily admit that the example came unfortunately *before* the rationale we are in the process of relating. It was indeed formative in the development of the approach. To the interviewer (Pawson) it came as a (minor methodological) eureka: after months of going round the houses, trading anecdotes about early educational expe-riences, the nature of crime, the likelihood of reoffence or rehabilitation, the influence of family, peers, teachers, Uncle Tom Cobbleigh and all, this simple formal schedule did the trick. Because it instigates a simple teacher–learner relationship into the act of data collection, all at once sub-jects are able to focus words about *their* world into the *researcher's* language.

Doing the business

A second example describes interviews conducted as part of an ongoing evaluation of a program attempting to reduce crime against small businesses in two areas in a city in the UK midlands. One element of that program is concerned with preventing reburglaries and the project leadership were familiar with the general ideas concerning repeat victimization (see Chapter 5). Moreover, a census of businesses undertaken in the project areas had revealed that their crime experience, including burglary, followed the familiar pattern, that is a heightened vulnerability to further crime following an incident, most particularly in the immediate term after that incident.

The practitioners had at their disposal a variety of burglary reduction measures, summarizable along a continuum from 'giving advice' to 'help with target hardening' to 'mobilizing attempts at detection'. They had also devised a system for scoring vulnerability to repeat victimization, since it was intended to target these different sets of responses to those deemed at low, medium or high risk of further burglary. The very idea of a targeted response is, of course, based on the realist canon that different program measures are appropriate for different subjects in different circumstances. This interview was based on the further assumption that, as they implemented this initiative, the practitioners would devise even more detailed 'folk theories' about what particular aspects of advice, target hardening and detection devices were salient to which aspects of the physical, social and cultural contexts in which the businesses operated. In short, the researchers were trying to elicit prototypical *CMR/CMO* theories. In line with the research design strategy outlined in Chapter 4, the plan is that these theories would identify hypotheses about 'within-program' differences which would then direct the data collection and analysis in the evaluation. The extracts shown below do not relate to the totality of folk theories used for assigning businesses to their respective risk levels, or to the full set of suppositions about how the various measures were expected to have their effects amongst differing businesses. For illustrative purposes, we limit discussion here to the pursuit of one sub-hypothesis, namely the decisions involved in implementing but one of the detection devices available – the 'autodialler'.

The interview followed a teacher–learner pattern. The interviewer teaches the subject – the practitioner – what the interview is designed to find out. The subject then teaches the interviewer the initiative's working theories concerning interventions to prevent repeat burglaries. The interviewer proceeds to formalize the theory for the subject who is then invited to comment upon and thus further refine that formalization. The interviewee is invited to present examples not as ends in themselves, but as a way of accessing and then making explicit forms of theory which may not have been fully articulated previously.

There follow four fragments from the interview transcript. In each, the right column explains what the realistic evaluator is doing in asking the questions and what they are making of the answers. Beneath each transcript is further text which explains in more general terms the contribution of the exchange to the teacher–learner and concept refinement functions. The respondents (R) are two members of the team whose particular responsibility lay with the burglary prevention work, with the final fragment coming from a more senior member of the team of practitioners. The interviewers (I) are Pawson and Tilley.

Transcript fragment A

	Significance for evaluator
I: We want you to tell us about your reasoning in deciding what to do to try to prevent reburglary. It is something peculiar in a way to work through your own reasoning, where I guess . . . I guess a lot of the time you are using hunches. We are asking you to speak your hunches out loud. This is not easy to do. And the best way to do it is through very concrete examples. So if you could recall a specific example?	The interviewer is explaining to the subject what is wanted from the interview and. suggesting discussion of examples as a vehicle for getting at it.

Fragment A, as the right-hand notes indicate, is the first shot at trying to establish a division of expertise within an interview. It simply indicates how an interviewer might begin to explain what is wanted from the interviewee, though in the abstract terms here it is probably not immediately understandable by all and it may take several stabs to convince that such everyday reasoning is the crux of the interview. Interviewees are invited to discuss their thinking through examples, partly because it is through these that detailed *CMO* configurations are most likely to emerge, partly because respondents often find it easier to develop their description of their thinking with examples, and partly because if the respondent is missing the point of the interview, it is relatively easy to get it on track with questions asked about an example.

Transcript fragment B

	Significance for evaluator
I: Can you just recall a 'high-risker'. What action you have decided on the basis of the assessment. Any example will do.	Interviewer makes further bid for an example and goes into 'learning mode'.
R: I visited yesterday a multi-occupied building yesterday. Entry had been gained via a flat roof of an adjoining property into a window and a fairly messy burglary had taken place. They'd obviously come with a crowbar and forced their way into the other three or four businesses that occupied that one building. They had also been very successful. They've only really got one good point of entry. The rest of the entries were fairly well covered with the old-fashioned really solid doors. Because there was only the one point of entry, you	Interviewer learns about measure to be adopted, and that the physical context has to be right for it. Elicits a 'technical answer' which leaves unspoken the mechanisms through which it will work, which leads the interviewer to . . .

could feasibly cover that with one of these
autodiallers which trips to noise and then offers
an audio verification channel for about 45
seconds. It would not take long for
somebody to break into that, trip it off and
for somebody listening in to pick it up very
quickly.

I: You will have to explain, I don't know   prompt for more
anything about these.   detail.

R: What it is is a cheap adaptation of an   Detailed explanation
answerphone. You leave a message on this   elicited of how the
answerphone device if you like, what it will   mechanism will be
do is work in reverse. It will dial out to a   triggered and will
number. You leave your answerphone or   then activate
message saying 'this is 23 Smith Lane.' The   response producing
alarm has now been tripped. It's actually got   an outcome giving
a sound-sensitive device in it when the sound   a greater chance
goes, over a certain threshold. 'The alarm has   of burglar
now been tripped, can you please listen for   apprehension.
the next 45 seconds to establish whether
there is an on-going break-in or burglary.'
This wouldn't be heard withinthe room. This
would go straight down the line and I'm trying
to get the police to buy into this. At last we are
getting some success, I think. They would
then be able to say 'yes there is a burglar on
the premises.' It gives them a level of audio
verification, they can listen into that room for
up to 45 seconds. Then if it really is an ongoing burglary the police will obviously give
it a grade 1 [immediate] response and attend
the scene and hopefully catch someone.

In fragment B, having been assured that his detailed everyday knowledge
really is the issue, the respondent launches into an example of a high risk-
business, and begins to explain why an 'autodialler would be appropriate'.
He describes one aspect of the physical context which is needed: a single
entry point which can be covered adequately by a single sensor. He also
explains the mechanism through which this device is deemed more reli-
ably than others to enable the police to determine whether a quick
response is liable to yield an arrest. An initial *CMO* configuration hypothesis is established.

Transcript fragment C

I: Are there any other characteristics of businesses which would tend to suggest to you that they might be good candidates or might not be good candidates?

Interviewer is asking about non-physical features of context, furnished by a business.

R: Very much so. The operating nature of the business. Obviously a bakery will have a completely different concept of working to a travel agency.

Respondent agrees in general terms that there are those features.

I: Why would that make any difference to the alarm system?

Prompt for detail.

R: It makes quite a huge difference to the alarm system. One guy said that he finds the problem with it is that he is running his business and he goes home at six o'clock and he rings up the police and says 'you can now set the alarm in my office because I've gone home', the police will do so and then if he wants to go back for something at seven o'clock it took him longer on the phone to get the police to work out which was his alarm and switch it off than it did to spend 2 minutes going in there. So eventually he didn't do that any more. He just had to make sure that when he left at six or whatever time it was, he was finished before he rang up and told the police. So you've got to be sensitive to the actual operational style of the business and I think sensitive to the management style as well. I think people who are looking for me to solve their crime problem are people I'm going to be very wary of. People who are aboard with what the initiative is trying to achieve and accept the fact that there might be a little bit of difficulty in . . . they are the ones I'm going to try and work towards.

Specification of some business habit and business orientation features of context needed for autodialler device successfully to be implemented to trigger mechanisms to produce preferred outcome patterns. The first contextual feature is specific to autodiallers, and the second is more generic for the implementation of crime prevention measures.

I: Just talk us through that in a bit more detail.

Prompt for detail.

R: I don't want to get tied down in detail at that stage. It's one of the things I've been thinking about while we've been going round doing dry runs without explaining to people who I am and what I'm doing.

Interviewers scent implicit theory and try further encouraging noises . . .

I: That's exactly what we are trying to tease out. Any other things you can think of that would make you think that autodiallers would be more effective in this business rather than this one.

. . . via a broader prompt

> *R*: There are certain management styles that I think would be prone to we saying that we are the initiative and we are trying to do this and you are in agreement. Because it will present problems for their operational style. . . . I don't know. It's too early to say. Bear in mind that this is a learning process.
>
> which only draws back the respondent to an earlier theme, at which point the interviewers move on.

In fragment C the interviewer prompts for other features of context that might be important in enabling the autodialler to be used to trigger rapid police presence and improved chances of an arrest. The respondent, by now accustomed to using examples, immediately describes some organizational contextual needs for the autodialler to be usable effectively to trigger its causal potential to bring the police quickly to apprehend the burglar, and so provide a further *CMO* configuration refinement. The extract also demonstrates the tendency for the program theories of the practitioner to lurk somewhat dormantly, and the corresponding need for the researchers to understand the need to explore across the 'learning processes' of a range of practitioners.

Transcript fragment D

Significance for evaluator

I: Are there any types of business which you think make them a good candidate for the autodialler?

Standard prompt for contextual condition.

R: Maybe they will be more effective in Scargrave.

Names one of the two chosen program areas.

I: Why?

Seeks theory.

R: We took advice from police in both areas. They thought we'd have a bigger effect in the Scargrave because a lot of burglaries use inside information, which staff pass on to associates who have a go at the premises. Because many businesses in the Scargrave are Asian family owned and operated it is less likely that information will be passed on deliberately or inadvertently. People wouldn't hear we'd put in these super-duper devices and be put off because this installation would give them away. If inside information is a big part in burglary and repeat burglary, less information gets to the outsider. If measures are put in place, burglars in Scargrave would not know they were there.

Respondent explains a conjectured economic/cultural condition for the autodiallers to be effective in triggering apprehension of offenders.

I: So, the burglaries are more likely to take place in Scargrave with the devices than in Midtown, because it is more probable that offenders will not know they are there and will not thereby be put off committing the offence, and if they do they are more likely to be able to evade the device?	Interviewer articulates the *CMO* configuration explicitly, inviting agreement.
R: Yes, the flip-side may well be the burglars aren't put off. As a last resort to catch burglars, however, the alarms may be more effective in Scargrave.	Respondent agrees and relates back to the general theory explaining use of autodiallers to catch burglars.

Finally, in fragment D, this time with the second respondent with wider responsibility for the initiative, we have a further and more sociological discussion of the contextual needs for the autodialler effectively to trigger the apprehension mechanism. Here, a theory of how burglars operate is given, and it is noted that they will operate rather differently in the two scheme target areas, since one area is predominantly Asian whilst the other is mostly white. Given the way Asian businesses are run – in particular the family involvement – scope for burglaries with the benefit of insider information is thought to be limited. Because of this they constitute a more promising context for autodialler effectiveness, since it is thought less likely that members of staff will leak information allowing the burglar to side-step detection either by avoid triggering the physical mechanism or by avoidance of the premises.

Each of these tiny fragments can be used to build testable *CMO* configurations. Collectively, they reveal how addressing an apparently simple problem using a straightforward physical measure involves a barrow-load of theory which needs to be understood if attention is appropriately to be directed to outcome patterns. Each suggests the collection of rather particular further data to inform an informative evaluation. Autodiallers, it is suggested, work best with 'single entry points', 'adjacent police', 'routinized work patterns', 'co-operative management styles' and 'close-knit staff structures'. In this instance, we omit discussion of how the evaluators are dealing with the perils of operationalization of such concepts, having discussed the issue in previous chapters!

Conclusion

In advocating the realist interview as an approach with general utility in data construction in evaluation research, we should make it clear that we are not simply putting some specific interviewing 'tricks' or 'techniques' up for inspection. The idea is not simply a matter of piling up a set of attitudinal statements and getting them explained as in the prison education example, or the process of painless tooth extraction described in the autodialler example. What we are actually counselling is the *information flow* as depicted in the model in Figure 6.4. Its key aspect is the creation of a situation in which the theoretical postulates and conceptual structures under investigation are open for inspection in a way that allows the respondent to make an informed and critical contribution to them. Much more could be said about when, why and for whom one would adopt and adapt the approach. Here we only need stress that the strategy involves a highly specific and carefully planned route march which goes between the quantitative and qualitative traditions.

This chapter has followed our basic methodological inclinations in that once again we declare ourselves 'conservative revolutionaries'. We have already concurred that the cycle of realistic evaluation conforms to the grand old wheel of science. We have acknowledged that realistic evaluation can utilize a range of research designs and so can be quantitative or qualitative, action- or outcome-oriented, contemporaneous or retroactive, and so on or so forth. We have already endorsed a conventional strategy for accumulating programming wisdom built around the idea of developing middle-range theory. What is innovative about our method, through all of these aspects of inquiry, is that knowledge acquisition is dominated by and organized around the development of realist propositions linking mechanisms, contexts and outcomes. And so it is with data collection. We still prefer the good old-fashioned way, with the researcher asking well-informed questions, placing the subject in a position to give even better-informed replies. All this comes to pass if research is organized around the development of *CMO* propositions.

7

NO SMOKING WITHOUT
FIRING MECHANISMS:
A 'REALISTIC' CONSULTATION

The following (fictional) dialogue is intended to demonstrate that the (realistic) arguments developed in this book are applicable beyond the criminal justice examples used so far in the text. Those who have followed us thus far will realize why competent and informative evaluations require a thorough understanding of the substantive fields in which evaluation studies are undertaken. The examples we have been using have been picked, therefore, to echo our own research experiences.

This chapter considers how a realistic approach could be applied to the evaluation of smoking cessation programs. In this instance, we make no pretence to full familiarity with the literature on health education. The chapter has, therefore, been given the form of a dialogue, to act as a piece of 'show and tell'. It shows how realistic evaluators, as they *learn* about smoking cessation research, can cast new light on intervention programs, and how that can lead to a distinctively different set of evaluation practices, which promise more useful findings.

We step forward to the year 2000. We present three protagonists who will introduce themselves. One of them holds views which we particularly admire. They are at their first meeting in a government health department.

Emma Bluestocking: Good morning, and thank you for coming. Let's begin with some introductions. I'm Emma Bluestocking, and I have policy responsibility for health promotion in the Department. Andrew, why don't you say what you do.

Dr Andrew Tissle: Hello. My name is Andrew Tissle. I'm a member of the Research Division, and part of my work includes the commissioning and oversight of evaluation studies in the health promotion field.

Professor Frank Candour: Well, I'm Frank Candour. I'm Professor of Evaluation Studies at Haleford. I'm here because you invited me to advise on a program of evaluations, but I don't have any details yet of what your problems are and of exactly what you want from me.

E.B.: OK. Let me put you in the picture. We are committed to reducing the level of smoking in this country. We want to cut the prevalence of smoking in men and women aged sixteen and over to no more than 20% in the next eight years, from the current levels of 31% and 28% respectively.[1] We clearly want to be as effective and economical as we can in achieving these reductions. We want to take advantage of existing research findings. We are intending also to fund a number of demonstration projects in the next two to three years to inform an effective program nation-wide. We are committed to the view that 'practices, interventions and integrated activity should be subject to rigorous and objective evaluation before widespread introduction.'[2] It is in that light that we're implementing the demonstration projects. We've asked you, Frank, to help us think through the evaluation needs of the work we are planning. I understand you're too busy actually to want to do any of the evaluation work yourself, and that suits us! You can act as an honest broker.

F.C.: Thanks, that's helpful. Smoking and its prevention is not the field in which I do evaluations myself, so even if I wasn't snowed under I wouldn't be your best bet. But I'm happy to advise on setting the evaluation agenda. I'm glad also to be asked at the outset: too often program evaluation is tacked on as an afterthought, when it's impossible to collect the data you really need. What do we know from previous research? That's always a good starting point.

A.T.: I should come in here. There have, of course, been masses of programs and a corresponding mass of evaluations. I'm reading myself in at the moment and to be honest it's hard to see the wood for the trees. Just to give you a clue – there are smoking prevention programs, smoking cessation programs, and relapse prevention programs. As to program content, you would not believe the diversity. There are public health programs: media campaigns, health warnings, self-help leaflets, information packs, education initiatives, task forces, community quitting contests, worksite bans, etc., etc. Then there are the more clinically based initiatives: face-to-face advice, counselling, therapy, acupuncture, nicotine gum and patches, sensory deprivation, coping skills training, craving management, hypnosis, etc., etc. Surrounding this is a mass of psychological testing and demographic research on who smokes and why. These lead to psychological profiles of 'psychosocial', 'indulgent', 'sensorimotor', 'stimulation', 'automatic', 'addictive' smokers and so forth. Then you've got the social and cultural contributions identifying the smoking rates within and between different social groups: sex, social class, age, race, education and so on.

F.C.: And what about the evaluations?

A.T.: Well this is 'medicine', so randomized controlled trials are, of course, favoured but increasingly other methods are gaining use.

F.C.: And the findings?

A.T.: Right now I'd have to say that a general sense of frustration comes over. First of all, I would say that results reported in smoking cessation trials vary widely and with little apparent consistency.[3] Then I note the very modest success of the blockbuster program and its evaluation.[4] And then I'm bemused by a rather problematic finding for those of us in public health which claims that most smokers quit on their own rather than in 'organised programs'.[5]

F.C.: Mmnnnn. Sounds like quite an agenda for us. Tell me about the 'Blockbuster'.

A.T.: The Americans have run a huge program. Their Year 2000 Cancer Control Objectives included a commitment to reduce the percentage of adults who smoke from 34% in 1983 to 15% or less, and of youths who smoke by age twenty from 36% to 15% or less. They have invested quite heavily in something called COMMIT, their community smoking intervention trial, spending some $45 million on the demonstration program in eleven cities. This began almost ten years ago, and is ongoing.

E.B.: We'd hoped for some useful pointers from COMMIT, for it was trying to do essentially what we are planning to do. But I'm afraid the evaluation conclusions make rather pessimistic reading. They don't help us decide what to do at all. They did not identify any pronounced effects.

F.C.: I thought Andrew said the program was ongoing. How have they changed it?

E.B.: They decided to continue with the program in 1991, before the evaluation findings became available. I gather they are spending even more money in even more states by way of follow-up.

F.C.: To something that produced no really positive finding?

E.B.: Afraid so. And that's one reason we are anxious to see if we can be a bit more effective in the program and in learning for future practice from its evaluation.

A.T.: The COMMIT program was evaluated very rigorously. It may, of course, just have been a weak program. But we would like at the end of our evaluation to be able to make some positive suggestions about ways of achieving reductions in smoking.

E.B.: And if that means adopting a different methodology we shall do so, provided, of course, we don't thereby sacrifice research standards.

F.C.: Tell me, then, a little more about COMMIT and its evaluation.

A.T.: A quasi-experimental evaluation was undertaken, using 22 communities (eleven experimental, eleven control) chosen to represent a cross-section of the US and Canada.[6] The communities were either small cities or well-defined portions of major metropolitan areas and each pair was chosen to be well matched on a range of variables: on population size as well as various sociodemographic factors including race/ethnicity, male/female ratio, age distribution, educational level, family income, mobility and migration patterns, extent of urbanization, number of worksites, estimated smoking prevalence rates and access to smoking intervention measures, age, gender, educational, social and religious background. A random sample was selected from each community to inform researchers of baseline smoking prevalence and to select cohorts of 'heavy smokers' (25 and more per day) and 'light-to-moderate-smokers' (less than 25 a day) to be tracked through the initiative. The intervention itself was delivered over four years through a community organization approach. So one had a virtual blitz of mandated activities, including public education programs, health care provision, worksite activities, cessation resources and networks (a total of 58 in all). The hypothesis was that by making it difficult to escape consistent and repeated messages about cessation, whilst simultaneously being provided with the opportunity to participate in cessation activities, smoking would be significantly reduced (especially amongst heavy smokers) in the intervention communities rather than in the controls.

F.C.: But Emma said the findings were disappointing?

A.T.: Yes, indeed. For the heavy smokers, the quit rate for all intervention and control communities was virtually identical, indeed with a minute advantage going to the communities without the intervention (0.180 versus 0.187). For the light to moderate smokers there was a small and just significant experimental-versus-control improvement (0.306 as opposed to 0.275) across all community pairs. Overall the intervention effect is not significant and the initiative as a totality comes in way below the policy targets.

F.C.: And that's that? What did they conclude?

A.T.: There's not much more. There is clearly huge disappointment all round. I think they are wondering if the initiative was too short and not intensive enough.[7] The project director concluded that, 'We have learned that with heavy smokers it may take something more to break their addiction.'[8] I think they're thinking about a more clinical approach again.

F.C.: What? Four years – too short? Fifty-eight initiatives – not intensive enough? I suppose they were a bit low on cash to make the thing work as well? I just don't believe this. Every program I have known has created some winners and losers. There must have been a community out of all that lot which made some progress. Which towns and cities were involved? Didn't the community variation shape the way interventions were received?

A.T.: The short answer to all your questions is that we don't know. The communities are named and profiled in the description of the research design,[9] but kept anonymous in the actual analysis.[10]

F.C.: Come again?

A.T.: In the presentation of the results, the comparison and quit rates are given for the experimental and control community in each matched pair, but each pair is designated by a number which doesn't correspond to the listing of actual community names given in other COMMIT publications.

F.C.: Come again?

E.B.: Don't sound so pious, Frank. You know there is always proper caution in naming names in this kind of enquiry.

A.T.: It doesn't matter anyway. The point is that each pair of communities is very well matched, and for the program to have an effect it needs to be shown to work across a broad range of them. So the COMMIT team are quite correct to look at the aggregate outcome.

F.C.: I'm afraid I couldn't disagree more, Andrew. Programs always work for certain subjects in certain situations and half the battle in evaluation is to find out *which*. I've done lots of work on community initiatives against crime. All of these communities have been different in their *appetite* for the initiatives. And if we are talking about small cities, there will likely be a difference in the reception given to the program *within* subsections of that community. My hunch is that there will have been plenty of variation in success rates as we move from COMMIT community pair to pair.

A.T.: Well yes, for the heavy smokers community pair 9 had a quit rate in the intervention at 0.215 as opposed to the control's 0.127. And then community pair 1 had the intervention achieving a quit rate of 0.139 against that of 0.205 for the control. Both are massively significant, but they receive no commentary in the analysis because they represent two ends of a continuum which cancels out in the round.[11]

F.C.: So the truth of the matter is that, far from being a program where not much happened, COMMIT triumphed in some places, flopped in others and didn't dawn in yet others. So there *is* a lot to be learned. Andrew, when you described the selection of towns you mentioned a list of fairly standard and readily measured attributes of cities and that the overall sample gave a good cross-section of these attributes. Was there any particular reason for picking these items as indicators of the local conditions in which the program was expected to work well?

A.T.: No. As far as I can tell the matching was done to ensure comparability using available data. There were not, I think, any particular reasons given for matching across *that set* of variables. The idea was simply to get equivalent experiment and control communities and to test whether the program worked across the cross-section.

F.C. One reason why there might have been such considerable differences in impact is because of real differences in communities. I take it, being a community-based initiative, that part of the way COMMIT was supposed to work was through a process of 'coming together', of 'networking', of 'joining forces' against a smoking threat. The chances of raising community spirit obviously depend on what kind of community we are dealing with in the first instance. The urban sociology of North America is not a speciality of mine, but applying the stereotypes, I guess that communities vary from 'the fenced enclave in which you drive to see the next-door neighbour if you happen to know them' to the 'teeming metropolitan suburb full of camaraderie and rivalry that comes from living cheek by jowl'.

E.B.: And what you are saying is that the particular COMMIT activities, such as 'magnet events' like the 'quit and win' contests, are going to constitute quite different attractions according to the existing community culture. Some communities will be far too lofty to engage in games and contests, whereas for others they may too busy contending with a range of more immediate life and death contests already.

F.C.: Exactly; if you use a magnet you need to point the north-seeking pole north. The kind of thing you really need from COMMIT is a knowledge of where dear old location 9 lies on the landscape of communities, so that you can learn about matching the action to the community. It doesn't appear that the outcome evaluation attended to the differences within and between communities. Was there any analysis of what the individual elements of the program did? I assume some kind of process analysis went on which actually monitored the implementation of the program?

A.T.: We are talking about a very big initiative here, so the whole thing was driven by a 'mobilization process', involving community boards, co-ordinators and resident task forces.[12] Control and co-ordination between the eleven sites was achieved via a master 'Smoking Control Plan' and a step-by-step 'Annual Action Plan'. In addition there was a tracking system to monitor the contaminating influence of extraneous variables such as, say, the death of a local dignitary from cancer or some new national legislation. And there was a cost tracking system too.

F.C.: But how do they know which of the 58 separate initiatives governed by these implementation directives actually contributed to the outcomes?

A.T.: I see, you're worried that such a complex intervention cannot be standardized properly and that the differences in outcome across the eleven sites are a sign of implementation failure? Such community programs have to strike a compromise between sticking to a strict program definition and offering practitioners flexibility to apply their local knowledge. There are reports of differences between the researchers and practitioners in this respect but I gather there was a clear basis to the partnership based on trying to 'develop processes which emphasized to community members the research nature and scientific requirements of the project'.[13] It's hard to tell from this distance, but from experience, I would say that huge efforts have gone into making sure the program has integrity.

F.C.: No, no I didn't mean that at all. Even if it were possible to standardize the initiative completely, it wouldn't help in understanding the way in which it worked. The *same* program can and will always work in different ways. It's like the old thing about trying to activate 'community crime initiatives'. Telling people about burglary can induce them to join together against it, but it can make them withdraw into their mini-fortresses in fear of crime. In the same way, I would imagine that creating 'smokers' networks' can bring people together to provide a bit of mutual support as they struggle with withdrawal, or, if significant numbers relapse, the groups might legitimate a form of mutual surrender. We have to see what the initiative fires in people's minds. This is what realists mean by mechanisms: we cannot simply treat programs as 'things', we have to follow them through into the choices made by the recipients.

A.T.: COMMIT did this too. They also did a 'receipt survey' which monitored the population in terms of whether they were 'aware of' or 'participated in' the activities.[14] For the light to moderate cohort there was a significant correlation between communities in terms of their 'quit rate' and the 'receipt index'.

F.C.: What's that, the more the program is noticed the more it is acted upon, provided you are a light smoker? That's fairly obvious but not quite what I had in mind. Evaluation has to try to follow *how* the program enters the subjects' reasoning. You could *notice* an anti-smoking program and say, 'Oh, how interesting,' *or*, 'Oh no, not that again.' My hunch about some of the big differences in impact of the initiative would in fact turn on a sequence of events in which such 'call to attention' mechanisms were crucial. First of all, if you think about context, you would have some communities with a fairly sophisticated understanding of public health messages for whom the ideas on offer would not be new. For other groups there will have been less community health resources and the program will have presented a much greater opportunity. Now this little scenario imagines just two types of community and just two types of subject choice. Of course, there will be many more subtle variations in context and mechanism than this and the point is that the aggregative experimental method systematically directs attention away from these pockets of program power.

E.B.: What do you think of this, Frank? [*She reads from a document in front of her.*] 'Faith in the randomized controlled trial is so firm amongst epidemiologists, clinical scientists and journals – not excluding this one – that it may justly be described as a shibboleth, if not a religion. Science, like freedom, dies of dogma; subversion is its lifeblood. We need a more rounded and complex perspective.'[15] This is a comment on COMMIT from an editorial in a recent issue of the *American Journal of Public Health*. The fact that others too are beginning to concede that fundamental questions may need to be asked about experimental evaluation has prompted us to consider an alternative method. That is, if we can find a coherent alternative.

F.C.: Absolutely, the concern is well placed and there is a better bet. What we have with COMMIT is a technically complex evaluation, with random allocation of subjects to ensure that there wasn't an undue number of people who were most likely to be open to the program effect. That would have been thought to be unrepresentative. Unfortunately, no programs are effective for everyone. The trick is to work out who will benefit from which types of intervention. *If the evaluation made a principled effort to avoid focusing on those most likely to benefit, it rather missed the point of evaluation*: to help the likes of Emma to decide how to target their efforts to most effect. And, as if this steam-rolling over community differences were not enough, the method also does its best to homogenize the initiative itself. So the process evaluation is all about delivering a standardized package, so that the evaluation can compare like with like. Even the receipt index only manages to find out *whether* subjects engaged with the program and not *how*. So the evaluation has skated over the other great requirement of understanding program effectiveness, which is to understand the pattern of choices created and followed. To find out who is going to benefit from which interventions, you have to develop and refine a set of ideas explaining how the intervention will work amongst its various possible subject groups, and to direct your evaluations accordingly. Sorry, I've gone into lecture mode.

A.T.: Before you air your views on how it *should* be done, could we check out with you your views on 'replication'? In the past we have tried to replicate some of the hottest anti-smoking initiatives from overseas, only for them to run cold here quite inexplicably.

E.B.: Ahhhh, the duplicity of duplication.

A.T.: Two of the potentially finest school smoking education projects in Britain are the Family Smoking Education project and Smoking and Me.[16] Unfortunately, though evaluations of these programs found them a solid success when they were first introduced respectively in Norway and Minnesota, USA, they failed to yield similar success in Britain.

F.C.: And how was the UK evaluation done?

A.T.: Thirty-nine mixed-sex comprehensive schools were selected and divided into four groups: ten formed a control group with no interventions, ten had only the Family Smoking Education project, nine had only the Smoking and Me project, and ten experienced Family Smoking Education followed by Smoking and Me.

F.C.: And the results?

A.T.: Absolutely flat across the treatments and controls. The overall finding was that 'two of the best school smoking education projects in Britain have not achieved better results than non-specific population wide approaches.'[17]

F.C.: And the explanation for this finding?

A.T.: It was thought 'very disappointing'; the failure was 'difficult to explain'.[18]

F.C.: Of course I don't know the details, but my guess is that it will be easy to explain. Mixed findings are the rule when the 'same' initiative is introduced in different places. So is the quizzical response. Your *bon mot* about duplication was actually spot on, Emma. If you think about the complexity of programs, it is folly to think that we can simply duplicate the dosage. The first typical problem is that it is quite rare that exactly the same is done. Were there any differences in this case?

A.T.: Well yes, there were some. Whilst it was thought 'straightforward' to translate the Norwegian Family Smoking Education initiative here, there were acknowledged developmental needs for the Minnesotan Smoking Prevention Programme on which Smoking and Me was based.[19]

F.C.: I'm not convinced that the Norwegian program would translate without tears, but let's settle for an example of a difference between the Minnesotan program and its British counterpart?

A.T.: OK. In Minnesota the pupils acted as peer opinion leaders, with 'full responsibility for each classroom intervention' under the supervision and observation of health professionals,[20] whilst in Britain, although the content remained the same, the teacher remained in control and there was no use of health professionals.[21] But the question is, does that matter?

F.C.: That's right. That is the question. Whether it matters or not depends on how the program worked and is supposed to work. We need a theory to tell us whether it mattered and how. Do we have one? Without the theory of what is important we are stuck with trying to duplicate the whole thing. And that's impossible. The Minnesotan classroom walls may have been lime-green as opposed to magnolia in the UK. Does it matter?

A.T.: Of course not.

F.C.: You know that because it is well outside *any* theory of smoking cessation. The question is – what *is* the theory under test?

A.T.: I'm not so sure what you mean by 'theory' in this context.

E.B.: Hear! Hear!

F.C.: We'll get there in a moment. Let's deal with the second major problem in replication, namely that the conditions present for the intervention often differ in ways which are significant for the intervention to have its effect. Are there any examples here?

A.T.: It's of course difficult again to know what might be significant. But, for example, the Norwegian experiment was undertaken when a Tobacco Act including a total ban on advertising was in force. There was no such total ban in Britain. Then there seems to be some confusion over the age group. The UK study was beamed at eleven- to twelve-year-olds, whereas the Norwegian project was directed at thirteen- to fourteen-year-olds. The UK study authors also note that the onset of smoking has for some groups fallen below even these tender years, so the possibility of 'too little too late' is raised in their 'discussion'.[22] They also talk about the relatively easy availability of cigarettes for the young in the UK. Perhaps that's a crucial difficulty, it's hard to say.

F.C.: Ah ha, the bright ideas of the dreaded 'post-match discussion'. Actually I agree. It is difficult to know what differences in context are significant in enabling a measure to have its potential impact. The presence or absence of advertisements for tobacco products may or may not be important. Age and availability might, perhaps, be crucial too. We're back to theory yet again. Without some theory which specifies the context for measures to produce their impacts in particular ways, we are at a loss in deciding whether the differences in what is done and the circumstances in which it is done are or are not significant. I suspect that both the failures of the COMMIT evaluation and the failures to replicate the Norwegian and Minnesotan projects have a common source. Neither began with a theory which explained how the measures introduced were expected to have their impact on which groups and in what conditions.

A.T.: Hang on a moment. I'm getting impatient with this talk of theory. The last thing we need in programming and evaluation is a bunch of theorists. They have so little to do with the practical job we're faced with. My instinct is always to get away from theory and be a bit more down to earth.

E.B.: Quite so, anti-smoking theories cover everything from breaking the conspiracy of tobacco capitalism to subjugate worker-smokers,[23] to seizing in a symbolic *rite de passage* that moment of individuality when a person's objectives for living are in the balance.[24]

F.C.: Hey look, we academics have a living to make too! But what I mean by theory need not be so rhapsodic, and it's a mistake to contrast theory and practice in the way you suggest. The theories I have in mind are program theories, the bright ideas which go into the construction of each new initiative. We all have to use theories, as I'm using that term here. The trouble is that practitioners and policy makers don't articulate or explain them enough and many evaluators only pick them up as an afterthought. All I'm suggesting is that we are upfront about our theories and use them in our evaluation work, since we're more likely in that way to come out with useful findings. What were the bright ideas which led to the development of the Family Smoking Education project and Smoking and Me?

A.T.: I'm not certain. I've only read the evaluations and, as you suggest, they don't dwell on the formative thinking behind the initiatives. But from what I can gather they used videos and classroom discussion to get over the anti-smoking message. The novelty is perhaps the picking up on *specific spheres of influence* on smoking. So one program uses a leaflet for parents to reinforce the program theme, the other places emphasis on refusal skills for managing social situations in which smoking occurs.

F.C.: Splendid, see – chock full of 'theories'. What's more they might relate *directly* to some of the worries as to the differences between the initial trials and the UK replications. Presumably the success of a refusal skills program depends on the verisimilitude of the social situations which are simulated – and this will turn crucially on the balance of input from child, teacher and health professional.

E.B.: And the *age* of the children may well also affect their ability imaginatively to reconstruct these situations.

F.C.: Exactly; we are guessing, but it is likely that the success of a refusal skills initiative depends on kids being young enough not to have started smoking and old enough to appreciate the reality of peer group pressure. That in turn requires considerable experience and ability from the teachers and health workers to draw some realism out of the kids. What needs research here is the question of putting this exact balance of ingredients in place rather than expecting to replicate the job lot and come up with the same results.

A.T.: And what are you saying about the advertising ban? That the UK family will find it more difficult to reinforce the anti-smoking message because they will forever be taking their kids to Benson & Hedges cup finals and walking to sweet shops past posters of Silk being Cut?

F.C.: Well perhaps, but that sounds rather tenuous to me. My best bet would be that a 'family reinforcement mechanism' would depend rather crucially on the type of family doing the reinforcing. Rather than just examine the results for the block of families which happened to be thrown up by the structure of the experimental design I would have kept a very close eye on the types of families which were able to add the reinforcement. It is by putting some detail on that theory you will begin to construct the transferable lessons.

A.T.: I can see that. So what is done in a smoking prevention program will trigger a mechanism effecting a change in smoking behaviour only if the surrounding circumstances are right. What you are saying is that in order to do our evaluations we need a theory anticipating which mechanisms are triggered in which situations to produce which outcomes. And that we need this theory to direct our research design and measurement efforts?

F.C.: That's right. What is useful in evaluation is the construction of what are called 'context–mechanism–outcome pattern configurations' or *CMO* configurations. In relation to smoking these would tell how the measures we introduce work (the mechanisms they activate) within specific circumstances (in their contextual conditions) to produce particular patterns of change in smoking behaviour (to generate well-defined outcome patterns). Over a series of evaluations, better and better specified *CMO* configurations need to be developed.

E.B.: In rather less fanciful language, what you are saying is that research should be all about discovering the right horse for the right course? The better this connection is defined, the more sharply focused we can make our interventions and the more effectively and economically we can attain our ends.

F.C.: That's it.

E.B.: OK, let us suppose for the minute that you have convinced us, in the abstract, that our evaluation should go about the business of progressively focusing down on which specific anti-smoking message will impact on which set of people. How do we actually put the principle into practice? Give us an example.

F.C.: I hope I can do better than that. I'm hoping that you can give me a few examples from what you know already. Let's start with the best known mechanism: telling people that smoking will give them respiratory and cardiovascular disease and will kill 'em off eventually. It seems quite a powerful bit of reasoning to me, but we presumably know by now that its impact has been limited.

A.T.: Yes, a number of studies have shown that non-smokers and smokers are very similar in their knowledge of the hazards of smoking.[25, 26]

F.C.: Yet there must be some contexts, there must be some people in some places for whom the medical message has hit home?

A.T.: Perhaps. For a start 38 million smokers visit a physician every year in the US,[27] so there are a lot of studies which have pursued the idea of smoking programs as an adjunct to the work of family practitioners. Then, as a more specific example, there is a US study showing that pregnant women smoked at only 70% of the rate of non-pregnant women in the same age range, with most of the difference being associated with quitting.[28] Even more esoteric is a study showing how the intervention of dental surgeons helped to snuff out the use of chewing tobacco.[29] Whilst these are totally different circumstances, presumably they all reflect increased sensitivity of particular groups of smokers to 'medical' lessons.

F.C.: So what you've given me here is a theory about an especially 'teachable moment' when mechanism meets context.[30]

A.T.: But wait a minute, studies also show that *unmarried* pregnant women actually smoke *more* than their non-pregnant counterparts[31] and that smoking cessation *after* pregnancy may be an unattainable goal for the majority of *working class mothers.*[32]

E.B.: Yes, and for that matter don't doctors smoke like the Queen Mary?[33]

F.C.: No no no, I'm not claiming a rigid law here that 'medical messages work on the medically attuned', I'm asking you to do the research on it. It is *often* the case that the 'vulnerable' are more conducive to the change suggested by a program. In the crime reduction field, lessons about the importance of guarding against 'repeat victimization' tend to work very well if your house has just been 'done'. But not for everyone. Some people just don't care. Some are fatalistic. Some need extra support to put measures in place. Some turn their houses into a fortress. I'm sure you'd get the same range of responses for health education messages to the vulnerable. You ought to think of your research agenda as one of trying to find out the best 'matches' of the medium and message and messenger and messagee!

E.B.: How?

F.C.: Let's see what's been done already. Andrew, you said there was a lot of work on anti-smoking interventions within general practice?

A.T.: Yes, enough to get us through to a meta-analysis or two[34, 35] They tend to concentrate on the most effective *form* of physician-led intervention – on whether the program is best delivered though leaflets at the surgery, through face-to-face counselling, through one session or several, through nicotine replacement advice, through some combined package of the aforementioned and so forth. But I'm not sure they offer much hope. Let me quote you something, 'We seem to have finally learned that minor differences in treatments will not lead to major differences in outcomes. Such studies have consistently failed to identify any one elusive "magic bullet" intervention component.'[36]

F.C.: That's very perceptive. But I bet it's talking again about experimental versus control group trials or factorial designs, so I doubt that any of the studies have pursued the question about *who* might be especially sensitive to the various messages. Before we go fiddling about trying to perfect the intervention for everyone, we have to start from the understanding that *any* single intervention works in different ways for different people. Let us imagine a simple session in which our doctor talks through with a patient the benefits of giving up smoking. Off the top of my head, there might be several different mechanisms which such an intervention might trigger. It might be taken (more) seriously because it carries state-of-the-art advice on novel steps to avoid smoking: let's call that the 'new tactics' mechanism (M_1). Then another reason that a doctor/patient exchange may also hit the target is because the practitioner carries rather a lot of clout. Let's call that the 'expert/exemplary status' mechanism (M_2). Can you help me with some more?

E.B.: Alternatively, the exchange might work by encouraging guilt from the patient because they sense that future relationships with their doctor might be jeopardized if they continue smoking.

F.C.: Brilliant, let's call that the 'contract guilt' mechanism (M_3).

A.T.: I'll give you – the 'cause for concern' mechanism (M_4). This is when the consultation makes a specific connection between smoking and a current medical condition of a patient. And then there's . . .

F.C.: . . . great, sorry Andrew, hold on a sec. There are indeed likely to be many more mechanisms but I want to try to lead you elsewhere now. The point is that the impact of all of these mechanisms will vary according to subject and circumstances. Clearly, for instance, the impact of 'cause for concern' warnings (M_4) about smoking and respiratory disease will vary with the 'complaint' (C_4), and so hit home if the patient is feeling a bit 'chesty' much more than if she has come in for ingrowing toenails.

A.T.: Yes, the dentists I've just mentioned were actually instructed to say, 'your use of smokeless tobacco is probably related to this precancerous lesion here in your mouth'.

F.C.: Good grief! But let's move on through the mechanisms. Many older working class patients still quake at the knees when faced with a consultant, whilst I often wonder whether our spotty young GP is still mugging it up from textbooks. So the 'exemplary status' mechanism (M_2) is constrained by the 'relative status' of the patient (C_2). Where am I up to?

A.T.: Well, I've often noticed that anti-smoking initiatives are all variations on a rather similar theme. So the efficacy of the 'novel' messages (M_1) will depend on whether the patient has just started smoking or is on the sixth relapse (C_1).

E.B.: OK, I've got it. My mechanism (M_3) is about 'guilt' induced by not following the doctor's advice. Let me see, this might differ according to how the patient understood their contractual relationship with a doctor. Patients might experience more or less guilt according to whether they are paying privately or using National Health resources (C_3).

F.C.: Excellent. In a couple of minutes of brainstorming there, we've come up with a little theory about what it is about smoking advice from a medic which might work for different patients in different circumstances. All initiatives contain dozens of highways and byways like this and evaluation has to follow them.

E.B.: Thank you for the flattery, Frank, but you are shooting yourself in the foot here. Without the benefit of research, you are telling us that there are many contexts in which physician-based interventions will not work. When the teenage patient arrives with acne or for the contraceptive pill, she will not cower at the promise of hard arteries at 50. So we give up?

F.C.: No, er well, yes and no. That little scene is quite plausible: kids and sensible advice often don't go together. But I'm not arguing that all highways and byways are known in advance and fixed in stone. My guess is that such scenarios have already been anticipated in some programs and that someone has come up with an idea to give young people 'cause for fear' with more upfront messages about the immediate physical effects of smoking. Andrew. Help!

A.T.: Nozu and Tsunoda argue that a concern with acute physiological problems is part of the life world of the young, so programs which demonstrate the immediate connection between smoking and, for instance, the rising of blood pressure and the constriction of blood vessels have found some success.[37]

F.C.: Yep. I'm sure that this little theory, too, is not a 'given', and there are groups of teenagers who might fret at high blood pressure, whilst others remain unmoved. The point is to put it to research. And the way to conceive evaluation research is the way we are developing it now. I began with some half-baked theories about *what it is about a certain intervention which might work for certain people in certain circumstances.* You added a couple more such propositions along the same formula. Andrew found another one for us from the Japanese literature. The health education literature would no doubt add a few dozen more. If we had some experienced anti-smoking 'practitioners' in on this discussion, they would probably amaze us with an armful of further program reasoning that had not begun to cross our minds. That's how programs get constructed. They are not things, they are composed of dozens of little hypotheses and the job of evaluation is to test them out systematically.

A.T.: OK, I'm half convinced but I'm not clear on how you would turn this blur of ideas into a research design.

E.B.: Yes, how do you get from here to some useful demonstration projects?

F.C.: I'm not sure that it is a 'blur' of ideas. There is a common thread about *reducing smoking by maximizing the capacity of the health warning mechanism by firing it with subjects and in contexts where it will be most telling.* As a general rule, I find it best to avoid blockbusters and choose or create a family of three or four programs which allow you to test out different hypotheses within a middle-range proposition like this.

E.B.: So, perhaps, we could look at the medical message theme beginning with a GP-based scheme; and then one at, say, a 'well women' clinic where we might piggyback smoking cessation messages on a specific class of health concerns; and then one based, perhaps, on hospital patients/outpatients where disquiet on health matters had become a stage more critical to potential subjects?

F.C.: That's right. For each you would introduce a tailored package of measures. Each might employ a core of materials/consultations about the deleterious consequences of smoking. Then, for each, there would be more targeted stuff, for instance about 'smoking and the foetus' or 'quitting and avoiding weight gain' or 'a girl's guide to blood pressure' at the women's clinic. And maybe some rather hard-hitting information in a chest clinic about . . .

A.T.: . . . Yes, but the design? We want your ideas on the evaluation.

E.B.: We normally consult with practitioners on program content, Frank.

F.C.: Actually that *was* research design and no, I'm not trying to usurp the practitioner's function. What I'm saying is that it is crucial to recognize and, if necessary, to *arrange* for the evaluation to tackle initiatives in which a well-circumscribed set of mechanisms is let loose on a well-circumscribed range of contexts. What is vital is to harvest together – from practitioners, policy makers, subjects, previous researchers, the current evaluation team, and even the methodological consultant – the dozens of available theories on why, for whom and in what circumstances the particular initiative might work best. In their making, programs are always envisaged in terms of subjects being receptive to a particular set of ideas. It's obvious that, in practice, this concordance between subjects and ideas will vary. Initiatives will thus always have 'winners' and 'losers' and the ideal way to find out how a program works is to identify the folks falling into each category. This requires that the research hypothesizes a range of salient subgroups of subjects and circumstances in advance of evaluation. The research then will track them through to outcome, with the aim of confirming, disconfirming and refining the purported pockets of program success.

A.T.: It's a good slogan, Frank, 'picking pockets of program progress'. Explain what you mean by it.

F.C.: Well, let's start from a crude initial supposition such as our hunch that 'medical messages' are invariably *lost* on 'apathetic adolescents'. I'm saying that evaluation is the process of refining such mechanism/context propositions. Thus after some well-focused research, this crude alliterative couplet might get refined as 'messages about smoking and immediate high blood pressure and poor skin quality and tricks to avoid compensatory eating' do *work* reasonably well on 'appearance-conscious, mutually supporting, working class girls, who are sufficiently concerned with some aspect of health to have gotten themselves into a clinic'. This is an example of my jargon about *CMO* configurations. Of course, I'm still making up all the categories and connections here myself. The point is that categories like this do not just spring forth out of the research. It requires somebody to 'think' them. This is the most crucial aspect of 'research design'. When and only when you have theorized such a matrix of program pockets can you do the research. As to the precise technical features of the research, I've little to teach you. You need evidence on mechanisms, outcomes and contexts. You need data on words, deeds and places. You need a pluralist approach.

E.B.: So these comparisons of subgroups of subjects internal to a program actually tell us how a program works best and then in future policy making and program-building we use the findings for ever more precise targeting?

F.C.: Exactly.

A.T.: But if you only use comparisons which are internal to a program and don't use control groups, how do you know that you have not just lit upon subjects who would have just stopped smoking anyway?

F.C.: I admire your devotion to treatment/control comparison. But what I am encouraging you to do is set up hundreds of comparisons. Remember I've already said that inter-programme comparisons are vital too. One way to widen our understanding of the contextual sensitivity of the 'medical messages' mechanism is by testing it out across a range of carefully chosen contexts. It is also quite easy to construct some other form of baseline to discover whether the program only works for people likely to stop anyway: you have already mentioned the mass of demographic data on patterns of smoking prevalence. But, above all, we need *intra-program comparisons*. As soon as research gets to the point of saying there is the program and there are the experimental and control groups, then the old black box mentality shrouds out any real chance of finding why and for whom certain program ideas might work.

E.B.: Point taken. I'm troubled about something else in your 'focusing process', Frank. It seems to make progress on a terribly narrow front. Look, I'm charged with bringing down smoking by a third.

F.C.: *CMO* focusing is a process of learning more and more about less and less. So it *is* slow. Given the choice, I would opt for making slow-but-sure progress on *several fronts* rather than seeking the same magic bullet to blow the cigarette out of the mouth of every smoker. Let us try to repeat the 'pickpocket' recipe with a completely different anti-smoking initiative. What else do you have in mind?

E.B.: We are very interested in worksite bans, which actually seek to forbid smoking across whole organizations . . .

We leave the discussion here as the players continue to carve out a research program on worksite bans, and take the reader to the very end of the play.

F.C.: Before we finish, I must ask you about the most obvious 'program' of the lot. Why don't you just quadruple the price of cigarettes?

E.B.: My dear Frank, there would be context–mechanism–outcome configurations involved of which you have never dreamt.

Notes

1 Department of Health (1992).
2 Magowan (1994, p. 82).
3 Kottke et al. (1988).
4 COMMIT Research Group (1991).
5 Fiore et al. (1990).
6 COMMIT Research Group (1991).
7 COMMIT Research Group (1995a).
8 Jencks et al. (1995, p. 344).
9 COMMIT Research Group (1991).
10 COMMIT Research Group (1995a).
11 Ibid.
12 COMMIT Research Group (1991).
13 Ibid.
14 COMMIT Research Group (1995b).
15 Susser (1995, p. 156).
16 Nutbeam et al. (1993, p. 106).
17 Ibid. (p. 106).
18 Ibid. (p. 106).
19 Ibid. (p. 102).
20 Arkin et al. (1981, p. 613).
21 Gray (1987, p. 16).
22 Nutbeam et al. (1993).
23 Stebbins (1991).
24 Willms (1991).
25 Lee et al. (1991).
26 Ben-Shlomo et al. (1991).
27 Cummings et al. (1989).
28 Williamson et al. (1989).
29 Stevens et al. (1995).
30 Vogt et al. (1989).
31 Williamson et al. (1989).
32 Graham (1993).
33 Dekker (1993).
34 Kottke et al. (1988).
35 Lichtenstein and Glasgow (1992).
36 Ibid.
37 Nozu and Tsunoda (1992).

8

EVALUATION, POLICY AND PRACTICE: REALIZING THE POTENTIAL

In earlier chapters we have had much to say about the wisdom of two groups of stakeholders – *practitioners* and *participants*. Living the everyday life of an initiative means that they know a lot but are not know-alls about their programs. This partial expertise is best put to use in a process of mutual teaching and learning with the realistic evaluator. In this penulti-mate chapter we turn to another key stakeholder, the *policy maker*, though we have just seen a rather caricatured version of her in the previous chap-ter. Policy makers are, of course, crucial. It is up to policy makers to agree or initiate a program. It is normally policy makers who commission or agree that an evaluation be undertaken. Policy makers are also often the prime recipients of an evaluation report and may undertake further program development with reference to it. Policy makers, consequently, see much but they too are not all-seeing. They too are locked in a division of expertise, and they too can be helped in realizing the potential of programs if they are engaged in a teacher–learner relationship with the evaluator.

What uses, then, ought policy makers to be able to make of evaluations? We can do no better in setting these purposes down than to quote the thoughts of Eleanor Chelimsky in her keynote address to the founding conference of the European Evaluation Society. On the basis of long expe-rience of the policy / research interface as a former Head of the US General Accounting Office's Program Evaluation and Methodology Division, she commends the enterprise of evaluation to the decision maker on three grounds:

> The first type of decision . . . is the formulation of a *new* policy or program. Why is evaluation useful here? Well, for three reasons. Evaluations of past initiatives can help a policymaker avoid reinventing wheels; they can spare policymakers later political embarrassment by showing early on that the evidence is just not there to warrant the implementation of some highly touted proposal; and they allow policymakers instead to build on earlier interventions that *have* been effec-tive, or are at least promising. The evaluator's role here is to bring the best available information to the decision maker on past experience with the problem to be addressed, and on strategies for addressing it.

A second way decision makers use evaluation well is for timely monitoring of how established programs are doing, and for determining whether the assumptions underlying the policies or programs appear to be correct, or at least not *wrong*.

Finally decision makers use evaluation to establish results of their initiatives, both short-term and long-term, not only to decide whether or how they should be modified, but also to be in a position to defend their own records. (Chelimsky, 1995, p.11)

Chelimsky acknowledges that evaluation does not always work quite in this way. Certainly not easily. In particular it can be difficult to get unwelcome messages across. She has a wide range of wise advice on how this can be done. She stresses, for example, that reports need to show independence, candour and appropriate self-criticism, balance, and manifest familiarity with what is already known and the need to anticipate potential attacks on findings. They also need to display precision, readability and clarity. With all this we concur. We want to add to it, by showing in this chapter how the approach we have been advocating not only is superior in the validity of the findings it generates, but also serves well the realistic purposes of evaluation set out by Chelimsky.

The chapter will discuss two main issues. First, we consider what the evaluator learns from and teaches to the policy maker when undertaking a realistic evaluation. Second, we summarize the full potential of realistic evaluation by bringing into one overall model the teaching and learning interactions between the evaluator and the practitioner and participant as well as the policy maker. Here we take the 'real' root of our method one stage/syllable further: we point out that what realistic evaluation offers is a means of program reali*zation*. As in previous chapters we develop the arguments though an example – in this case the British Safer Cities program.

Drawing the policy maker into the teacher–learner cycle

In order to conduct evaluations along the lines advocated in this book, the evaluator has some distinctive learning to do from the policy maker. Let us begin by marking the point of distinction with some simple contrasts.

To the experimentalist a program is a set of required behaviours designed by the policy maker and implemented by practitioners. The presence or absence of these behaviours determines whether or not the program has 'integrity' (see Chapter 2). Once this is established the program may be evaluated by reference to associated changes in the targeted behaviour. To the constructivist the conduct of a program is a perpetual act of negotiation and the policy maker's account of that program is merely one amongst many, all of which need to be considered and reconciled (see Chapter 1). *To the realistic evaluator the policy maker's account, like that of others, has a rather specific significance as a source of testable theory, which takes the form of an explicit or reconstructible context–mechanism–outcome pattern configuration.*

Policy makers self-evidently know a great deal about the programs for which they have responsibility. The policy maker's thinking is critical in the formulation of the program. It will characteristically be with the *program as a whole*, rather than with the minutiae of daily practice. The program may not be the original idea of the policy maker, of course, but the policy maker has to be persuaded that the program will yield (or will have a fair chance of yielding) desired outcomes. However embryonic they might be, the policy maker will have some notions about how the program will generate positive benefits. This is the policy maker's overarching *program theory*.

A program can thus be construed as a conjecture. The evaluation is a test of it. Unless the evaluator has a good grasp of the details of the conjecture, the evaluation will be ill-informed, or only very partially informed. The researcher's life would be simple if the conjecture was the straightforward proposition 'if *X* is done then *Y* will follow', along lines assumed in experimental evaluation. Policy makers' thinking, in our experience, is always more ambitious and never so crude. The decision to initiate or maintain a program is thus the result of judgement and debate, which chain of thought might be more accurately rendered 'all things considered the expected benefits make the investment worthwhile'. Whilst the decision making process can be eclectic and indeed eccentric, it will always sustain sets of finely nuanced notions about *how* a program should be marshalled in order for its effects to work through. And the evaluator needs to be *au fait* with such thinking if data collection is to be adequate to the policy makers' program theory.

Let us give a brief example of how the researcher can weave the decision maker's theories into the process of realistic evaluation. The initiative in question is the British Safer Cities program which was announced in 1988. Formally speaking it had three aims: to reduce crime, to lessen the fear of crime and to create safer cities in which economic enterprise and community life could flourish. We attempt to draw out the methodological lessons from the work of one of the present authors, in a study commissioned to look at one specific organizational aspect of Safer Cities, namely its success in catalysing provision for longer term strategic attention to crime prevention in the cities targeted, once Safer Cities status was withdrawn (Tilley, 1992).

Safer Cities was run by the Home Office and sprang in part from a funding opportunity created by Action for Cities – a much larger program aiming to regenerate cities which were in economic and social decline. The idea was that allocating some seed-corn funding (£250,000 per annum), appointing local staff (three of them), providing a profile of the recorded crime patterns in the areas, and forming multi-agency steering committees (as a condition for the grant) would catalyse collaborative crime prevention efforts that would be adequately resourced and targeted, and be effective in generating ameliorations in the crime problem. Such a bald description of the mechanics and aspirations of the program gives us no clue about how to evaluate its capacity for crime prevention, and the evaluator's first contact with the policy makers is to reconstruct the formative thinking and thus to learn the assumed, implicit, or latent *CMO* configurations. Any effort to evaluate the long term potential of Safer Cities needs to begin with the theory of what it is that the program is expected to do in the contexts in which it is introduced to have its intended impacts.

As we have seen with other stakeholders, such theories often lie dormant and half-articulated and it is the evaluator's task to bring them vibrantly to life. In the present case this involved doing the rounds of key decision making personnel, attending meetings, inspecting files etc., all the time utilizing the principles described in Chapter 6 to encourage the policy makers to articulate, refine, formalize and reformulate their notions of the program theory. Tables 8.1 and 8.2 attempt to reconstruct this theory in the by now familiar realistic format. The first of these concentrates on the *organizational assumptions* underpinning the initiative and describes a complex

Table 8.1   *Safer Cities implicit organizational theory*

Context	+	Mechanism	=	Outcome
Cities with . . . High crime rates		Hard data on the patterns of local crime inform decisions to allocate effort where needs are greatest		Reduced crime levels, where need is greatest
Low level of interagency co-operation in attempting to reduce crime; responsibility assigned to the police only		Injection of cash buys multi-agency attention to crime prevention		Reduced fear of crime
Reasonable interagency trust		Local staff with expertise and understanding of local context bring capacity to catalyse action and co-operation where possible		Improvements in community life and improvements
Willingness of local authority to work with national government department		Local steering group fosters mutual shaming into commitment to co-operate in crime prevention		in the economy
Crime and fear of crime undermining community confidence and local economy				

Table 8.2 *Underlying crime prevention program theory*

Context	+	Mechanism	=	Outcome
Communities with wide range of opportunities for crime: easy pickings at low risk to the offender		'Situational' measures increase *risk and difficulty*, and reduce prospective rewards from from offending		More failed crimes; lower yields from crimes; more apprehensions of offenders
		Visible situational measures alter prospective offenders' *perception* of the risks, efforts and rewards from crime, and alter their cost–benefit calculations of the utility of crimes		Reduced rate of attempted crimes

set of tactical expectations about how, in order to work, the initiative must weave its way through a web of national and local agencies and on into the community.

Table 8.2 concentrates on the theory behind the *measures* to be implemented and how they were supposed to work. Within the Home Office, from which the Safer Cities program originated, there prevailed a rather specific 'situational' theory of crime regularities and their reduction, and the same theories undergirded the initiative. The situational measures referred to might include, for example, reductions in amounts of cash held on buses or in shops, improvements in lighting, reducing the height of fencing, widening aisles in street markets, and improvements in physical security. As we have explained in Chapter 5, these measures are assumed to work by affecting the levels of perceived risk, effort and reward facing the prospective offender. Most programs have this marriage of an organizational and an operational theory, it being clear to policy makers in the present case that the key to success was that a variety of different agencies would be needed to implement such measures, and that to do so these agencies would need to be adequately motivated.

We have sermonized throughout the book about interventions always having winners and losers, about how the success of programs is always contingent on them being implemented in the right conditions and so forth. This brings us to the next step of the teacher–learner process with the policy maker, which is to coax out (cf. Chapter 6) their views on what may *differentiate* the impact of a program across its differing settings. In fact twenty 'safer cities' were selected for funding for an unspecified but limited period of at least three years, and in practice the officials involved had subtle ideas about the differing conditions in these cities which might or might not lead some to achieve success and others not to do so. These officials adhered generally to the theory outlined in Table 8.1, but recognized that cities were selected for participation for a variety of reasons, not all to do with the theoretically specified conducive context. Hence, there was a political basis to the inclusion of some, where either the crime rate or the state of interagency relationships was less hospitable according to the theory. Built in to the implicit program theory was a sense of different program platforms, which in some cases heralded rather pessimistic expectations about the impact on crime.

There was also less than universal commitment within the Home Office (and indeed amongst Safer Cities staff) to the theory of crime prevention outlined in Table 8.2, with a belief that alternative approaches might be generated with a less 'situational' and more 'social' approach to crime prevention. Moreover, it was assumed within the Home Office that the experience and intellectual backgrounds of the staff appointed to the projects might also have an impact on the pattern of intervention attempted, with commensurate effects on the nature of the impact which would be felt. As with all programs we thus begin to anticipate a series of *within-program* differences in the underlying generative process (cf. Chapter 4) and this suite of policy maker theories constitutes a significant resource for the evaluator.

We now reach the next stage in the realist evaluation cycle in which the gathering group of *CMO* configuration theories is put to the test against actual program progress in the field, examined using some of the data collection methods outlined in Chapter 6, interviewing local program personnel. This confirmed that Safer Cities initial contexts varied substantially: for example by crime rate, by levels of interagency trust, by population, and by the orientation of the staff appointed (Tilley, 1992; 1993d). It followed that the programs also differed markedly by levels of activity, some becoming mired in interagency battles, some in financial opportunism. The investigation, however, also revealed a gap in the policy makers' original organizational theory of the program; they knew much but were not know-alls. Unacknowledged contextual conditions had led Safer Cities to trigger unexpected causal mechanisms generating unexpected outcome patterns.

What was unearthed was that the willingness of local authorities, key participants in local crime prevention partnerships, to take part in Safer Cities was something of a Hobson's choice for many of them. Central government was commonly resented for reducing local revenue raising powers. Accordingly, there was a need for alternative sources of money, and the program offered the prospect of some. Safer Cities was therefore invited but was nevertheless still resented as an 'intrusion' from central government. The funds offered were initially seen as a way of supporting activity the local authority had had to abandon owing to financial constraints imposed by central government. The local Home Office appointees to the individual Safer Cities projects thus faced suspicion, which they had to struggle to overcome in order to persuade agencies to work cooperatively with the projects and their aims. These appointees also needed to create sufficient credibility to persuade local agencies to work together to develop and implement longer term crime prevention and community safety strategies. Ironically, once the initial suspicion had been overcome, the 'outsider' or 'stranger' status of local Safer Cities appointees (combined with their grant giving powers) provided them with a set of distinctive opportunities for partnership and long term strategy development which would not have been present for members of local agencies.

Table 8.3 is a drastic summary in realistic terms of what was discovered. It sees Safer Cities passing through five stages. In the course of these, initial suspicions are overcome. The outsider status of the projects and their workers is then exploited in various ways to generate longer term strategies before the projects finally constitute an irritating intrusion a second time, once local capacity has been fully built. At each stage differing mechanisms

Table 8.3 *Realistic evaluation findings about Safer Cities development*

Context	+	Mechanism	=	Outcome
Central government removing discretionary power of local authorities		1 Safer Cities resented as central government intrusion. Efforts to appropriate available grants to make up shortfall in revenue		1 Safer Cities operates as 'suspicious'
Central government reducing local authority revenue raising opportunities		2 Safer Cities becomes part of local institutional landscape, builds local capacity for crime prevention and is found useful for money provided, advice given, and demonstration that agencies working together could achieve more than working in isolation		2 Safer Cities acts as 'honest broker'
Reduced opportunities for local authority to provide financial support for voluntary groups		3 Local agency leaders open to suggestion from Safer Cities that they consider longer term locally owned, funded and administered crime prevention		3 Safer Cities acts as 'necessary catalyst' to initial poorly planned crime prevention measures
		4 Safer Cities convenient and available to service local crime prevention strategy group		4 Safer Cities acts as 'faithful servant'
		5 Safer Cities irritant when self-sufficiency is established		5 Safer Cities functions as 'the guest who stayed too long'

are triggered producing new outcomes furnishing conditions for further development, though the broad context within which Safer Cities operated remained unchanged. As realistic evaluation would expect also, there were some variations on the general pattern according to the detailed differing local contexts furnished by individual Safer Cities projects. These had to do, for example, with the presence or absence of existing arrangements to deal with crime prevention, the political complexion of the local authority, the composition of the steering group and so on.

What the realistic evaluator teaches back to the policy makers in this case is a refinement to parts of their original theory about how the program would develop. Policy makers are then in a position to make adjustments within the existing Safer Cities program or make plans for future programs which take into account this undulating platform created by 'outsider' provision. The original organizational theory was not quite correct but, as in Chelimsky's phrase, 'at least not wrong' and decision making is assisted in the manner she suggests.

The teacher–learner cycle completed

We now come to the culmination of the program teaching and learning that takes place in realistic evaluation as we have described it. We engage in a bit of conceptual housekeeping here, bringing together the various elements described in this book into a single, unified model. This presents a *realistic evaluation and policy-making cycle*, incorporating all the various research relationships described to this point. It is a rotation of activities in which there are well-defined roles for the evaluator, policy-maker, practitioner and participant. The key to the model is the researcher acting as 'go-between', seeking mutual enlightenment with each set of stakeholders.

Realistic evaluation involves the researcher learning the policy, practitioner and participant ideas that constitute the program and govern its impact. These theories are not just constructions: they describe understandings of real social forces affecting the thinking and action of agents. We have stressed that these theories can be reconstructed in realistic terms: that is to say, even where they are implicit (and sometimes quite deeply buried) they can be framed in terms of what is thought to work for whom in what circumstances. These 'folk theories' give us a seed bed of 'context–mechanism–outcome pattern configurations'. These inform data collection which in turn allows the evaluator to test, arbitrate and, above all, refine the theories. The evaluator then feeds back findings, which constitute a consolidation of what has been learned, to the policy maker and practitioner. The improved and substantiated realist theory then comprises a basis for further cycles of improvement in policy making and practice.

Figure 8.1 shows the model diagrammatically. A few words of explanation might be needed! At the heart of the program are three nested ovals.

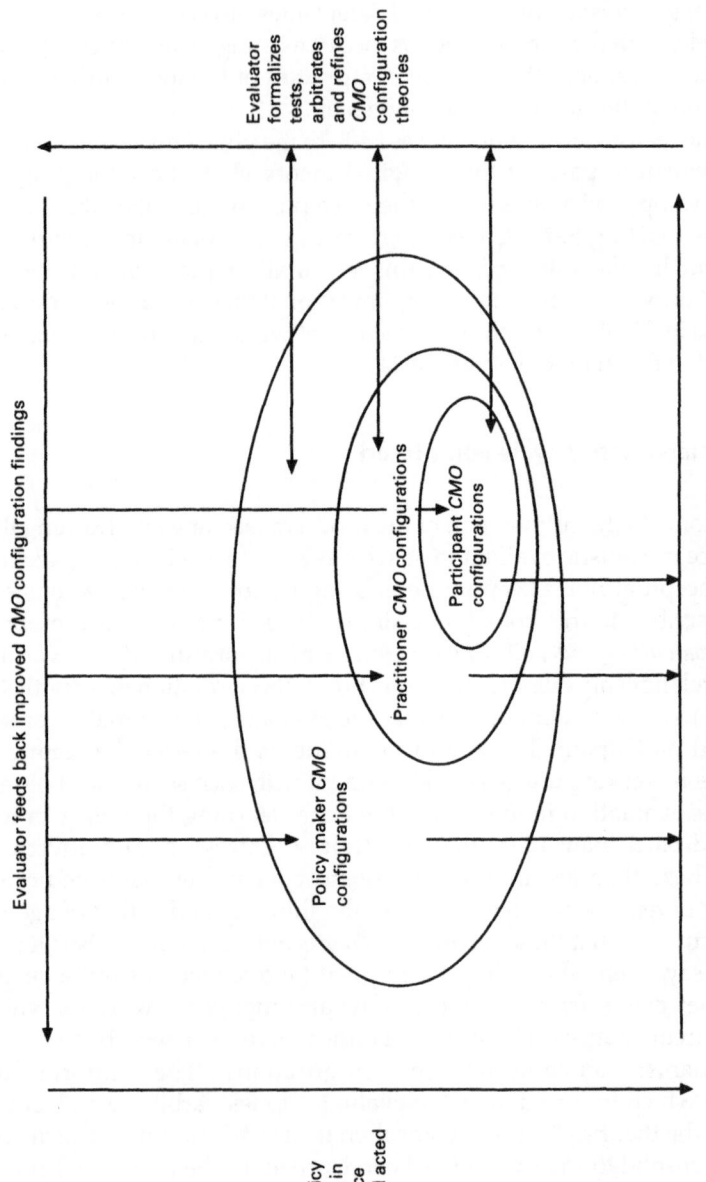

Figure 8.1 *The realistic evaluation and policy making cycle*

The outer oval describes the working context of the policy maker, who devises, maintains, modifies or cancels programs. As we have stressed already, the policy maker's decisions are made for a host of reasons, amongst which is a view that the program will achieve something. This view will be based on some notion of how the program will deliver its intended benefits. Indeed, differing policy makers may support the program with differing ideas about how it will work, and any single policy maker may have quite complex ideas about how the program will pan out in the conditions in which it is implemented. The policy maker, of course, does not devise programs in a vacuum. There will be a variety of acknowledged and unacknowledged conditions for policy development decisions. In this sense we could, in principle, have included yet a further oval describing the contextual conditions for policy decision making!

The policy maker is temporally ahead of the practitioner whose working context is set (at least in part) by the policy maker whose program ideas the practitioner tries to enact. The practitioner thus occupies the middle oval. The practitioner will both have a good deal of scope for discretion in shaping how the policy maker's program is delivered and develop views as to its potential. In exercising discretion, the original policy maker's intentions may be contradicted. They will almost always be modified. The practitioner will also have more closely textured ideas about how the program works amongst varying target subgroups. Implementation will characteristically generate unintended consequences as compared with the policy maker's original decisions.

The participant comes last in the temporal ordering of program experience. Participants normally experience only one moment or one slice of a program, but they know a great deal about that. They are important sources for validating, arbitrating, and refining others' theories about why they will or will not change their behaviour. They may also be sources for supplementary theories about how the program has its impact amongst some (their) subgroups.

Farrell and Pease (1993) have used the phrase 'getting the grease to the squeak' to describe the targeting of a program. As we move from the policy maker through to the practitioner we are, so to speak, channelling the grease to the squeak, which is represented by the participant. This metaphor constitutes, if you like, our program standard. The vertical line to the left of the nested ovals, running from top to bottom, describes the movement from the grease to the squeak. The better the program, the more effectively it gets to and applies the grease where it is needed.

The evaluator feeds off and feeds into programs. Feeding off programs has the sense of trying to elicit the reasoning incorporated into the program. The horizontal line going from left to right below the ovals, with lines coming down from the policy maker, practitioner and participant to the evaluator, describes the evaluator's work in eliciting *CMO* configuration theories incorporated into the program, methods for which are described in Chapter 6. The policy maker's and practitioner's theories are, of course, fallible. Even where intended outcomes are achieved, their thinking may fail to capture what it is that the program is doing to produce its consequences. It may thus need to be supplemented by other theorizing drawn from the evaluator's familiarity with relevant literature, imagination and so on. In Chapter 4 we described an exemplary study of the impact of property marking where the evaluator's conclusions about the context–mechanism–outcome configuration was at some distance from property marker practitioners' thinking.

The vertical line going upwards on the right-hand side of the ovals, fed with two-way relationships with the policy maker, practitioner and participant, describes the evaluator formalizing, arbitrating between, and garnering sharply defined evidence to test the conjectured program *CMO* configurations generated by the policy maker, practitioner, participant and independent evaluator.

Finally the horizontal line going from right to left above the ovals describes the evaluator feeding back or teaching *CMO* configuration findings. These are unlikely at any point to be the last word, since evidence is always limited, theories are complex and the ideas within programs are too numerous. Provided the program continues, the process can then recommence with the downward left vertical. The refined theories can then inform program development for both policy makers and practitioners, better to help them accomplish program intentions, and better also to allow participants to attain their legitimate aims. The process is potentially endless, since the revisions can then be evaluated once more, following exactly the same formula, and the program developed (or brought to a close) accordingly.

The dividend from the relationship of realistic evaluation to program and policy development can be described by extending the 'real' root to our method one syllable further with the term 'realization'. Overall, thus, realistic evaluation construes the achievement of the purposes of evaluation through a process of program *realization*. We have argued throughout the book that the basic task of evaluation research is one of *CMO* configuration focusing, learning in greater and greater detail the three Ws – *what* works for *whom* in *what* circumstances. Our argument in this chapter is simple, namely that exactly the same process lies at the heart of best practice when it comes to the development and implementation of initiatives. We can summarize the ideal in terms of the 'three phases of realization' as follows:

1 *Realization as understanding of how change is brought about.* Realistic evaluators come to realize (understand) how the causal powers triggered by the programme generate their outcomes in specifiable contexts.
2 *Realization as actualization of some potential – the process of making it real.* Realistic evaluation recognizes that policy objectives are attained through a program's realization (actualization) of the latent causal potential in the situations in which intervention takes place.

3 *Realization as accomplishment of some objective.* Realistic evaluation is undertaken to improve the realization (accomplishment) of policy and program objectives.

This brings us to the final piece of teaching and learning which is needed if realistic evaluation cycles, and the growth of mutual understanding within them, are to be set in motion. This has to do with methodology itself. Policy makers set the context for evaluation, reflecting their understanding of what evaluation can teach them and what use they make of it. Policy makers often have erroneous, even perverse, understandings of what constitutes a researchable question. Policy makers often want simple answers. Learning methodology is not normally a priority!

We acknowledge, therefore, that getting realistic methodological lessons across will not be easy. It is probably only possible to do so on a case-by-case basis. The difficulty is illustrated by this policy maker riposte to an earlier effort at methodological enlightenment:

> Our task is to prevent crime and we must go about it in a common-sense fashion that commands public support. I am not convinced that this *treatise on replication* serves any practical purpose whatsoever.

Government researchers, whose stock in trade is not only to do research but to commission and explain it to policy makers, have an important role to play in eliciting and, where necessary, rewriting and reinterpreting evaluations and series of evaluations in realistic terms. They may have more direct opportunities for enlightenment. The following government researcher's response to the policy maker just quoted is a welcome opportunist effort at teaching a robust methodological lesson:

> Public support is, of course, important, but so too is that of experienced thinking practitioners . . . If innovatory projects are subsequently rubbished by inept, unthinking and uncritical attempts at replication, then the credibility of the [government department's] . . . efforts and the energy and commitment of the . . . service are brought into question. This report is aimed at helping those trying to elicit lessons from past experience to use it to good effect in their own work.

Evaluators themselves also have this wider role to play in including, in their proposals for evaluations, explanations of how realistic evaluation will yield valid and usable results in ways other methodologies will not.

Conclusion: being realistic about realistic evaluation

This book has been about how to improve evaluation research. With this (awe)-inspiring vision of evaluating one's way through nested *CMO* configurations, we reach the end of our account of how to do *realistic evaluation*. The path that we have just drawn from research to policy is, unquestionably, an *ideal*. We appreciate, of course, that the policy making process also operates in a larger realm – the world of *realpolitik*.

Programmes live and die for a host of reasons other than the deliberations of evaluators. Researchers and policy makers have a whole range of relationships other than the mutual admiration born out of collaborative teaching and learning. In these concluding thoughts, we wish to concede this ground, show that realists are as capable of cynicism as anyone else, *but* then go on to show why the ideal is worth clinging to.

Thinking back to Safer Cities, it is fair to say that it typifies most initiatives in that it tossed about on a sea of financial and political change with a clumsy evaluation backwash. Funding and staffing arrangements were subject to the customary budgetary stop–start. The customary round of self-appraisal brought forth the usual rose-coloured spectacle assessment from local participants. Considerable sums were spent on an aggregative outcome analysis, of limited usefulness – not least because its results came too late to influence the major modification enacted in the second phase of the initiative. Within the initial twenty cities, the program took on its own separate life with its own dynamics once it had come into being. The policy makers were in no position to anticipate or regulate the subsequent developments (Tilley, 1992; 1993d). Each set of practitioners developed suites of ideas about how their interventions were being received and were producing their effects amongst the intended beneficiaries. Whilst Safer Cities made some use of realistic evaluation – the CCTV study described in Chapter 3 is an example – it did not infuse the program with it and many teaching and learning opportunities were lost. A realistic understanding of evaluation amongst policy makers could have elicited much more which would have been of use to program realization.

And so it is with all programs. Having spent several years as onlookers to policy making in the politically tender fields of policing and prisons we have, indubitably and inevitably, seen political caprice in action. We know of quick decisions, in boardroom and cabinet room, born of short term expediency. We know of decision makers whose daily work involves removing from their life's agenda the uncertainties so typically raised by research. We know well the symptoms of 'myopia', 'selective vision', and indeed the 'blind eye' that afflict many policy makers when they do actually confront evaluation documents. On the other side of the coin, we know of the endless futile hours given to the extraction of lame and self-serving assessments from practitioners acting as lay evaluators. We know of the problem of evaluators keeping their heads well down and out of danger, producing expensive, safe and technically obscure answers to half-baked questions. We also know of the spasmodic capacity of evaluation to generate political power, and have seen the elevation of some researchers turned decision makers on the basis of skilful promulgation of dubious evaluations of pet programs.

In short, we know of some rather appetizing 'tales from the field' about the ragged relationship between policy and evaluation, and one day if Sage offers us another 100,000 words, we will spend some time in their telling. But for the time being, we have a rather less garrulous and much more important point to make. This is a book about bringing objectivity to evaluation. And it is only because we acknowledge that there is a vantage point from which to learn the real lessons from real programs that we feel confident in passing the judgements just made about the sticky ends of much evaluation research. Moreover, it is because we have already seen and identified many examples of good practice (such as in Chapters 4 and 5) that the existence of the blatantly false trails leaves us with a healthy scepticism rather than wholesale cynicism about the policy potential of evaluation research.

Thus, in acknowledging the presence of power play in policy making, we do not suppose that 'power' always overwhelms 'knowledge'. Evaluators can never achieve perfect control of the uses of evaluations, but what they can try to perfect are the tools of their own trade. There is no need for modesty about the power of well-crafted research. Realistic evaluation is not only for 'engineering' but can serve the ends of 'enlightenment' and 'advocacy' as well (Weiss, 1987). Indeed we see the proposition *what works for whom in what circumstances* as the basic proposition of 'political arithmetic' (Abrams, 1985). And as a way of dealing with 'true believers', we can do no better than to offer a further insight from Chelimsky:

> We have to persuade true believers that something they absolutely 'know' to be true is in fact hyperbole, myth, unsupported by evidence, or even an outright lie. Spinoza wrote that it is the fact of error that needs explaining, not the discovery of truth. But in policymaking, the truth is often that error has been made and that the policy maker has invested in that error. So for evaluators trying to re-establish facts, it is, alas, the truth that needs, not only explanation, but also *very* persuasive arguments and data support. (1995, p. 15)

Alas, elements within the enterprise of evaluation have recently shown signs of heading in the opposite direction and following much of sociology and cultural studies in heeding the siren calls to 'value subjectivity' and to 'embrace the postmodern narrative'. One after another of evaluation's truth claims, scope claims and consensus claims have bitten the dust, as another group of true believers have become convinced that their own is but one of many truths, constituted in discourse (Everitt, 1996). This is no place to offer a rebuttal, or even a howl of disbelief (but see Pawson, 1996). Suffice to say that it is essential to the most modest ambition of evaluation that it is able to provide *criteria* for calling into question the claims for a particular intervention (Stern, 1996). The whole point of the book has been to show that there will always be differences in opinion about 'how programs work', but providing that this question is posed in a properly circumscribed way, then it *is* possible to furnish grounds for why one account can be preferred. Thus, we steadfastly refuse to sign up to the 'your truth is as good as my truth, your lie is as good as my lie' analysis of policy making.

9

THE NEW RULES OF REALISTIC EVALUATION

This chapter is a brief recapitulation of the argument of the book.

Learning a paradigm, as Kuhn once said, is like learning a language. This summary takes the form of a final bombardment of realist research terminology, and so is presented as a glossary of the 'key terms'. We have faced a temptation, in writing this book, to introduce a whole raft of realist neologisms and to wreak havoc on some of the established evaluation usages. By the end, though, we find that we have been more influenced by our self-imposed injunction to be 'realistic'. Evaluation is, after all, *applied* research. And although we have called throughout for injections of 'theory' into every aspect of evaluation design and analysis, the goal has never been to construct theory *per se*; rather it has been to develop the theories of practitioners, participants and policy makers. The proof of this realist pudding thus lies, not so much with the question of what realism can do for evaluation, but with the issue of what realist evaluation can do for programming and policy making. The upshot is that we have avoided being terminological terrorists and have tried instead to be conceptual captivators in smuggling the realist paradigm ever so gently into the existing language of evaluation. We remain true to this spirit in this final statement of the essence of our ideas. Accordingly, this *realistic evaluation thesaurus* is the ultimate pocket reference, and what we feign as a 'bombardment' is in fact a little coruscation of just eight terms.

Each concept is introduced with an associated *rule* for the conduct of evaluation research. With backgrounds in sociology we are naturally super-sensitive to the expression 'rules of inquiry'. The very idea of laying down the law on social science method has remained controversial ever since the famous attempt by Durkheim (1962). Gallons of methodological blood have been spilled subsequently with regard to the extent that one can pre-specify, in abstract and general terms, pathways of investigation which are, by definition, novel, time tied, and location specific. Our usage of 'rules' is not meant to imply we are involved in the production of some axiomatic truths as set down by the realist thought-police, nor is meant ironically. Methodological rules actually develop in the way we have generated them in this book – by going between principle and practice (Diesing, 1972), by traversing logic-in-use and reconstructed logic (Kaplan,

1964). Methodological rules are not written in stone but are the medium and outcome of research practice (Pawson, 1989, Chapter 1).

Methodological progress can actually be charted in much the same way as we trace the success of a program. The same realist explanatory principles apply. Our baseline argument throughout has been not that programs are 'things' that may (or may not) 'work'; rather they contain certain ideas which work for certain subjects in certain situations. We hardly have to change terminology at all to come to the appreciation that methodological rules contain ideas which work for certain investigations of certain processes. These ideas on the scope and salience of methodological rules do not simply descend from metaphysical heaven but are established by being tried and tested in research practice. In the beginning, the great epistemological and ontological principles act as high totems inspiring the research practitioner to certain broad and prized objectives. Success in a specific investigation may be claimed as an embodiment of these principles – but that particular inquiry will necessarily have a range of distinctive features which allowed it to meet the goals. It is the task of the methodologist to elucidate these features, so that the research community can copy the practice. And that practice, having been imitated across a range of inquiries with mixed success, then enables the research community to reflect back on the principles (and allows the methodologist a little carve of the totem). Over time there develops a picture of the research *contexts* in which the particular investigative *mechanisms* work best to generate the desired methodological *outcomes*. Methodological rules, like program theories, are thus under a process of continual refinement. This book has attempted to distil the process by acting as go-between, connecting up the ideas of a half-dozen philosophers and a handful of evaluators. The following statements will thus only gain currency if many more evaluators adopt the rules by adapting them.

Rule 1: generative causation

Evaluators need to attend to how and why social programs have the potential to cause change. Causation is not to be understood 'externally' and so the basic evaluation task is *not* to hypothesize or demonstrate the constant conjunction whereby programme X produces outcome Y. The change generated by social interventions should be viewed 'internally' and takes the form of the release of underlying causal powers of individuals and communities. Realists do not conceive that programs 'work', rather it is the action of stakeholders that makes them work, and the causal potential of an initiative takes the form of providing reasons and resources to enable program participants to change. The capacity for change of natural and social phenomena is only triggered in conducive circumstances. The evaluator needs to understand the conditions required for the programs' causal potential to be released and whether this has been released in practice.

Rule 2: ontological depth

Evaluators need to penetrate beneath the surface of observable inputs and outputs of a program. Social (and physical) reality is stratified. That which we can observe, including the most manifest and routine regularities, is produced by the operation of underlying generative forces which may not be immediately observable. Interventions are always embedded in a range of attitudinal, individual, institutional, and societal processes, and thus program outcomes are generated by a range of macro and micro social forces. In social life, the choice making behaviour of individuals in their different situations is fundamental to understanding their manifest patterns of behaviour. In social interventions the stakeholders' capacity for choice making is, of course, subject to social constraint and is always limited by the power and resources of their 'stakeholding'. Program evaluations need to grasp how the changes introduced inform and alter the balance of the constrained choices of participants.

Rule 3: Mechanisms

Evaluators need to focus on how the causal mechanisms which generate social and behavioural problems are removed or countered through the alternative causal mechanisms introduced in a social program. Realist evaluators seek to understand 'why' a program works through an understanding of the action of mechanisms. Mechanisms refer to the choices and capacities which lead to regular patterns of social behaviour. Causal mechanisms are at work in generating those patterns of behaviour which are deemed 'social problems' and which are the rationale for a program. Programs are often prolonged social encounters and even the simplest initiative will offer subjects considerable compass for decision making. A key aspect of evaluation research design is thus to anticipate the diversity of potential program mechanisms involved and a key analytic task is to discover whether they have disabled or circumvented the mechanisms responsible for the original problem.

Rule 4: Contexts

Evaluators need to understand the contexts within which problem mechanisms are activated and in which program mechanisms can be successfully fired. Realist evaluators seek to understand 'for whom and in what circumstances' a program works through the study of contextual conditioning. The operation of mechanisms is always contingent on context; subjects will only act upon the resources and choices offered by a program if they are in conducive settings. Context refers to the spatial and institutional locations of social situations together, crucially, with the norms, values, and interrelationships found in them. Just as programs involve multiple mechanisms, they will, characteristically, also include multiple contexts. Another key act of design and analysis is thus to try to identify the people and situations for whom the initiative will be beneficial by drawing on success and failure rates of different subgroups of subjects *within* and *between* interventions.

Rule 5: Outcomes

Evaluators need to understand what are the outcomes of an initiative and how they are produced. Outcomes provide the key evidence for the realist evaluator in any recommendation to mount, monitor, modify or mothball a program. Programs cannot be understood as undifferentiated wholes, as 'things' with some simple brute facticity. They fire multiple mechanisms having different effects on different subjects in different situations, and so produce *multiple outcomes*. Realist evaluators thus examine outcome patterns in a *theory testing* role. Outcomes are not inspected simply in order to see if programs work, but are analysed to discover if the conjectured mechanism/context theories are confirmed.

Rule 6: CMO *configurations*

In order to develop transferable and cumulative lessons from research, evaluators need to orient their thinking to context–mechanism–outcome pattern configurations (CMO configurations). A *CMO* configuration is a proposition stating what it is about a program which works for whom in what circumstances. The conjectured *CMO* configuration is the starting point for an evaluation, and the refined *CMO* configuration is the finding of an evaluation. Whilst realists know that the same program will often work in different ways in different circumstances, they appreciate that sequences of evaluations oriented to one another can improve the understanding of *CMO* configurations. Rather than replicate interventions in anticipation of the same results, the realist evaluator sees subsequent trials as an opportunity for *CMO configuration focusing*, a process in which the relatively well-known action of a program mechanism is fine-tuned to adapt it to local circumstances. Rather than anticipating the cumulation of program wisdom in the form of discovering representative programs which work universally, the realist evaluator seeks to generalize about programs through a process of *CMO configuration abstraction*, the creation of middle range theories which provide analytic frameworks to interpret similarities and differences between families of programs.

Rule 7: Teacher–learner processes

In order to construct and test context–mechanism–outcome pattern explanations, evaluators need to engage in a teacher–learner relationship with program policy makers, practitioners and participants. These stakeholders clearly have an insider understanding of the programs in which they are implicated and so constitute key informants in the research process. Programs, however, are embedded in a diversity of individual and institutional forces. Accordingly, there will be limitations to the understanding of any particular group of stakeholders, and the evaluator needs to be attentive to the unintended consequences and unacknowledged conditions of their decisions. Realist evaluators neither assume that stakeholders should act as 'respondents' providing answers to the predetermined questions of the researcher, nor assume that their task is the faithful 'reproduction' of the privileged views of stakeholders. This division of expertise requires a teacher–learner relationship to be developed between researcher and informant in which the medium of exchange is the *CMO* theory and the function of that relationship is to refine *CMO* theories. The research act thus involves 'learning' the stakeholder's theories, formalizing them, 'teaching' them back to the informant, who is then in a position to comment upon, clarify and further refine the key ideas. Such a process, repeated over many evaluations, feeds into the wider cycle of 'enlightenment' between the research and policy fields.

Rule 8: Open systems

Evaluators need to acknowledge that programs are implemented in a changing and permeable social world, and that program effectiveness may thus be subverted or enhanced through the unanticipated intrusion of new contexts and new causal powers. Unlike the physics laboratory – where empirical systems can approximate theoretical models fairly well, and specified mechanisms can be triggered in well-controlled conditions to produce specifiable regularities – in the changing environment of social programs, empirical closure is chronically compromised. Stakeholders always learn from their experience of interventions and emergent causal forces threaten even well-established *CMO* configurations. The sudden failure of a hitherto successful program is, of course, subject to realist explanation by 'reconstructing' the action of the hitherto unconsidered mechanisms and contexts. But this open system character of social life means that all *CMO* configurations are *ceteris paribus* where *ceteris* are, and can never be, *paribus*.

Evaluation is a craft and in this work we have sought to apply a touch of *intellectual craft* to the endeavour. This phrase, of course, belongs to C. Wright Mills and, as our finale, we can apply one of his favourite tricks to our own work. Mills worried over the tendency for social scientists to tread a well-worn pathway to eminence which went from bright ideas to rigorous scholarship to massive erudition to over-blown pomposity. His antidote was to show how the 300,000 word monographs of some key thinkers could be reduced to the odd pithy paragraph (Mills, 1959). We close with the ritual humiliation of reducing our own ideas to a single sentence. In Chapter 1, we used the same diagrammatic matrix in an attempt to summarize the guiding themes of experimental, pragmatic, and naturalistic evaluation (Figures 1.2, 1.3, 1.4). We rely on the same grid in order to make our final summary statement of the rules of realistic evaluation as in Figure 9.1.

This diagram does, of course, have a more prosaic purpose as well. Comparing it with the other evaluation paradigms, one can see at a glance that the directional flow of our ideas is foundational in that the fountainhead is with methodological fundamentals. In this respect, we have sought to recapture some of the spirit of the evaluation pioneers, whilst swapping the idealism of their motto of the 'experimental method for the experimenting society' for the harsher realism of a 'realist-method-for-a-realistic-world'. On the other hand, as compared with the constructivists and pragmatists, we remain wantonly idealist in refusing to accept that the consequence of programs being peopled and political is that researchers become mere palliators and pundits.

We believe, in short, that *the strength of evaluation research depends on the perspicacity of its view of explanation.* This is perhaps the one methodological rule from which we will not be budged.

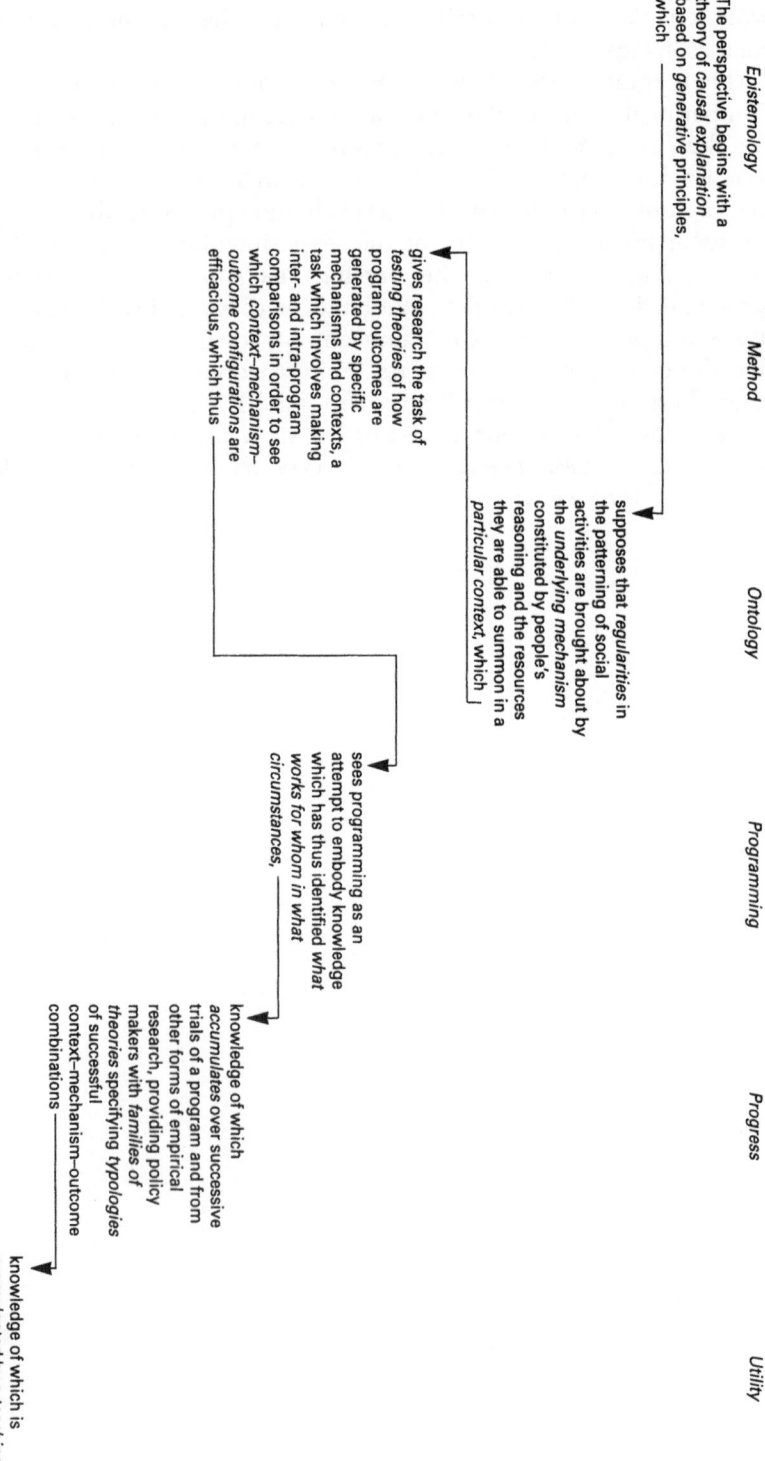

Methodological strategy

Epistemology

The perspective begins with a theory of *causal explanation* based on *generative principles*, which ———

Method

gives research the task of testing theories of how program outcomes are generated by specific mechanisms and contexts, a task which involves making inter- and intra-program comparisons in order to see which context–mechanism– outcome configurations are efficacious, which thus ———

Ontology

supposes that *regularities* in the patterning of social activities are brought about by the *underlying mechanism* constituted by people's reasoning and the resources they are able to summon in a *particular context*, which ┘

Programming

sees programming as an attempt to embody knowledge which has thus identified *what works for whom in what circumstances*, ———

Policy implementation

Progress

knowledge of which *accumulates* over successive trials of a program and from other forms of empirical research, providing policy makers with *families of theories* specifying *typologies* of successful context-mechanism–outcome combinations ———

Utility

knowledge of which is promulgated by a *teaching and learning* process in which the stakeholders' fragmentary expertise is marshalled by the researcher

Figure 9.1   *An overview of realistic evaluation*

REFERENCES

Abrams, P. (1985) 'The uses of British sociology', in M. Bulmer (ed.), *Essays on the History of British Sociological Research*. Cambridge: Cambridge University Press.

Anderson, D., Chenery, S. and Pease, K. (1995) *Biting Back: Tackling Repeat Burglary and Car Crime*. Crime Prevention and Detection Series Paper 58, London: Home Office.

Andrews, D., Bonta, J. and Hoge, R. (1990) 'Classification for effective rehabilitation', *Criminal Justice and Behavior*, 17: 19–52.

Archer, M. (1995) *Realist Social Theory: the Morphogenic Approach*. Cambridge: Cambridge University Press.

Arkin, R., Roemhild, H., Johnson, C., Luepker, R. and Murray, D. (1981) 'The Minnesota smoking prevention program: a seventh grade health curriculum supplement', *The Journal of School Health*, 11: 611–616.

Becker, H. (1971) *Sociological Work: Method and Substance*. Chicago: Aldine.

Bell, C. and Newby, H. (eds) (1972) *Community Studies*. London: Unwin.

Bell, C. and Newby, H. (eds) (1977) *Doing Sociological Research*. London: Unwin.

Bell, W. (1983) *Contemporary Social Welfare*. New York: Macmillan.

Bennett, T. (1989) *Contact Patrols in Birmingham and London: an Evaluation of a Fear Reducing Strategy*. Report to the Home Office Research and Planning Unit.

Bennett, T. (1991) 'The effectiveness of a police-initiated fear-reducing strategy', *British Journal of Criminology*, 31: 1–14.

Bennett, T. (1996) 'What's new in evaluation research?', *British Journal of Criminology*, 36: 567–573.

Ben-Shlomo, Y., Sheiham, A. and Marmot, M. (1991) 'Smoking and health', in R. Jowell, L. Brook, B. Taylor and G. Prior (eds), *British Social Attitudes: 8th Report*. Aldershot: Dartmouth.

Bhaskar, R. (1975) *A Realist Theory of Science*. Brighton: Harvester.

Bhaskar, R. (1979) *The Possibility of Naturalism*. Brighton: Harvester.

Blumer, H. (1969) *Symbolic Interactionism*. Englewood Cliffs, NJ: Prentice-Hall.

Bogatz, G. and Ball, S. (1971) *The Second Year of Sesame Street: a Continuing Evaluation*. Princeton, NJ: Educational Testing Service.

Bos, H. (1980) *Studies on Christiaan Huygens*. Lisse: Swets and Zeitlinger.

Bottoms, A.E., Mawby, R. and Xanthos, P. (1989) 'A tale of two estates', in D. Downes (ed.), *Crime and the City*. London: Macmillan.

Bottoms, A.E. and Wiles, P. (1986) 'Housing tenure and residential community crime careers in Britain', in A. Reiss and M. Tonry (eds), *Communities and Crime*. Chicago: University of Chicago Press.

Boudon, R. (1974) *Education, Opportunity and Social Inequality*. New York: Wiley.

Boudon, R. (1980) *The Crisis in Sociology*. London: Macmillan.

Bridgeman, C. and Sampson, A. (1994) *Wise after the Event: Tackling Repeat Victimisation*. A Report by the National Board for Crime Prevention, London: Home Office.

Brown, B. (1995) *Closed Circuit Television in Town Centres: Three Case Studies*. Crime Prevention and Detection Series Paper 73, London: Home Office.

Bryman, A. (1988) *Quantity and Quality in Social Research*. London: Unwin Hyman.

Burns, I. (1990) 'Foreword', in D. Forrester, S. Frenz, M. O'Connell and K. Pease (eds), *The Kirkholt Burglary Prevention Project: Phase II*. Crime Prevention Unit Paper 23, London: Home Office.

Burquest, R., Farrell, G. and Pease, K. (1992) 'Lessons from schools', *Policing*, 6: 148–155.

Campbell, D. (1969) 'Reforms as experiments', *American Psychologist*, 24: 409–429.

Campbell, D. and Stanley, J. (1963) *Experimental and Quasi-Experimental Evaluations in Social Research*. Chicago: Rand McNally.

Chelimsky, E. (1995) 'Where we stand today in the practice of evaluation', *Knowledge and Policy*, 8: 8–19.

Chen, H. (1990) *Theory-Driven Evaluation*. Beverly Hills, CA: Sage.

Chen, H. and Rossi, P. (1981) 'The multi-goal theory-driven approach to evaluation: a model linking basic and applied social science', in H. Freeman and M. Soloman (eds), *Evaluation Studies Review Annual*, vol. 6. Beverly Hills, CA: Sage. pp. 38–54.

Chen, H. and Rossi, P. (1983) 'Evaluating with sense: the theory-driven approach', *Evaluation Review*, 7: 283–302.

Chenery, S., Ellingworth, D., Tseloni, A. and Pease, K. (1996) 'Crimes which repeat: undigested evidence from the British Crime Survey 1992', *International Journal of Risk, Security and Crime Prevention*, 1: 207–216.

Clarke, R. (1992) 'Introduction', in R. Clarke (ed.), *Situational Crime Prevention: Successful Case Studies*. New York: Harrow and Heston.

Cohen, L. and Felson, M. (1979) 'Social change and crime rate trends: a routine activity approach', *American Sociological Review*, 44: 588–608.

Cohen, S. and Taylor, L. (1972) *Psychological Survival*. Harmondsworth: Penguin.

COMMIT Research Group (1991) 'Community Intervention Trial for Smoking Cessation (COMMIT): summary of design and intervention', *Journal of the National Cancer Institute*, 83: 1620–1628.

COMMIT Research Group (1995a) 'Community Intervention Trial for Smoking Cessation (COMMIT). I: Cohort results from a four-year trial', *American Journal of Public Health*, 85: 183–192.

COMMIT Research Group (1995b) 'Community Intervention Trial for Smoking Cessation (COMMIT). II: Changes in adult cigarette smoking prevalence', *American Journal of Public Health*, 85: 193–200.

Cook, T. D. and Campbell, D. T. (1979) *Quasi-Experimentation*. Chicago: Rand McNally.

Cook, T., Appleton, H., Conner, R., Shaffer, A., Tamkin, G. and Weber, S. (eds) (1975) *'Sesame Street' Revisited*. New York: Russell Sage Foundation.

Cook, T., Cooper, H., Cordray, D., Hartman, H., Hedges, L., Light, R., Louis, T. and Mosteller, F. (1992) *Meta-Analysis for Explanation*. New York: Russell Sage Foundation.

Costner, H. (1991) Review of Chen, H. (1990), *Contemporary Sociology*, 20: 92–94.

Cronbach, L. (1963) 'Course improvement through evaluation', *Teachers College Record*, 64: 672–683.

Cronbach, L. (1982) *Designing Evaluations of Educational and Social Programs*. San Francisco: Jossey-Bass.

Cummings, S., Rubin, S. and Oster, G. (1989) 'The cost-effectiveness of counselling smokers to quit', *Journal of the American Medical Association*, 261: 75–79.

Dekker, H. (1993) 'Prevalence of smoking in physicians and medical students in the Netherlands', *Social Science and Medicine*, 36: 817–822.

Department of Health (1992) *The Health of a Nation: a Summary of the Strategy for Health in England*. London: HMSO.

Department of Health (1993) *Code of Practice for the Commissioning and Management of Research and Development*. London: HMSO.

Diesing, P. (1972) *Patterns of Discovery in the Social Sciences*. London: Routledge.

Duguid, S., Hawkey, C. and Pawson, R. (1996) 'Using recidivism to evaluate prison education programs', *Journal of Correctional Education*, 47: 74–85.

Duguid, S., Hawkey, C. and Knights, W. (1997) 'Measuring the impact of education: preliminary findings of the prison education program', *Canadian Journal of Criminology*, forthcoming.

Durkheim, E. (1951) *Suicide*. New York: Free Press.

Durkheim, E. (1962) *The Rules of Sociological Method*. New York: Free Press.

Elwood, J. (1988) *Causal Relations in Medicine*. Oxford: Oxford University Press.

Everitt, A. (1996) 'Developing critical evaluation', *Evaluation*, 2: 173–188.

Fabiano, E., Robinson, D. and Porporino, F. (1990) *Preliminary Assessment of the Cognitive Skills Training Program*. Ottawa: Correctional Services of Canada.

Farrell, G. and Pease, K. (1993) *Once Bitten, Twice Bitten: Repeat Victimisation and its Implications for Crime Prevention*. Crime Prevention Unit Paper 46, London: Home Office.

Farrell, G., Phillips, C. and Pease, K. (1995) 'Taking like candy', *British Journal of Criminology*, 35: 384–399.

Farrington, D. (1992) 'Was the Kirkholt Burglary Prevention Project Effective?', unpublished paper.

Felson, M. (1994) *Crime and Everyday Life*. Thousand Oaks, CA: Pine Forge Press.

Fiore, M., Novothy, T., Pierce, J., Giovino, G., Hatziandrean, E., Newcombe, P., Surawicz, T. and Davis R. (1990) 'Methods used to quit smoking in the United States: do cessation programs help?', *Journal of the American Medical Association*, 263: 2760–2765.

Forrester, D., Chatterton, M. and Pease, K. (1988) *The Kirkholt Burglary Prevention Project, Rochdale*. Crime Prevention Unit Paper 13, London: Home Office.

Forrester, D., Frenz, S., O'Connell, M. and Pease, K. (1990) *The Kirkholt Burglary Prevention Project: Phase II*. Crime Prevention Unit Paper 23, London: Home Office.

Foster, J. (1995) 'Informal social control and community crime prevention', *British Journal of Criminology*, 35: 563–583.

Foster, J. and Hope, T. (1993) *Housing, Community and Crime: the Impact of the Priority Estates Project*. London: HMSO.

Gendreau, P. and Ross, R. (1987) 'The revivification of rehabilitation', *Justice Quarterly*, 4: 349–408.

Giddens, A. (1984) *The Constitution of Society*. Cambridge: Polity.

Gordon, S. (1992) *History and Philosophy of Social Science*. London: Routledge.

Gottfredson, D. and Tonry, M. (1987) *Prediction and Classification*. Chicago: Chicago University Press.

Graham, H. (1993) *When Life's a Drag*. Department of Health, London: HMSO.

Gray, E. (1987) *Smoking and Me: a Teacher's Guide*. London: Health Education Authority.

Greenwood, J. (1994) *Realism, Identity and Emotion*. London: Sage.

Guba, Y. and Lincoln, E. (1981) *Effective Evaluation: Improving the Usefulness of Evaluation Results through Responsive and Naturalistic Approaches*. San Francisco: Jossey-Bass.

Guba, Y. and Lincoln, E. (1989) *Fourth Generation Evaluation*. London: Sage.

Hammersley, M. (1992) *What's Wrong with Ethnography*. London: Routledge.

Hammersley, M. and Scarth, J. (1993) 'Beware of wise men bearing gifts', in R. Gomm and P. Woods (eds), *Educational Research in Action*. London: Paul Chapman.

Harré, R. (1972) *The Philosophies of Science*. Oxford: Oxford University Press.

Harré, R. (1978) *Social Being*. Oxford: Blackwell.

Harré, R. (1986) *Varieties of Realism*. Oxford: Blackwell.

Heller, N., Stenzel, W., Gill, A., Klode, R. and Schimerman, S. (1975) *Operation Identification Projects: Assessment of Effectiveness*. National Institute of Law Enforcement and Criminal Justice.

Hesse, M. (1974) *The Structure of Scientific Inference*. London: Macmillan.

Hirschi, T. and Selvin, H. (1973) *Principles of Survey Analysis*. New York: Free Press.

Hope, T. and Foster, J. (1992) 'Conflicting forces: changing the dynamics of crime and community on a "problem" estate', *British Journal of Criminology*, 32: 488–504.

Hume, D. (1739) *A Treatise of Human Nature*. London: John Noon.

Husain, S. (1988) *Neighbourhood Watch in England and Wales: a Locational Analysis*. Crime Prevention Unit Paper 47, London: Home Office.

Jencks, S. and Anderson, L. (1995) 'COMMIT anti-smoking program shows modest success', *Journal of the National Cancer Institute*, 87: 343–344.

Joint Committee on Standards for Educational Evaluation (1994) *The Program Evaluation Standards* (2nd edn). Thousand Oaks, CA: Sage.

Julnes, G. (1996) 'Neo-realist evaluation', paper presented at the ISA Social Science Methodology Conference, Essex University.

Kaplan, A. (1964) *The Conduct of Inquiry*. New York: Chandler.

Keat, R. and Urry, J. (1975) *Social Theory as Science*. London: Routledge.

Knuttsen, J. (1984) *Operation Identification – a Way to Prevent Burglaries?* Report 14, Stockholm: National Swedish Council for Crime Prevention.

Kottke, T., Battista, R., De Friese, G. and Brekke, M. (1988) 'Attributes of successful smoking cessation interventions in medical practice', *Journal of the American Medical Association*, 295: 2883–2889.

Koyré, A. (1968) *Metaphysics and Measurement*. London: Chapman and Hall.

Kuhn, T. (1961) 'The function of measurement in modern physical science', in H. Woolf (ed.), *Quantification*. Indianapolis: Bobbs-Merill.

Lakatos, I. (1970) 'Falsification and the methodology of scientific research programmes', in I. Lakatos and A. Musgrave (eds), *Criticism and the Growth of Knowledge*. Cambridge: Cambridge University Press.

Laycock, G. (1985) *Property Marking: a Deterrent to Domestic Burglary?* Crime Prevention Unit Paper 3, London: Home Office.

Laycock, G. (1992) 'Operation Identification, or the power of publicity', in R. Clarke (ed.), *Situational Crime Prevention: Successful Case Studies*. New York: Harrow and Heston, pp. 230–238.

Laycock, G. and Tilley, N. (1995) *Policing and Neighbourhood Watch: Strategic Issues*. Crime Prevention and Detection Series Paper 60, London: Home Office.

Layder, D. (1990) *The Realist Image in Social Science*. London: Macmillan.

Layder, D. (1993) *New Strategies in Social Research*. Cambridge: Polity.

Lee, A.J., Crombie, I., Smith, W. and Tunstall-Pedoe, H. (1991) 'Cigarette smoking and employment status', *Social Science and Medicine*, 33: 1309–1312.

Lichtenstein, E. and Glasgow, R. (1992) 'Smoking cessation: what have we learned over the past decade?', *Journal of Consulting and Clinical Psychology*, 60: 518–527.

Lipsey, M. (1995) 'What do we learn from 400 research studies on the effectiveness of treatment with juvenile delinquents?' in J. McGuire (ed.), *What Works? Reducing Reoffending*. Chichester: John Wiley.

Lloyd, S., Farrell, G. and Pease, K. (1994) *Preventing Repeated Domestic Violence: a Demonstration Project*. Crime Prevention Unit Paper 49, London: Home Office.

Löesel, F. (1995) 'The efficacy of correctional treatment', in J. McGuire (ed.), *What Works? Reducing Reoffending*. Chichester: John Wiley.

Magowan, R. (1994) *Smoking*. Health Gain Investment Programme Technical Review Document, Trent Regional Health Authority.

Martinson, R. (1974) 'What works? Questions and answers about prison reform', *Public Interest*, 35: 22–45.

Martinson, R. (1979) 'New findings, new views: a note of caution regarding sentencing reform', *Hofstra Law Review*, 7: 243–258.

Mayhew, P., Aye Maung, N. and Mirrlees-Black, C. (1993) *The 1992 British Crime Survey*. Home Office Research Study 132, London: HMSO.

Merton, R. (1968) *Social Theory and Social Structure*. New York: Free Press.

Mill, J.S. (1961) *A System of Logic*. London: Longman.

Mills, C.W. (1959) *The Sociological Imagination*. New York: Oxford University Press.

Mirrlees-Black, C. and Ross, R. (1995) *Crime against Retail and Manufacturing Premises: Findings from the 1994 Commercial Victimisation Survey*. Home Office Research Study 146, London: Home Office.

Mitchell, J. (1983) 'Case study and situational analysis', *Sociological Review*, 31: 187–211.

Nathan, R. (1989) *Social Science in Government: Uses and Misuses*. New York: Basic Books.

Nozu, Y. and Tsunoda, H. (1992) 'A review of studies on school-based smoking prevention programmes', *Nippon Koshu Eisei Zassi*, 39: 307–318.

Nuffield, J. (1982) *Parole Decision-Making in Canada*. Ottawa: Solicitor General of Canada.

Nutbeam, D., Macaskill, P., Smith, C., Simpson, J. and Catford, J. (1993) 'Evaluation of two school smoking educational programmes under normal classroom conditions', *British Medical Journal*, 306: 102–107.

Nuttall, C. (1992) 'What works?', in *Proceedings of the Annual Conference of the Association of Chief Officers of Probation*. Wakefield: Association of Chief Officers of Probation.

Olson, M. (1965) *The Logic of Collective Action*. Cambridge, MA: Harvard University Press.

Palmer, T. (1975) 'Martinson revisited', *Journal of Research in Crime and Delinquency*, July: 133–152.

Patton, M. (1978) *Utilisation-Focused Evaluation*. Beverly Hills, CA: Sage.

Patton, M. (1980) *Qualitative Evaluation Methods*. Beverly Hills, CA: Sage.

Patton, M. (1982) *Practical Evaluation*. Beverly Hills, CA: Sage.

Patton, M. (1990) 'The evaluator's responsibility for utilisation', in M. Alkin (ed.), *Debates on Evaluation*. Newbury Park, CA: Sage.

Pawson, R. (1989) *A Measure for Measures: a Manifesto for an Empirical Sociology*. London: Routledge.

Pawson, R. (1996) 'Three steps to constructivist heaven', *Evaluation*, 2: 213–220.

Pawson, R. and Tilley, N. (1994) 'What works in evaluation research?', *British Journal of Criminology*, 34: 291–306.

Pawson, R. and Tilley, N. (1996) 'What's crucial in evaluation research: a reply to Bennett', *British Journal of Criminology*, 36: 574–578.

Pease, K. (1992) 'Preventing burglary on a British public housing estate', in R. Clarke (ed.), *Situational Crime Prevention: Successful Case Studies*. New York: Harrow and Heston. pp. 223–229.

Peirce, C. (1931) *Collected Papers*, vol. 5. Cambridge, MA: Belknap Press.

Polvi, N., Looman, T., Humphries, C. and Pease, K. (1991) 'The time course of repeat burglary victimisation', *British Journal of Criminology*, 31: 411–414.

Popper, K. (1945) *The Open Society and its Enemies*. London: Routledge.

Popper, K. (1957) *The Poverty of Historicism*. London: Routledge.

Popper, K. (1959) *The Logic of Scientific Discovery*. London: Hutchinson.

Porporino, F. and Robinson, D. (1995) 'An evaluation of the reasoning and rehabilitation program with Canadian federal offenders', in R. Ross and R. Ross (eds), *Thinking Straight*. Ottawa: Air Training Publications.

Ragin, C. (1994) *Constructing Social Research*. Thousand Oaks, CA: Pine Forge Press.

Roethlisberger, F. and Dickson, W. (1939) *Management and the Worker*. Cambridge MA: Harvard University Press.

Rosenbaum, D. (1988) 'Community crime prevention: a review and synthesis of the literature', *Justice Quarterly*, 5: 325–395.

Ross, R. and Fabiano, E. (1985) *Time to Think: a Cognitive Model of Delinquency Prevention and Offender Rehabilitation*. Johnson City, TN: Institute of Social Sciences and the Arts.

Ross, R. and Gendreau, P. (1980) *Effective Correctional Treatment*. Toronto: Butterworths.

Rossi, P. and Freeman, H. (1985) *Evaluation: a Systematic Approach*. Beverly Hills, CA: Sage.

Rossi, P. and Lyall, K. (1978) 'An overview of the NIT experiment', in T. D. Cook, M. DelRosario, K. Hennigan, M. Mark and W. Trochin (eds), *Evaluation Studies Annual Review*, vol. 3. Beverly Hills, CA: Sage.

Sacks, H. (1972) 'An initial investigation of the usability of conversational data for doing sociology', in D. Sudnow (ed.), *Studies in Social Interaction*. New York: Free Press.

Safe Neighbourhoods Unit (1993) *Crime Prevention on Council Estates*. Prepared for the Department of the Environment. London: HMSO.

Sampson, A. and Phillips, C. (1992) *Multiple Victimisation: Racial Attacks on an East London Estate*. Crime Prevention Unit Paper 36, London: Home Office.

Sayer, A. (1984) *Method in Social Science: a Realist Approach*. London: Hutchinson.

Schnur, A. (1948) 'The educational treatment of prisoners and recidivism', *American Journal of Sociology*, 54: 142–147.

Schuman, H. and Presser, S. (1981) *Questions and Answers in Attitude Surveys*. New York: Academic Press.

Scott, W. (1842) *Fortunes of Nigel* (The Waverley novels), London and Edinburgh: Abbortsford.

Scriven, M. (1980) *The Logic of Evaluation*. Inverness, CA: Edgepress.

Scriven, M. (1991) *Evaluation Thesaurus* (4th edn). Newbury Park, CA: Sage.

Shadish, W.R., Cook, T. and Leviton, L. (1991) *Foundations of Program Evaluation*. Beverly Hills, CA: Sage.

Skogan, W. (1992) 'Community policing in the United States', paper presented at the Crime Reduction Conference, Paris.

Spelman, W. (1995) 'Once bitten, then what? Cross-sectional and time-course explanations of repeat victimisation', *British Journal of Criminology*, 35(3): 366–383.

Stebbins, K. (1991) 'Tobacco, politics and economics: implications for global health', *Social Science and Medicine*, 33: 1317–1326.

Stern, E. (1995) 'Editorial', *Evaluation*, 1: 5–9.

Stern, E. (1996) 'Editorial', *Evaluation*, 2: 131–133.

Stevens, V., Severson, H., Lichtenstein, E., Little, S. and Leben, J. (1995) 'Making the most of a teachable moment: a smokeless-tobacco cessation intervention in the dental office', *American Journal of Public Health*, 85: 231–235.

Stinchcombe, A. (1968) *Constructing Social Theories*. New York: Harcourt, Brace and World.

Stufflebeam, D. (1980) 'An interview with Daniel L. Stufflebeam', *Educational Evaluation and Policy Analysis*, 2(4).

Susser, M. (1995) 'Editorial: the tribulations of trials – intervention in communities', *American Journal of Public Health*, 85: 156–158.

Tilley, N. (1992) *Safer Cities and Community Safety Strategies*. Crime Prevention Unit Paper 38, London: Home Office.

Tilley, N. (1993a) *Understanding Car Parks, Crime and CCTV*. Crime Prevention Unit Paper 42, London: Home Office.

Tilley, N. (1993b) *After Kirkholt: Theory, Method and Results of Replication Evaluations*. Crime Prevention Unit Paper 47, London: Home Office.

Tilley, N. (1993c) *The Prevention of Crime against Small Businesses: the Safer Cities Experience*. Crime Prevention Unit Paper 45, London: Home Office.

Tilley, N. (1993d) 'Crime prevention and the Safer Cities story', *Howard Journal of Criminal Justice*, 32: 40–57.

Tilley, N. (1996) 'Demonstration, exemplification, duplication and replication in evaluation research', *Evaluation*, 2: 35–50.

Trickett, A., Osborn, D., Seymour, J. and Pease, K. (1992) 'What is different about high crime areas?', *British Journal of Criminology*, 32: 81–90.

Vogt, T., Lichtenstein, E., Ary, D., Biglan, A., Danielson, R., Glasgow, R., Hollis, J., Hornbrook, M., Lando, H., Mullooly, J., Severson, H. and Stevens, V. (1989) 'Integrating tobacco intervention into a health maintenance organization: the TRACC program', *Health Education Research*, 4: 1570–1574.

Wallace, W. (1971) *The Logic of Science in Sociology*. New York: Aldine.

Weiss, C. (1972) *Evaluation Research: Methods for Assessing Program Effectiveness*. Englewood Cliffs, NJ: Prentice-Hall.

Weiss, C. (1976) 'Using research in the policy process: potential and constraints', *Policy Studies Journal*, 4: 224–228.

Weiss, C. (1980) 'Knowledge creep and decision accretion', *Knowledge: Creation, Diffusion, Utilisation*, 1: 381–404.

Weiss, C. (1981) 'Doing research or doing policy', *Evaluation and Program Planning*, 4: 297–402.

Weiss, C. (1987) 'The circuitry of enlightenment', *Knowledge: Creation, Diffusion, Utilisation*, 8: 274–281.

Weiss, C. (1990) 'Evaluation for decisions', in M. Alkin (ed.), *Debates on Evaluation*. Newbury Park, CA: Sage.

Weiss, C. and Bucuvalas, M. (1980) *Social Science Research and Decision-Making*. New York: Columbia University Press.

Williamson, D., Serdula, J., Kendrick, J. and Binkin, N. (1989) 'Comparing the prevalence of smoking in pregnant and nonpregnant women', *Journal of the American Medical Association*, 261: 71–74.

Willms, D. (1991) 'A new stage, a new life: individual success in quitting smoking', *Social Science and Medicine*, 33: 1365–1371.

Znaniecki, F. (1934) *The Method of Sociology*. New York: Farrar and Rinehart.

INDEX

Entries in *italic* indicate diagrams and tables.